THE STANDARD E
COMPLETE PSYCHO
OF SIGMUND FREUD

VOLUME XIX

THE FIRST APPEARANCE OF THE DEVIL TO
CHRISTOPH HAIZMANN

The Standard Edition of the Complete Psychological Works of Sigmund Freud

Volume XIX
(1923 – 1925)
The Ego and the Id
and
Other Works

TRANSLATED FROM THE GERMAN UNDER
THE GENERAL EDITORSHIP OF
James Strachey

IN COLLABORATION WITH
Anna Freud

ASSISTED BY
Alix Strachey and Alan Tyson

VINTAGE BOOKS
London

THE HOGARTH PRESS
AND THE INSTITUTE OF PSYCHOANALYSIS

Published by Vintage 2001

17

Translation and editorial matter
Copyright © The Institute of Psychoanalysis 1961

First published in Great Britain in 1961 by
The Hogarth Press

Vintage
Random House, 20 Vauxhall Bridge Road,
London SW1V 2SA

www.vintage-books.co.uk

Addresses for companies within The Random House Group Limited
can be found at: www.randomhouse.co.uk/offices.htm

The Random House Group Limited Reg. No. 954009

A CIP catalogue record for this book
is available from the British Library

ISBN 9780099426745

Penguin Random House is committed to a sustainable future for
our business, our readers and our planet. This book is made from
Forest Stewardship Council® certified paper.

Printed and bound in Great Britain by Clays Ltd, St Ives plc

CONTENTS

VOLUME NINETEEN

THE EGO AND THE ID
(1923)

A SEVENTEENTH-CENTURY DEMONOLOGICAL NEUROSIS (1923 [1922])

REMARKS ON THE THEORY AND PRACTICE OF DREAM-INTERPRETATION (1923 [1922])

SOME ADDITIONAL NOTES ON DREAM-INTERPRETATION AS A WHOLE (1925)

ILLUSTRATIONS

*From the Trophaeum Mariano-Cellense, MS. 14,086 in the Austrian
National Library. Reproduced by kind permission of the Keeper of the
Department of Manuscripts.*

THE EGO AND THE ID
(1923)

EDITOR'S INTRODUCTION

DAS ICH UND DAS ES

(a) GERMAN EDITIONS:
1923   Leipzig, Vienna and Zurich: Internationaler Psycho-
            analytischer Verlag.   Pp. 77.
1925   *G.S.*, 6, 351–405.
1931   *Theoretische Schriften*, 338–91.
1940   *G.W.*, 13, 237–289.

(b) ENGLISH TRANSLATION:
The Ego and the Id
1927   London: Hogarth Press and Institute of Psycho-
            Analysis. Pp. 88. (Tr. Joan Riviere.)

The present is a very considerably modified version of the
one published in 1927.

This book appeared in the third week of April, 1923, though
it had been in Freud's mind since at least the previous July
(Jones, 1957, 104). On September 26, 1922, at the Seventh
International Psycho-Analytical Congress, which was held in
Berlin and was the last he ever attended, he read a short paper
with the title 'Etwas vom Unbewussten [Some Remarks on the
Unconscious]', in which he foreshadowed the contents of the
book. An abstract of this paper (which was never itself published)
appeared that autumn in the *Int. Zeitschrift Psychoanal.*, 5 (4),
486,[1] and, although there is no certainty that it was written
by Freud himself, it is worth while recording it:

'Some Remarks on the Unconscious'

'The speaker repeated the familiar history of the development
of the concept "unconscious" in psycho-analysis. "Unconscious"
was in the first instance a purely descriptive term which accordingly included what is temporarily latent. The dynamic view

[1] A translation was published in the *Int. J. Psycho-Anal.* the next year,
4 (3), 367. (The date of the reading of the paper is there misprinted
'Sept. 25'.) It is reprinted here in a slightly modified form.

of the process of repression made it necessary, however, to give the unconscious a systematic sense, so that the unconscious had to be equated with the repressed. What is latent and only temporarily unconscious received the name of "preconscious" and, from the systematic point of view, was brought into close proximity to the conscious. The double meaning of the term "unconscious" undoubtedly involved disadvantages, though they were of little significance and were difficult to avoid. It has turned out, however, that it is not practicable to regard the repressed as coinciding with the unconscious and the ego with the preconscious and conscious. The speaker discussed the two facts which show that in the ego too there is an unconscious, which behaves dynamically like the repressed unconscious: the two facts of a resistance proceeding from the ego during analysis and of an unconscious sense of guilt. He announced that in a book which was shortly to appear—*The Ego and the Id*—he had made an attempt to estimate the influence which these new discoveries must have upon our view of the unconscious.'

The Ego and the Id is the last of Freud's major theoretical works. It offers a description of the mind and its workings which is at first sight new and even revolutionary; and indeed all psycho-analytic writings that date from after its publication bear the unmistakable imprint of its effects—at least in regard to their terminology. But, in spite of all its fresh insights and fresh syntheses, we can trace, as so often with Freud's apparent innovations, the seeds of his new ideas in earlier, and sometimes in far earlier, writings.

The forerunners of the present general picture of the mind had been successively the 'Project' of 1895 (Freud, 1950a), the seventh chapter of *The Interpretation of Dreams* (1900a) and the metapsychological papers of 1915. In all of these, the inter-related problems of mental functioning and mental structure were inevitably considered, though with varying stress upon the two aspects of the question. The historical accident that psycho-analysis had its origin in connection with the study of hysteria led at once to the hypothesis of repression (or, more generally, of defence) as a mental function, and this in turn to a topographical hypothesis—to a picture of the mind as including two portions, one repressed and the other repressing. The quality of 'consciousness' was evidently closely involved in these hypotheses; and it was easy to equate the repressed part of the mind with what was 'unconscious' and the repressing part with what was 'conscious'. Freud's earlier pictorial diagrams of the mind, in *The Interpretation of Dreams* (*Standard Ed.*, **5,** 537–41) and in his letter to Fliess of December 6, 1896 (Freud, 1950*a*, Letter 52), were representations of this view of the position. And this apparently simple scheme underlay all of Freud's earlier theoretical ideas: functionally, a repressed force endeavouring to make its way into activity but held in check by a repressing force, and structurally, an 'unconscious' opposed by an 'ego'.

Nevertheless, complications soon became manifest. It was quickly seen that the word 'unconscious' was being used in two senses: the 'descriptive' sense (which merely attributed a particular *quality* to a mental state) and the 'dynamic' sense (which attributed a particular *function* to a mental state). This distinction was already stated, though not in these terms, in *The Interpretation of Dreams* (*Standard Ed.*, **5,** 614–15). It was stated much more clearly in the English paper written for the Society for Psychical Research (1912*g*, ibid., **12,** 262). But from the first another, more obscure notion was already involved (as was plainly shown by the pictorial diagrams)—the notion of 'systems' in the mind. This implied a topographical or structural division oi the mind based on something more than function, a division into portions to which it was possible to attribute a number of differentiating characteristics and methods of operating. Some such idea was no doubt already implied in the phrase 'the unconscious', which appeared very early (e.g. in a footnote to the *Studies on Hysteria*, 1895*d*, *Standard Ed.*, **2,** 76). The concept of a 'system' became explicit in *The Interpretation of Dreams* (1900*a*), ibid., **5,** 536–7. From the terms in which it was there introduced, topographical imagery was at once suggested, though Freud gave a warning against taking this literally. There were a number of these 'systems' (mnemic, perceptual, and so on) and among them 'the unconscious' (ibid., 541), which 'for simplicity's sake' was to be designated as 'the system *Ucs.*'. In these earlier passages all that was overtly meant by this unconscious system was the repressed, until we reach the final section of *The Interpretation of Dreams* (ibid., **5,** 611 ff.), where something with a much wider scope was indicated. Thereafter the question remained in abeyance until the S.P.R. paper (1912*g*) already referred to, where (besides the clear differentiation between the descriptive and dynamic uses of the term 'unconscious'), in the last sentences of the paper, a third, 'systematic', use was defined. It may be noted that in this passage (ibid., **12,** 266), it was only for this 'systematic' unconscious that Freud proposed to use the symbol '*Ucs.*'. All this seems very straightforward, but, oddly enough, the picture was blurred once more in the metapsychological paper on 'The Unconscious' (1915*e*). In Section II of that paper (ibid., **14,** 172 ff.) there were no longer *three* uses of the term 'unconscious' but only two. The 'dynamic' use disappeared, and was presumably subsumed into the 'systematic' one,[1] which was still to be called the '*Ucs.*', though it now included the repressed. Finally, in Chapter I of the present work (as well as in Lecture XXXI of the *New Introductory Lectures*, 1933*a*) Freud reverted to the threefold distinction and classification, though at the end of the chapter he applied the abbreviation '*Ucs.*', inadvertently perhaps, to all three kinds of 'unconscious' (p. 18).

But the question now arose whether, as applied to a *system*, the term 'unconscious' was at all appropriate. In the structural picture of the mind what had from the first been most clearly differentiated from 'the unconscious' had been 'the ego'. And it now began to appear that the ego itself ought partly to be described as 'unconscious'. This was pointed out in *Beyond the Pleasure Principle*, in a sentence which read in the first edition (1920*g*): 'It may be that much of the ego is itself unconscious[2]; only a part of it, probably, is covered by the term "preconscious".' In the second edition, a year later, this sentence was altered to: 'It is certain that much of the ego is itself unconscious . . .; only a small part of it is covered by the term "preconscious".'[3] And this discovery and the grounds for it were stated with still greater insistence in the first chapter of the present work.

It had thus become apparent that, alike as regards 'the

---

[1] The two terms seem to be definitely equated in *Beyond the Pleasure Principle* (1920*g*), ibid., **18,** 20.

[2] [I.e. not merely in the descriptive but also in the dynamic sense.]

[3] Freud had actually already spoken in the opening sentence of his second paper on 'The Neuro-Psychoses of Defence' (1896*b*) of the psychical mechanism of defence as being 'unconscious'.

unconscious' and as regards 'the ego', the criterion of consciousness was no longer helpful in building up a structural picture of the mind. Freud accordingly abandoned the use of consciousness in this capacity: 'being conscious' was henceforward to be regarded simply as a quality which might or might not be attached to a mental state. The old 'descriptive' sense of the term was in fact all that remained. The new terminology which he now introduced had a highly clarifying effect and so made further clinical advances possible. But it did not in itself involve any fundamental changes in Freud's views on mental structure and functioning. Indeed, the three newly presented entities, the id, the ego and the super-ego, all had lengthy past histories (two of them under other names) and these will be worth examining.

The term '*das Es*',[1] as Freud himself explains below (p. 23), was derived in the first instance from Georg Groddeck, a physician practising at Baden-Baden, who had recently become attached to psycho-analysis and with whose wide-ranging ideas Freud felt much sympathy. Groddeck seems in turn to have derived '*das Es*' from his own teacher, Ernst Schweninger, a well-known German physician of an earlier generation. But, as Freud also points out, the use of the word certainly goes back to Nietzsche. In any case, the term was adapted by Freud to a different and more precise meaning than Groddeck's. It cleared up and in part replaced the ill-defined uses of the earlier terms 'the unconscious', 'the *Ucs.*' and 'the systematic unconscious'.[2]

The position in regard to '*das Ich*' is a good deal less clear. The term had of course been in familiar use before the days of Freud; but the precise sense which he himself attached to it in his earlier writings is not unambiguous. It seems possible to detect two main uses: one in which the term distinguishes a person's self as a whole (including, perhaps, his body) from

---

[1] There was to begin with a good deal of discussion over the choice of an English equivalent. 'The id' was eventually decided upon in preference to 'the it', so as to be parallel with the long-established 'ego'.

[2] The symbol '*Ucs.*' disappears after the present work, except for a single belated occurrence in *Moses and Monotheism* (1939a), Chapter III, Part 1 (E), where oddly enough it is used in the 'descriptive' sense. Freud continued to use the term 'the unconscious', though with diminishing frequency, as a synonym for 'the id'.

other people, and the other in which it denotes a particular part of the mind characterized by special attributes and functions. It is in this second sense that the term was used in the elaborate account of the 'ego' in Freud's early 'Project' of 1895 (Freud, 1950a, Part I, Section 14); and it is in this same sense that it is used in the anatomy of the mind in *The Ego and the Id*. But in some of his intervening works, particularly in connection with narcissism, the 'ego' seems to correspond rather to the 'self'. It is not always easy, however, to draw a line between these two senses of the word.[1]

What is quite certain, however, is that, after the isolated attempt in the 'Project' of 1895 at a detailed analysis of the structure and functioning of the ego, Freud left the subject almost untouched for some fifteen years. His interest was concentrated on his investigations of the unconscious and its instincts, particularly the sexual ones, and in the part they played in normal and abnormal mental behaviour. The fact that repressive forces played an equally important part was, of course, never overlooked and was always insisted on; but the closer examination of them was left to the future. It was enough for the moment to give them the inclusive name of 'the ego'.

There were two indications of a change, both round about the year 1910. In a paper on psychogenic disturbances of vision (1910i), there comes what seems to be a first mention of 'ego-instincts' (*Standard Ed.*, **11**, 214), which combine the functions of repression with those of self-preservation. The other and more important development was the hypothesis of narcissism which was first proposed in 1909 and which led the way to a detailed examination of the ego and its functions in a variety of connections—in the study on Leonardo (1910c), in the Schreber case history (1911c), in the paper on the two principles of mental functioning (1911b), in the paper on 'Narcissism' itself (1914c) and in the metapsychological paper on 'The Unconscious' (1915e). In this last work, however, a

[1] In a few places in the *Standard Edition* where the sense seemed to demand it, '*das Ich*' has been translated by 'the self'. There is a passage in *Civilization and its Discontents* (1930a), towards the beginning of the fourth paragraph of Chapter I, in which Freud himself explicitly equates '*das Selbst*' and '*das Ich*'. And, in the course of a discussion of the moral responsibility for dreams (1925i), p. 133, below, he makes a clear distinction between the two uses of the German word '*Ich*'.

further development occurred: what had been described as the ego now became the 'system' *Cs.* (*Pcs.*).[1] It is this system which is the progenitor of the 'ego' as we have it in the new and corrected terminology, from which, as we have seen, the confusing connection with the quality of 'consciousness' has been removed.

The functions of the system *Cs.* (*Pcs.*), as enumerated in 'The Unconscious', *Standard Ed.*, 14, 188, include such activities as censorship, reality-testing, and so on, all of which are now assigned to the 'ego'. There is one particular function, however, whose examination was to lead to momentous results—the self-critical faculty. This and the correlated 'sense of guilt' attracted Freud's interest from early days, chiefly in connection with the obsessional neurosis. His theory that obsessions are 'transformed self-reproaches' for sexual pleasure enjoyed in childhood was fully explained in Section II of his second paper on 'The Neuro-Psychoses of Defence' (1896*b*) after being outlined somewhat earlier in his letters to Fliess. That the self-reproaches may be unconscious was already implied at this stage, and was stated specifically in the paper on 'Obsessive Actions and Religious Practices' (1907*b*), *Standard Ed.*, 9, 123. It was only with the concept of narcissism, however, that light could be thrown on the actual mechanism of these self-reproaches. In Section III of his paper on narcissism (1914*c*) Freud began by suggesting that the narcissism of infancy is replaced in the adult by devotion to an ideal ego set up within himself. He then put forward the notion that there may be 'a special psychical agency' whose task it is to watch the actual ego and measure it by the ideal ego or ego ideal—he seemed to use the terms indiscriminately (*Standard Ed.*, 14, 95). He attributed a number of functions to this agency, including the normal conscience, the dream-censorship and certain paranoic delusions. In the paper on 'Mourning and Melancholia' (1917*e* [1915]) he further made this agency responsible for pathological states of mourning (ibid., 14, 247) and insisted more definitely that it is something apart from the rest of the ego, and this was made still more clear in *Group Psychology* (1921*c*). It must be noticed, however, that here the distinction between the 'ego ideal' itself and the 'agency' concerned with its enforcement had been dropped: the

[1] These abbreviations (like the '*Ucs.*') go back to *The Interpretation of Dreams* (1900*a*), *Standard Ed.*, 5, 540 *n*.

'agency' was specifically called the 'ego ideal' (*Standard Ed.*, **18,** 109–10). It is as an equivalent to the 'ego ideal' that '*das Über-Ich*' [1] makes its first appearance (p. 28 below), though its aspect as an enforcing or prohibiting agency predominates later. Indeed, after *The Ego and the Id* and the two or three shorter works immediately following it, the 'ego ideal' disappears almost completely as a technical term. It makes a brief re-emergence in a couple of sentences in the *New Introductory Lectures* (1933*a*), Lecture XXXI; but here we find a return to the original distinction, for 'an important function' attributed to the super-ego is to act as 'the vehicle of the ego ideal by which the ego measures itself'—almost the exact terms in which the ego ideal was first introduced in the paper on narcissism (*Standard Ed.*, **14,** 93).

But this distinction may seem to be an artificial one when we turn to Freud's account of the genesis of the super-ego. This account (in Chapter III) is no doubt the part of the book second in importance only to the main thesis of the threefold division of the mind. The super-ego is there shown to be derived from a transformation of the child's earliest object-cathexes into identifications: it takes the place of the Oedipus complex. This mechanism (the replacement of an object-cathexis by an identification and the introjection of the former object) had been first applied by Freud (in his study of Leonardo, 1910*c*) to the explanation of one type of homosexuality, in which a boy replaces his love for his mother by identifying himself with her (*Standard Ed.*, **11,** 100). He next applied the same notion to states of depression in 'Mourning and Melancholia' (1917*e*), ibid., **14,** 249. Further and more elaborate discussions of these various kinds of identifications and introjections were pursued in Chapters VII, VIII and XI of *Group Psychology* (1921*c*), but it was only in the present work that Freud arrived at his final views on the derivation of the super-ego from the child's earliest object-relations.

Having once established his new account of the anatomy of the mind, Freud was in a position to examine its implications, and this he already does in the later pages of the book—the

---

[1] Jones (1957, 305 *n.*) remarks that the term had been used earlier by Münsterberg (1908), though, he adds, it was in a different sense and it is unlikely that Freud had come across the passage.

relation between the divisions of the mind and the two classes of instincts, and the interrelations between the divisions of the mind themselves, with special reference to the sense of guilt. But many of these questions, and in particular the last one, were to form the subject of other writings which followed in rapid succession. See, for instance, 'The Economic Problem of Masochism' (1924*c*), 'The Dissolution of the Oedipus Complex' (1924*d*), the two papers on neurosis and psychosis (1924*b* and 1924*e*), and the one on the anatomical distinction between the sexes (1925*j*), all in the present volume, as well as the still more important *Inhibitions, Symptoms and Anxiety* (1926*d*), published only a little later. Finally, a further long discussion of the super-ego, together with an interesting examination of the proper use of the terms 'super-ego', 'conscience', 'sense of guilt', 'need for punishment' and 'remorse' will be found in Chapters VII and VIII of *Civilization and its Discontents* (1930*a*).

Extracts from the earlier (1927) translation of this work were included in Rickman's *General Selection from the Works of Sigmund Freud* (1937, 245–74).

THE EGO AND THE ID

[PREFACE]

THE present discussions are a further development of some trains of thought which I opened up in *Beyond the Pleasure Principle* (1920g), and to which, as I remarked there,[1] my attitude was one of a kind of benevolent curiosity. In the following pages these thoughts are linked to various facts of analytic observation and an attempt is made to arrive at new conclusions from this conjunction; in the present work, however, there are no fresh borrowings from biology, and on that account it stands closer to psycho-analysis than does *Beyond the Pleasure Principle*. It is more in the nature of a synthesis than of a speculation and seems to have had an ambitious aim in view. I am conscious, however, that it does not go beyond the roughest outline and with that limitation I am perfectly content.

In these pages things are touched on which have not yet been the subject of psycho-analytic consideration, and it has not been possible to avoid trenching upon some theories which have been put forward by non-analysts or by former analysts on their retreat from analysis. I have elsewhere always been ready to acknowledge what I owe to other workers; but in this instance I feel burdened by no such debt of gratitude. If psycho-analysis has not hitherto shown its appreciation of certain things, this has never been because it overlooked their achievement or sought to deny their importance, but because it followed a particular path, which had not yet led so far. And finally, when it has reached them, things have a different look to it from what they have to others.

[1] [*Standard Ed.*, 18, 59.]

CONSCIOUSNESS AND WHAT IS UNCONSCIOUS

IN this introductory chapter there is nothing new to be said and it will not be possible to avoid repeating what has often been said before.

The division of the psychical into what is conscious and what is unconscious is the fundamental premiss of psycho-analysis; and it alone makes it possible for psycho-analysis to understand the pathological processes in mental life, which are as common as they are important, and to find a place for them in the framework of science. To put it once more, in a different way: psychoanalysis cannot situate the essence of the psychical in consciousness, but is obliged to regard consciousness as a quality of the psychical, which may be present in addition to other qualities or may be absent.

If I could suppose that everyone interested in psychology would read this book, I should also be prepared to find that at this point some of my readers would already stop short and would go no further; for here we have the first shibboleth of psycho-analysis. To most people who have been educated in philosophy the idea of anything psychical which is not also conscious is so inconceivable that it seems to them absurd and refutable simply by logic. I believe this is only because they have never studied the relevant phenomena of hypnosis and dreams, which—quite apart from pathological manifestations —necessitate this view. Their psychology of consciousness is incapable of solving the problems of dreams and hypnosis.

'Being conscious' [1] is in the first place a purely descriptive term, resting on perception of the most immediate and certain

---

[1] ['*Bewusst sein*' (in two words) in the original. Similarly in Chapter II of *Lay Analysis* (1926e), *Standard Ed.*, **20**, 197. '*Bewusstsein*' is the regular German word for 'consciousness', and printing it in two words emphasizes the fact that '*bewusst*' is in its form a passive participle—'being conscioused'. The English 'conscious' is capable of an active or a passive use; but in these discussions it is always to be taken as passive. Cf. a footnote at the end of the Editor's Note to Freud's metapsychological paper on 'The Unconscious', *Standard Ed.*, **14**, 165.]

character. Experience goes on to show that a psychical element (for instance, an idea) is not as a rule conscious for a protracted length of time. On the contrary, a state of consciousness is characteristically very transitory; an idea that is conscious now is no longer so a moment later, although it can become so again under certain conditions that are easily brought about. In the interval the idea was—we do not know what. We can say that it was *latent*, and by this we mean that it was *capable of becoming conscious* at any time. Or, if we say that is was *unconscious*, we shall also be giving a correct description of it. Here 'unconscious' coincides with 'latent and capable of becoming conscious'. The philosophers would no doubt object: 'No, the term "unconscious" is not applicable here; so long as the idea was in a state of latency it was not anything psychical at all.' To contradict them at this point would lead to nothing more profitable than a verbal dispute.

But we have arrived at the term or concept of the unconscious along another path, by considering certain experiences in which mental *dynamics* play a part. We have found—that is, we have been obliged to assume—that very powerful mental processes or ideas exist (and here a quantitative or *economic* factor comes into question for the first time) which can produce all the effects in mental life that ordinary ideas do (including effects that can in their turn become conscious as ideas), though they themselves do not become conscious. It is unnecessary to repeat in detail here what has been explained so often before.[1] It is enough to say that at this point psycho-analytic theory steps in and asserts that the reason why such ideas cannot become conscious is that a certain force opposes them, that otherwise they could become conscious, and that it would then be apparent how little they differ from other elements which are admittedly psychical. The fact that in the technique of psycho-analysis a means has been found by which the opposing force can be removed and the ideas in question made conscious renders this theory irrefutable. The state in which the ideas existed before being made conscious is called by us *repression*, and we assert that the force which instituted the repression and maintains it is perceived as *resistance* during the work of analysis.

[1] [See, for instance, 'A Note on the Unconscious' (1912*g*), *Standard Ed.*, **12**, 262 and 264.]

Thus we obtain our concept of the unconscious from the theory of repression. The repressed is the prototype of the unconscious for us. We see, however, that we have two kinds of unconscious—the one which is latent but capable of becoming conscious, and the one which is repressed and which is not, in itself and without more ado, capable of becoming conscious. This piece of insight into psychical dynamics cannot fail to affect terminology and description. The latent, which is unconscious only descriptively, not in the dynamic sense, we call *preconscious*; we restrict the term *unconscious* to the dynamically unconscious repressed; so that now we have three terms, conscious (*Cs.*), preconscious (*Pcs.*), and unconscious (*Ucs.*), whose sense is no longer purely descriptive. The *Pcs.* is presumably a great deal closer to the *Cs.* than is the *Ucs.*, and since we have called the *Ucs.* psychical we shall with even less hesitation call the latent *Pcs.* psychical. But why do we not rather, instead of this, remain in agreement with the philosophers and, in a consistent way, distinguish the *Pcs.* as well as the *Ucs.* from the conscious psychical? The philosophers would then propose that the *Pcs.* and the *Ucs.* should be described as two species or stages of the 'psychoid', and harmony would be established. But endless difficulties in exposition would follow; and the one important fact, that these two kinds of 'psychoid' coincide in almost every other respect with what is admittedly psychical, would be forced into the background in the interests of a prejudice dating from a period in which these psychoids, or the most important part of them, were still unknown.

We can now play about comfortably with our three terms, *Cs.*, *Pcs.*, and *Ucs.*, so long as we do not forget that in the descriptive sense there are two kinds of unconscious, but in the dynamic sense only one.[1] For purposes of exposition this distinction can in some cases be ignored, but in others it is of course indispensable. At the same time, we have become more or less accustomed to this ambiguity of the unconscious and have managed pretty well with it. As far as I can see, it is impossible to avoid this ambiguity; the distinction between conscious and unconscious is in the last resort a question of perception, which must be answered 'yes' or 'no', and the act of perception itself tells us nothing of the reason why a thing is or

[1] [Some comments on this sentence will be found in Appendix A (p. 60).]

is not perceived. No one has a right to complain because the actual phenomenon expresses the dynamic factor ambiguously.[1]

In the further course of psycho-analytic work, however, even

[1] This may be compared so far with my 'Note on the Unconscious in Psycho-Analysis' (1912g). [Cf. also Sections I and II of the metapsychological paper on 'The Unconscious' (1915e).] A new turn taken by criticisms of the unconscious deserves consideration at this point. Some investigators, who do not refuse to recognize the facts of psycho-analysis but who are unwilling to accept the unconscious, find a way out of the difficulty in the fact, which no one contests, that in consciousness (regarded as a phenomenon) it is possible to distinguish a great variety of gradations in intensity or clarity. Just as there are processes which are very vividly, glaringly, and tangibly conscious, so we also experience others which are only faintly, hardly even noticeably conscious; those that are most faintly conscious are, it is argued, the ones to which psycho-analysis wishes to apply the unsuitable name 'unconscious'. These too, however (the argument proceeds), are conscious or 'in consciousness', and can be made fully and intensely conscious if sufficient attention is paid to them.

In so far as it is possible to influence by arguments the decision of a question of this kind which depends either on convention or on emotional factors, we may make the following comments. The reference to gradations of clarity in consciousness is in no way conclusive and has no more evidential value than such analogous statements as: 'There are so very many gradations in illumination—from the most glaring and dazzling light to the dimmest glimmer—therefore there is no such thing as darkness at all'; or, 'There are varying degrees of vitality, therefore there is no such thing as death.' Such statements may in a certain way have a meaning, but for practical purposes they are worthless. This will be seen if one tries to draw particular conclusions from them, such as, 'there is therefore no need to strike a light', or, 'therefore all organisms are immortal'. Further, to include 'what is unnoticeable' under the concept of 'what is conscious' is simply to play havoc with the one and only piece of direct and certain knowledge that we have about the mind. And after all, a consciousness of which one knows nothing seems to me a good deal more absurd than something mental that is unconscious. Finally, this attempt to equate what is unnoticed with what is unconscious is obviously made without taking into account the dynamic conditions involved, which were the decisive factors in forming the dsycho-analytic view. For it ignores two facts: first, that it is exceedingly difficult and requires very great effort to concentrate enough attention on something unnoticed of this kind; and secondly, that when this has been achieved the thought which was previously unnoticed is not recognized by consciousness, but often seems entirely alien and opposed to it and is promptly disavowed by it. Thus, seeking refuge from the unconscious in what is scarcely noticed or unnoticed is after all only a derivative of the preconceived belief which regards the identity of the psychical and the conscious as settled once and for all.

these distinctions have proved to be inadequate and, for practical purposes, insufficient. This has become clear in more ways than one; but the decisive instance is as follows. We have formed the idea that in each individual there is a coherent organization of mental processes; and we call this his *ego*. It is to this ego that consciousness is attached; the ego controls the approaches to motility—that is, to the discharge of excitations into the external world; it is the mental agency which supervises all its own constituent processes, and which goes to sleep at night, though even then it exercises the censorship on dreams. From this ego proceed the repressions, too, by means of which it is sought to exclude certain trends in the mind not merely from consciousness but also from other forms of effectiveness and activity. In analysis these trends which have been shut out stand in opposition to the ego, and the analysis is faced with the task of removing the resistances which the ego displays against concerning itself with the repressed. Now we find during analysis that, when we put certain tasks before the patient, he gets into difficulties; his associations fail when they should be coming near the repressed. We then tell him that he is dominated by a resistance; but he is quite unaware of the fact, and, even if he guesses from his unpleasurable feelings that a resistance is now at work in him, he does not know what it is or how to describe it. Since, however, there can be no question but that this resistance emanates from his ego and belongs to it, we find ourselves in an unforeseen situation. We have come upon something in the ego itself which is also unconscious, which behaves exactly like the repressed—that is, which produces powerful effects without itself being conscious and which requires special work before it can be made conscious. From the point of view of analytic practice, the consequence of this discovery is that we land in endless obscurities and difficulties if we keep to our habitual forms of expression and try, for instance, to derive neuroses from a conflict between the conscious and the unconscious. We shall have to substitute for this antithesis another, taken from our insight into the structural conditions of the mind—the antithesis between the coherent ego and the repressed which is split off from it.[1]

For our conception of the unconscious, however, the consequences of our discovery are even more important. Dynamic

[1] Cf. *Beyond the Pleasure Principle* (1920g) [*Standard Ed.*, 18, 19].

considerations caused us to make our first correction; our insight into the structure of the mind leads to the second. We recognize that the *Ucs.* does not coincide with the repressed; it is still true that all that is repressed is *Ucs.*, but not all that is *Ucs.* is repressed. A part of the ego, too—and Heaven knows how important a part—may be *Ucs.*, undoubtedly is *Ucs.*[1] And this *Ucs.* belonging to the ego is not latent like the *Pcs.*; for if it were, it could not be activated without becoming *Cs.*, and the process of making it conscious would not encounter such great difficulties. When we find ourselves thus confronted by the necessity of postulating a third *Ucs.*, which is not repressed, we must admit that the characteristic of being unconscious begins to lose significance for us. It becomes a quality which can have many meanings, a quality which we are unable to make, as we should have hoped to do, the basis of far-reaching and inevitable conclusions. Nevertheless we must beware of ignoring this characteristic, for the property of being conscious or not is in the last resort our one beacon-light in the darkness of depth-psychology.

[1] [This had already been stated not only in *Beyond the Pleasure Principle* (loc. cit.) but earlier, in 'The Unconscious' (1915*e*), *Standard Ed.*, **14**, 192–3. Indeed, it was implied in a remark at the beginning of the second paper on 'The Neuro-Psychoses of Defence' (1896*b*).]

THE EGO AND THE ID

PATHOLOGICAL research has directed our interest too exclusively to the repressed. We should like to learn more about the ego, now that we know that it, too, can be unconscious in the proper sense of the word. Hitherto the only guide we have had during our investigations has been the distinguishing mark of being conscious or unconscious; we have finally come to see how ambiguous this can be.

Now all our knowledge is invariably bound up with consciousness. We can come to know even the *Ucs.* only by making it conscious. But stop, how is that possible? What does it mean when we say 'making something conscious'? How can that come about?

We already know the point from which we have to start in this connection. We have said that consciousness is the *surface* of the mental apparatus; that is, we have ascribed it as a function to a system which is spatially the first one reached from the external world—and spatially not only in the functional sense but, on this occasion, also in the sense of anatomical dissection.[1] Our investigations too must take this perceiving surface as a starting-point.

All perceptions which are received from without (sense-perceptions) and from within—what we call sensations and feelings—are *Cs.* from the start. But what about those internal processes which we may—roughly and inexactly—sum up under the name of thought-processes? They represent displacements of mental energy which are effected somewhere in the interior of the apparatus as this energy proceeds on its way towards action. Do they advance to the surface, which causes consciousness to be generated? Or does consciousness make its way to them? This is clearly one of the difficulties that arise when one begins to take the spatial or 'topographical' idea of mental life seriously. Both these possibilities are equally unimaginable; there must be a third alternative.[2]

[1] *Beyond the Pleasure Principle* [*Standard Ed.*, **18**, 26].
[2] [This had been discussed at greater length in the second section of 'The Unconscious' (1915*e*), *Standard Ed.*, **18**, 173–6.]

I have already, in another place,[1] suggested that the real difference between a *Ucs.* and a *Pcs.* idea (thought) consists in this: that the former is carried out on some material which remains unknown, whereas the latter (the *Pcs.*) is in addition brought into connection with word-presentations. This is the first attempt to indicate distinguishing marks for the two systems, the *Pcs.* and the *Ucs.*, other than their relation to consciousness. The question, 'How does a thing become conscious?' would thus be more advantageously stated: 'How does a thing become preconscious?' And the answer would be: 'Through becoming connected with the word-presentations corresponding to it.'

These word-presentations are residues of memories; they were at one time perceptions, and like all mnemic residues they can become conscious again. Before we concern ourselves further with their nature, it dawns upon us like a new discovery that only something which has once been a *Cs.* perception can become conscious, and that anything arising from within (apart from feelings) that seeks to become conscious must try to transform itself into external perceptions: this becomes possible by means of memory-traces.

We think of the mnemic residues as being contained in systems which are directly adjacent to the system *Pcpt.-Cs.*, so that the cathexes of those residues can readily extend from within on to the elements of the latter system.[2] We immediately think here of hallucinations, and of the fact that the most vivid memory is always distinguishable both from a hallucination and from an external perception;[3] but it will also occur to us at once that when a memory is revived the cathexis remains in the mnemic system, whereas a hallucination, which is not distinguishable from a perception, can arise when the cathexis does not merely spread over from the memory-trace on to the *Pcpt.* element, but passes over to it *entirely*.

Verbal residues are derived primarily from auditory perceptions,[4] so that the system *Pcs.* has, as it were, a special

---

[1] 'The Unconscious' [ibid., 201 ff.].

[2] [Cf. Chapter VII (B) of *The Interpretation of Dreams* (1900a), *Standard Ed.*, 5, 538.]

[3] [This view had been expressed by Breuer in his theoretical contribution to *Studies on Hysteria* (1895d), *Standard Ed.*, 2, 188.]

[4] [Freud had arrived at this conclusion in his monograph on aphasia (1891b) on the basis of pathological findings (ibid., 92–4). The point

sensory source. The visual components of word-presentations are secondary, acquired through reading, and may to begin with be left on one side; so may the motor images of words, which, except with deaf-mutes, play the part of auxiliary indications. In essence a word is after all the mnemic residue of a word that has been heard.

We must not be led, in the interests of simplification perhaps, to forget the importance of optical mnemic residues, when they are of *things*, or to deny that it is possible for thought-processes to become conscious through a reversion to visual residues, and that in many people this seems to be the favoured method. The study of dreams and of preconscious phantasies as shown in Varendonck's observations[1] can give us an idea of the special character of this visual thinking. We learn that what becomes conscious in it is as a rule only the concrete subject-matter of the thought, and that the relations between the various elements of this subject-matter, which is what specially characterizes thoughts, cannot be given visual expression. Thinking in pictures is, therefore, only a very incomplete form of becoming conscious. In some way, too, it stands nearer to unconscious processes than does thinking in words, and it is unquestionably older than the latter both ontogenetically and phylogenetically.

To return to our argument: if, therefore, this is the way in which something that is in itself unconscious becomes preconscious, the question how we make something that is repressed (pre)conscious would be answered as follows. It is done by supplying *Pcs.* intermediate links through the work of analysis. Consciousness remains where it is, therefore; but, on the other hand, the *Ucs.* does not rise into the *Cs.*

Whereas the relation of *external* perceptions to the ego is quite perspicuous, that of *internal* perceptions to the ego requires special investigation. It gives rise once more to a doubt whether we are really right in referring the whole of consciousness to the single superficial system *Pcpt.-Cs.*

Internal perceptions yield sensations of processes arising in the most diverse and certainly also in the deepest strata of the

is represented in the diagram reproduced from that work in Appendix C to the paper on 'The Unconscious', *Standard Ed.*, 14, 214.]

[1] [Cf. Varendonck (1921), a book to which Freud contributed an introduction (1921b).]

mental apparatus. Very little is known about these sensations and feelings; those belonging to the pleasure-unpleasure series may still be regarded as the best examples of them. They are more primordial, more elementary, than perceptions arising externally and they can come about even when consciousness is clouded. I have elsewhere[1] expressed my views about their greater economic significance and the metapsychological reasons for this. These sensations are multilocular, like external perceptions; they may come from different places simultaneously and may thus have different or even opposite qualities.

Sensations of a pleasurable nature have not anything inherently impelling about them, whereas unpleasurable ones have it in the highest degree. The latter impel towards change, towards discharge, and that is why we interpret unpleasure as implying a heightening and pleasure a lowering of energic cathexis.[2] Let us call what becomes conscious as pleasure and unpleasure a quantitative and qualitative 'something' in the course of mental events; the question then is whether this 'something' can become conscious in the place where it is, or whether it must first be transmitted to the system *Pcpt*.

Clinical experience decides for the latter. It shows us that this 'something' behaves like a repressed impulse. It can exert driving force without the ego noticing the compulsion. Not until there is resistance to the compulsion, a hold-up in the discharge-reaction, does the 'something' at once become conscious as unpleasure. In the same way that tensions arising from physical needs can remain unconscious, so also can pain—a thing intermediate between external and internal perception, which behaves like an internal perception even when its source is in the external world. It remains true, therefore, that sensations and feelings, too, only become conscious through reaching the system *Pcpt*.; if the way forward is barred, they do not come into being as sensations, although the 'something' that corresponds to them in the course of excitation is the same as if they did. We then come to speak, in a condensed and not entirely correct manner, of 'unconscious feelings', keeping up an analogy with unconscious ideas which is not altogether justifiable. Actually the difference is that, whereas with *Ucs. ideas* connecting links must be created before they can be

[1] [*Beyond the Pleasure Principle* (1920g), *Standard Ed.*, 18, 29.]
[2] [Ibid., 8.]

brought into the *Cs.*, with *feelings*, which are themselves transmitted directly, this does not occur. In other words: the distinction between *Cs.* and *Pcs.* has no meaning where feelings are concerned; the *Pcs.* here drops out—and feelings are either conscious or unconscious. Even when they are attached to word-presentations, their becoming conscious is not due to that circumstance, but they become so directly.[1]

The part played by word-presentations now becomes perfectly clear. By their interposition internal thought-processes are made into perceptions. It is like a demonstration of the theorem that all knowledge has its origin in external perception. When a hypercathexis of the process of thinking takes place, thoughts are *actually* perceived—as if they came from without—and are consequently held to be true.

After this clarifying of the relations between external and internal perception and the superficial system *Pcpt.-Cs.*, we can go on to work out our idea of the ego. It starts out, as we see, from the system *Pcpt.*, which is its nucleus, and begins by embracing the *Pcs.*, which is adjacent to the mnemic residues. But, as we have learnt, the ego is also unconscious.

Now I think we shall gain a great deal by following the suggestion of a writer who, from personal motives, vainly asserts that he has nothing to do with the rigours of pure science. I am speaking of Georg Groddeck, who is never tired of insisting that what we call our ego behaves essentially passively in life, and that, as he expresses it, we are 'lived' by unknown and uncontrollable forces.[2] We have all had impressions of the same kind, even though they may not have overwhelmed us to the exclusion of all others, and we need feel no hesitation in finding a place for Groddeck's discovery in the structure of science. I propose to take it into account by calling the entity which starts out from the system *Pcpt.* and begins by being *Pcs.* the 'ego', and by following Groddeck in calling the other part of the mind, into which this entity extends and which behaves as though it were *Ucs.*, the 'id'.[3]

---

[1] [Cf. Section III of 'The Unconscious' (1915e), *Standard Ed.*, 14, 177–8.]   [2] Groddeck (1923).

[3] [See Editor's Introduction, p. 7.]—Groddeck himself no doubt followed the example of Nietzsche, who habitually used this grammatical term for whatever in our nature is impersonal and, so to speak, subject to natural law.

We shall soon see whether we can derive any advantage from this view for purposes either of description or of understanding. We shall now look upon an individual as a psychical id, unknown and unconscious, upon whose surface rests the ego, developed from its nucleus the *Pcpt.* system. If we make an effort to represent this pictorially, we may add that the ego does not completely envelop the id, but only does so to the extent to which the system *Pcpt.* forms its [the ego's] surface, more or less as the germinal disc rests upon the ovum. The ego is not sharply separated from the id; its lower portion merges into it.

But the repressed merges into the id as well, and is merely a part of it. The repressed is only cut off sharply from the ego by the resistances of repression; it can communicate with the ego through the id. We at once realize that almost all the lines of demarcation we have drawn at the instigation of pathology relate only to the superficial strata of the mental apparatus—the only ones known to us. The state of things which we have been describing can be represented diagrammatically (Fig. 1);[1] though it must be remarked that the form chosen has no pretensions to any special applicability, but is merely intended to serve for purposes of exposition.

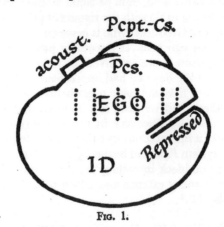

Fig. 1.

[1] [Compare the slightly different diagram near the end of Lecture XXXI of the *New Introductory Lectures* (1933*a*). The entirely different one in *The Interpretation of Dreams* (1900*a*), *Standard Ed.*, 5, 541, and its predecessor in a letter to Fliess of December 6, 1896 (Freud, 1950*a*, Letter 52), are concerned with function as well as structure.]

We might add, perhaps, that the ego wears a 'cap of hearing' [1] —on one side only, as we learn from cerebral anatomy. It might be said to wear it awry.

It is easy to see that the ego is that part of the id which has been modified ·by the direct influence of the external world through the medium of the *Pcpt.-Cs.*; in a sense it is an extension of the surface-differentiation. Moreover, the ego seeks to bring the influence of the external world to bear upon the id and its tendencies, and endeavours to substitute the reality principle for the pleasure principle which reigns unrestrictedly in the id. For the ego, perception plays the part which in the id falls to instinct. The ego represents what may be called reason and common sense, in contrast to the id, which contains the passions. All this falls into line with popular distinctions which we are all familiar with; at the same time, however, it is only to be regarded as holding good on the average or 'ideally'.

The functional importance of the ego is manifested in the fact that normally control over the approaches to motility devolves upon it. Thus in its relation to the id it is like a man on horseback, who has to hold in check the superior strength of the horse; with this difference, that the rider tries to do so with his own strength while the ego uses borrowed forces. The analogy may be carried a little further. Often a rider, if he is not to be parted from his horse, is obliged to guide it where it wants to go;[2] so in the same way the ego is in the habit of transforming the id's will into action as if it were its own.

Another factor, besides the influence of the system *Pcpt.*, seems to have played a part in bringing about the formation of the ego and its differentiation from the id. A person's own body, and above all its surface, is a place from which both external and internal perceptions may spring. It is *seen* like any other object, but to the *touch* it yields two kinds of sensations, one of which may be equivalent to an internal perception. Psychophysiology has fully discussed the manner in which a person's own body attains its special position among other objects in the world of perception. Pain, too, seems to play a part in the process, and the way in which we gain new knowledge of our organs

---

[1] ['*Hörkappe.*' I.e. the auditory lobe. Cf. footnote 4, p. 20 above.]
[2] [This analogy appears as an association to one of Freud's dreams in *The Interpretation of Dreams, Standard Ed.*, 4, 231.]

during painful illnesses is perhaps a model of the way by which in general we arrive at the idea of our body.

The ego is first and foremost a bodily ego; it is not merely a surface entity, but is itself the projection of a surface.[1] If we wish to find an anatomical analogy for it we can best identify it with the 'cortical homunculus' of the anatomists, which stands on its head in the cortex, sticks up its heels, faces backwards and, as we know, has its speech-area on the left-hand side.

The relation of the ego to consciousness has been entered into repeatedly; yet there are some important facts in this connection which remain to be described here. Accustomed as we are to taking our social or ethical scale of values along with us wherever we go, we feel no surprise at hearing that the scene of the activities of the lower passions is in the unconscious; we expect, moreover, that the higher any mental function ranks in our scale of values the more easily it will find access to consciousness assured to it. Here, however, psycho-analytic experience disappoints us. On the one hand, we have evidence that even subtle and difficult intellectual operations which ordinarily require strenuous reflection can equally be carried out preconsciously and without coming into consciousness. Instances of this are quite incontestable; they may occur, for example, during the state of sleep, as is shown when someone finds, immediately after waking, that he knows the solution to a difficult mathematical or other problem with which he had been wrestling in vain the day before.[2]

There is another phenomenon, however, which is far stranger. In our analyses we discover that there are people in whom the faculties of self-criticism and conscience—mental activities, that is, that rank as extremely high ones—are unconscious and unconsciously produce effects of the greatest importance; the example of resistance remaining unconscious during analysis is

---

[1] [I.e. the ego is ultimately derived from bodily sensations, chiefly from those springing from the surface of the body. It may thus be regarded as a mental projection of the surface of the body, besides, as we have seen above, representing the superficies of the mental apparatus.— This footnote first appeared in the English translation of 1927, in which it was described as having been authorized by Freud. It does not appear in the German editions.]

[2] I was quite recently told an instance of this which was, in fact, brought up as an objection against my description of the 'dream-work'. [Cf. *The Interpretation of Dreams, Standard Ed.*, 4, 64, and 5, 564.]

therefore by no means unique. But this new discovery, which compels us, in spite of our better critical judgement, to speak of an 'unconscious sense of guilt',[1] bewilders us far more than the other and sets us fresh problems, especially when we gradually come to see that in a great number of neuroses an unconscious sense of guilt of this kind plays a decisive economic part and puts the most powerful obstacles in the way of recovery.[2] If we come back once more to our scale of values, we shall have to say that not only what is lowest but also what is highest in the ego can be unconscious. It is as if we were thus supplied with a proof of what we have just asserted of the conscious ego: that it is first and foremost a body-ego.

[1] [This phrase had already appeared in Freud's paper on 'Obsessive Actions and Religious Practices' (1907b), *Standard Ed.*, 9, 123. The notion was, however, foreshadowed much earlier, in Section II of the first paper on 'The Neuro-Psychoses of Defence' (1894a).]
[2] [This is further discussed below, p. 49 ff.]

THE EGO AND THE SUPER-EGO (EGO IDEAL)

IF the ego were merely the part of the id modified by the influence of the perceptual system, the representative in the mind of the real external world, we should have a simple state of things to deal with. But there is a further complication.

The considerations that led us to assume the existence of a grade in the ego, a differentiation within the ego, which may be called the 'ego ideal' or 'super-ego', have been stated elsewhere.[1] They still hold good.[2] The fact that this part of the ego is less firmly connected with consciousness is the novelty which calls for explanation.

At this point we must widen our range a little. We succeeded in explaining the painful disorder of melancholia by supposing that [in those suffering from it] an object which was lost has been set up again inside the ego—that is, that an object-cathexis has been replaced by an identification.[3] At that time, however, we did not appreciate the full significance of this process and did not know how common and how typical it is. Since then we have come to understand that this kind of substitution has a great share in determining the form taken by the ego and that it makes an essential contribution towards building up what is called its 'character'.[4]

---

[1] [See Editor's Introduction, pp. 9–10.] Cf. 'On Narcissism: an Introduction' (1914c), and *Group Psychology and the Analysis of the Ego* (1921c).

[2] Except that I seem to have been mistaken in ascribing the function of 'reality-testing' to this super-ego—a point which needs correction. [See *Group Psychology* (1921c), *Standard Ed.*, **18**, 114 and *n.* 2, and the Editor's Note to the metapsychological paper on dreams (1917d), **14**, 220.] It would fit in perfectly with the relations of the ego to the world of perception if reality-testing remained a task of the ego itself. Some earlier suggestions about a 'nucleus of the ego', never very definitely formulated, also require to be put right, since the system *Pcpt.-Cs.* alone can be regarded as the nucleus of the ego. [In *Beyond the Pleasure Principle* (1920g) Freud had spoken of the unconscious part of the ego as its nucleus (*Standard Ed.*, **18**, 19); and in his later paper on 'Humour' (1927d) he referred to the super-ego as the nucleus of the ego.]

[3] 'Mourning and Melancholia' (1917e) [*Standard Ed.*, **14**, 249].

[4] [Some references to other passages in which Freud has discussed

At the very beginning, in the individual's primitive oral phase, object-cathexis and identification are no doubt indistinguishable from each other.[1] We can only suppose that later on object-cathexes proceed from the id, which feels erotic trends as needs. The ego, which to begin with is still feeble, becomes aware of the object-cathexes, and either acquiesces in them or tries to fend them off by the process of repression.[2]

When it happens that a person has to give up a sexual object, there quite often ensues an alteration of his ego which can only be described as a setting up of the object inside the ego, as it occurs in melancholia; the exact nature of this substitution is as yet unknown to us. It may be that by this introjection, which is a kind of regression to the mechanism of the oral phase, the ego makes it easier for the object to be given up or renders that process possible. It may be that this identification is the sole condition under which the id can give up its objects. At any rate the process, especially in the early phases of development, is a very frequent one, and it makes it possible to suppose that the character of the ego is a precipitate of abandoned object-cathexes and that it contains the history of those object-choices. It must, of course, be admitted from the outset that there are varying degrees of capacity for resistance, which decide the extent to which a person's character fends off or accepts the influences of the history of his erotic object-choices. In women who have had many experiences in love there seems to be no difficulty in finding vestiges of their object-cathexes in the traits of their character. We must also take into consideration cases of simultaneous object-cathexis and identification—cases, that

character-formation will be found in an Editor's footnote at the end of the paper on 'Character and Anal Erotism' (1908b), Standard Ed., 9, 175.]

[1] [Cf. Chapter VII of Group Psychology (1921c), Standard Ed., 18, 105.]

[2] An interesting parallel to the replacement of object-choice by identification is to be found in the belief of primitive peoples, and in the prohibitions based upon it, that the attributes of animals which are incorporated as nourishment persist as part of the character of those who eat them. As is well known, this belief is one of the roots of cannibalism and its effects have continued through the series of usages of the totem meal down to Holy Communion. [Cf. Totem and Taboo (1912–13), Standard Ed., 13, 82, 142, 154–5, etc.] The consequences ascribed by this belief to oral mastery of the object do in fact follow in the case of the later sexual object-choice.

is, in which the alteration in character occurs before the object
has been given up. In such cases the alteration in character has
been able to survive the object-relation and in a certain sense
to conserve it.

From another point of view it may be said that this transformation of an erotic object-choice into an alteration of the
ego is also a method by which the ego can obtain control over
the id and deepen its relations with it—at the cost, it is true,
of acquiescing to a large extent in the id's experiences. When
the ego assumes the features of the object, it is forcing itself,
so to speak, upon the id as a love-object and is trying to make
good the id's loss by saying: 'Look, you can love me too—I am
so like the object.'

The transformation of object-libido into narcissistic libido
which thus takes place obviously implies an abandonment of
sexual aims, a desexualization—a kind of sublimation, therefore. Indeed, the question arises, and deserves careful consideration, whether this is not the universal road to sublimation, whether all sublimation does not take place through the
mediation of the ego, which begins by changing sexual object-
libido into narcissistic libido and then, perhaps, goes on to give
it another aim.[1] We shall later on have to consider whether
other instinctual vicissitudes may not also result from this
transformation, whether, for instance, it may not bring about
a defusion of the various instincts that are fused together.[2]

Although it is a digression from our aim, we cannot avoid
giving our attention for a moment longer to the ego's object-
identifications. If they obtain the upper hand and become too
numerous, unduly powerful and incompatible with one another,
a pathological outcome will not be far off. It may come to a
disruption of the ego in consequence of the different identifications becoming cut off from one another by resistances; perhaps

[1] Now that we have distinguished between the ego and the id, we
must recognize the id as the great reservoir of libido indicated in my
paper on narcissism (1914c) [Standard Ed., 14, 75]. The libido which
flows into the ego owing to the identifications described above brings
about its 'secondary narcissism'. [The point is elaborated below on
p. 46.]

[2] [Freud returns to the subject of this paragraph below, on pp. 45
and 54. The concept of the fusion and defusion of instincts is explained
on pp. 41–2. The terms had been introduced already in an encyclopaedia article (1923a), Standard Ed., 18, 258.]

the secret of the cases of what is described as 'multiple personality' is that the different identifications seize hold of consciousness in turn. Even when things do not go so far as this, there remains the question of conflicts between the various identifications into which the ego comes apart, conflicts which cannot after all be described as entirely pathological.

But, whatever the character's later capacity for resisting the influences of abandoned object-cathexes may turn out to be, the effects of the first identifications made in earliest childhood will be general and lasting. This leads us back to the origin of the ego ideal; for behind it there lies hidden an individual's first and most important identification, his identification with the father in his own personal prehistory.[1] This is apparently not in the first instance the consequence or outcome of an object-cathexis; it is a direct and immediate identification and takes place earlier than any object-cathexis.[2] But the object-choices belonging to the first sexual period and relating to the father and mother seem normally to find their outcome in an identification of this kind, and would thus reinforce the primary one.

The whole subject, however, is so complicated that it will be necessary to go into it in greater detail. The intricacy of the problem is due to two factors: the triangular character of the Oedipus situation and the constitutional bisexuality of each individual.

In its simplified form the case of a male child may be described as follows. At a very early age the little boy develops an object-cathexis for his mother, which originally related to the mother's breast and is the prototype of an object-choice on the anaclitic model;[3] the boy deals with his father by identifying himself with him. For a time these two relationships proceed

[1] Perhaps it would be safer to say 'with the parents'; for before a child has arrived at definite knowledge of the difference between the sexes, the lack of a penis, it does not distinguish in value between its father and its mother. I recently came across the instance of a young married woman whose story showed that, after noticing the lack of a penis in herself, she had supposed it to be absent not in all women, but only in those whom she regarded as inferior, and had still supposed that her mother possessed one. [Cf. a footnote to 'The Infantile Genital Organization' (1923e), p. 145 below.]—In order to simplify my presentation I shall discuss only identification with the father.

[2] [See the beginning of Chapter VII of *Group Psychology* (1921c), *Standard Ed.*, **18**, 105.]

[3] [See the paper on narcissism (1914c), *Standard Ed.*, **14**, 87 ff.]

side by side, until the boy's sexual wishes in regard to his mother become more intense and his father is perceived as an obstacle to them; from this the Oedipus complex originates.[1] His identification with his father then takes on a hostile colouring and changes into a wish to get rid of his father in order to take his place with his mother. Henceforward his relation to his father is ambivalent; it seems as if the ambivalence inherent in the identification from the beginning had become manifest. An ambivalent attitude to his father and an object-relation of a solely affectionate kind to his mother make up the content of the simple positive Oedipus complex in a boy.

Along with the demolition of the Oedipus complex, the boy's object-cathexis of his mother must be given up. Its place may be filled by one of two things: either an identification with his mother or an intensification of his identification with his father. We are accustomed to regard the latter outcome as the more normal; it permits the affectionate relation to the mother to be in a measure retained. In this way the dissolution of the Oedipus complex[2] would consolidate the masculinity in a boy's character. In a precisely analogous way,[3] the outcome of the Oedipus attitude in a little girl may be an intensification of her identification with her mother (or the setting up of such an identification for the first time)—a result which will fix the child's feminine character.

These identifications are not what we should have expected [from the previous account (p. 29)], since they do not introduce the abandoned object into the ego; but this alternative outcome may also occur, and is easier to observe in girls than in boys. Analysis very often shows that a little girl, after she has had to relinquish her father as a love-object, will bring her masculinity into prominence and identify herself with her father (that is, with the object which has been lost), instead of with her mother. This will clearly depend on whether the masculinity in her disposition—whatever that may consist in— is strong enough.

[1] Cf. *Group Psychology* (1921c), loc. cit.

[2] [Cf. the paper bearing this title (1924d) in which Freud discussed the question more fully. (P. 173 below.)]

[3] [The idea that the outcome of the Oedipus complex was 'precisely analogous' in girls and boys was abandoned by Freud not long after this. See 'Some Psychical Consequences of the Anatomical Distinction between the Sexes' (1925j), p. 248 below.]

It would appear, therefore, that in both sexes the relative strength of the masculine and feminine sexual dispositions is what determines whether the outcome of the Oedipus situation shall be an identification with the father or with the mother. This is one of the ways in which bisexuality takes a hand in the subsequent vicissitudes of the Oedipus complex. The other way is even more important. For one gets an impression that the simple Oedipus complex is by no means its commonest form, but rather represents a simplification or schematization which, to be sure, is often enough justified for practical purposes. Closer study usually discloses the more complete Oedipus complex, which is twofold, positive and negative, and is due to the bisexuality originally present in children: that is to say, a boy has not merely an ambivalent attitude towards his father and an affectionate object-choice towards his mother, but at the same time he also behaves like a girl and displays an affectionate feminine attitude to his father and a corresponding jealousy and hostility towards his mother. It is this complicating element introduced by bisexuality that makes it so difficult to obtain a clear view of the facts in connection with the earliest object-choices and identifications, and still more difficult to describe them intelligibly. It may even be that the ambivalence displayed in the relations to the parents should be attributed entirely to bisexuality and that it is not, as I have represented above, developed out of identification in consequence of rivalry.[1]

In my opinion it is advisable in general, and quite especially where neurotics are concerned, to assume the existence of the complete Oedipus complex. Analytic experience then shows that in a number of cases one or the other constituent disappears, except for barely distinguishable traces; so that the

---

[1] [Freud's belief in the importance of bisexuality went back a very long way. In the first edition of the *Three Essays* (1905*d*), for instance, he wrote: 'Without taking bisexuality into account I think it would scarcely be possible to arrive at an understanding of the sexual manifestations that are actually to be observed in men and women.' (*Standard Ed.*, 7, 220.) But still earlier we find a passage in a letter to Fliess (who influenced him greatly on this subject) which seems almost to foreshadow the present paragraph (Freud, 1950*a*, Letter 113, of August 1, 1899): 'Bisexuality! I am sure you are right about it. And I am accustoming myself to regarding every sexual act as an event between four individuals.']

result is a series with the normal positive Oedipus complex at one end and the inverted negative one at the other, while its intermediate members exhibit the complete form with one or other of its two components preponderating. At the dissolution of the Oedipus complex the four trends of which it consists will group themselves in such a way as to produce a father-identification and a mother-identification. The father-identification will preserve the object-relation to the mother which belonged to the positive complex and will at the same time replace the object-relation to the father which belonged to the inverted complex: and the same will be true, *mutatis mutandis*, of the mother-identification. The relative intensity of the two identifications in any individual will reflect the preponderance in him of one or other of the two sexual dispositions.

The broad general outcome of the sexual phase dominated by the Oedipus complex may, therefore, be taken to be the forming of a precipitate in the ego, consisting of these two identifications in some way united with each other. This modification of the ego retains its special position; it confronts the other contents of the ego as an ego ideal or super-ego.

The super-ego is, however, not simply a residue of the earliest object-choices of the id; it also represents an energetic reaction-formation against those choices. Its relation to the ego is not exhausted by the precept: 'You *ought to be* like this (like your father).' It also comprises the prohibition: 'You *may not be* like this (like your father)—that is, you may not do all that he does; some things are his prerogative.' This double aspect of the ego ideal derives from the fact that the ego ideal had the task of repressing the Oedipus complex; indeed, it is to that revolutionary event that it owes its existence. Clearly the repression of the Oedipus complex was no easy task. The child's parents, and especially his father, were perceived as the obstacle to a realization of his Oedipus wishes; so his infantile ego fortified itself for the carrying out of the repression by erecting this same obstacle within itself. It borrowed strength to do this, so to speak, from the father, and this loan was an extraordinarily momentous act. The super-ego retains the character of the father, while the more powerful the Oedipus complex was and the more rapidly it succumbed to repression (under the influence of authority, religious teaching, schooling and reading), the stricter will be the domination of the super-ego over the ego later on—in the form of conscience or perhaps of an unconscious sense of guilt. I shall presently [p. 48] bring forward a suggestion about the source of its power to dominate in this way —the source, that is, of its compulsive character which manifests itself in the form of a categorical imperative.

If we consider once more the origin of the super-ego as we have described it, we shall recognize that it is the outcome of two highly important factors, one of a biological and the other of a historical nature: namely, the lengthy duration in man of his childhood helplessness and dependence, and the fact of his Oedipus complex, the repression of which we have shown to be connected with the interruption of libidinal development by the latency period and so with the diphasic onset of man's sexual life.[1] According to one psycho-analytic hypothesis,[2] the last-mentioned phenomenon, which seems to be peculiar to man, is a heritage of the cultural development necessitated by the glacial epoch. We see, then, that the differentiation of the super-ego from the ego is no matter of chance; it represents the most important characteristics of the development both of the individual and of the species; indeed, by giving permanent expression to the influence of the parents it perpetuates the existence of the factors to which it owes its origin.

Psycho-analysis has been reproached time after time with ignoring the higher, moral, supra-personal side of human nature. The reproach is doubly unjust, both historically and methodologically. For, in the first place, we have from the very beginning attributed the function of instigating repression to the moral and aesthetic trends in the ego, and secondly, there has been a general refusal to recognize that psycho-analytic

[1] [In the German editions this sentence reads as follows: 'If we consider once more the origin of the super-ego as we have described it, we shall recognize that it is the outcome of two highly important biological factors: namely, the lengthy duration in man of his childhood helplessness and dependence, and the fact of his Oedipus complex, which we have traced back to the interruption of libidinal development by the latency period and so to the diphasic origin of man's sexual life.' The slightly different version given in the text above was inserted by Freud's express orders in the English translation in 1927. For some reason the emendations were not included in the later German editions.]

[2] [The idea was put forward by Ferenczi (1913). Freud seems to accept it rather more definitely near the end of Chapter X of *Inhibitions, Symptoms and Anxiety* (1926d), *Standard Ed.*, **20**, 155.]

research could not, like a philosophical system, produce a complete and ready-made theoretical structure, but had to find its way step by step along the path towards understanding the intricacies of the mind by making an analytic dissection of both normal and abnormal phenomena. So long as we had to concern ourselves with the study of what is repressed in mental life, there was no need for us to share in any agitated apprehensions as to the whereabouts of the higher side of man. But now that we have embarked upon the analysis of the ego we can give an answer to all those whose moral sense has been shocked and who have complained that there must surely be a higher nature in man: 'Very true,' we can say, 'and here we have that higher nature, in this ego ideal or super-ego, the representative of our relation to our parents. When we were little children we knew these higher natures, we admired them and feared them; and later we took them into ourselves.'

The ego ideal is therefore the heir of the Oedipus complex, and thus it is also the expression of the most powerful impulses and most important libidinal vicissitudes of the id. By setting up this ego ideal, the ego has mastered the Oedipus complex and at the same time placed itself in subjection to the id. Whereas the ego is essentially the representative of the external world, of reality, the super-ego stands in contrast to it as the representative of the internal world, of the id. Conflicts between the ego and the ideal will, as we are now prepared to find, ultimately reflect the contrast between what is real and what is psychical, between the external world and the internal world.

Through the forming of the ideal, what biology and the vicissitudes of the human species have created in the id and left behind in it is taken over by the ego and re-experienced in relation to itself as an individual. Owing to the way in which the ego ideal is formed, it has the most abundant links with the phylogenetic acquisition of each individual—his archaic heritage. What has belonged to the lowest part of the mental life of each of us is changed, through the formation of the ideal, into what is highest in the human mind by our scale of values. It would be vain, however, to attempt to localize the ego ideal, even in the sense in which we have localized the ego,[1] or to

---

[1] [The super-ego is accordingly not included in the diagram on p. 24. Nevertheless it is given a place in the later diagram in Lecture XXXI of the *New Introductory Lectures* (1933a).]

work it into any of the analogies with the help of which we have tried to picture the relation between the ego and the id.

It is easy to show that the ego ideal answers to everything that is expected of the higher nature of man. As a substitute for a longing for the father, it contains the germ from which all religions have evolved. The self-judgement which declares that the ego falls short of its ideal produces the religious sense of humility to which the believer appeals in his longing. As a child grows up, the role of father is carried on by teachers and others in authority; their injunctions and prohibitions remain powerful in the ego ideal and continue, in the form of conscience, to exercise the moral censorship. The tension between the demands of conscience and the actual performances of the ego is experienced as a sense of guilt. Social feelings rest on identifications with other people, on the basis of having the same ego ideal.

Religion, morality, and a social sense—the chief elements in the higher side of man[1]—were originally one and the same thing. According to the hypothesis which I put forward in *Totem and Taboo*[2] they were acquired phylogenetically out of the father-complex: religion and moral restraint through the process of mastering the Oedipus complex itself, and social feeling through the necessity for overcoming the rivalry that then remained between the members of the younger generation. The male sex seems to have taken the lead in all these moral acquisitions; and they seem to have then been transmitted to women by cross-inheritance. Even to-day the social feelings arise in the individual as a superstructure built upon impulses of jealous rivalry against his brothers and sisters. Since the hostility cannot be satisfied, an identification with the former rival develops. The study of mild cases of homosexuality confirms the suspicion that in this instance, too, the identification is a substitute for an affectionate object-choice which has taken the place of the aggressive, hostile attitude.[3]

With the mention of phylogenesis, however, fresh problems arise, from which one is tempted to draw cautiously back. But

[1] I am at the moment putting science and art on one side.

[2] [Freud (1912–13), *Standard Ed.*, **13**, 146 ff.]

[3] Cf. *Group Psychology* (1921c) [*Standard Ed.*, **18**, 120] and 'Some Neurotic Mechanisms in Jealousy, Paranoia and Homosexuality' (1922b) [ibid., 231].

there is no help for it, the attempt must be made—in spite of a fear that it will lay bare the inadequacy of our whole effort. The question is: which was it, the ego of primitive man or his id, that acquired religion and morality in those early days out of the father-complex? If it was his ego, why do we not speak simply of these things being inherited by the ego? If it was the id, how does that agree with the character of the id? Or are we wrong in carrying the differentiation between ego, super-ego, and id back into such early times? Or should we not honestly confess that our whole conception of the processes in the ego is of no help in understanding phylogenesis and cannot be applied to it?

Let us answer first what is easiest to answer. The differentiation between ego and id must be attributed not only to primitive man but even to much simpler organisms, for it is the inevitable expression of the influence of the external world. The super-ego, according to our hypothesis, actually originated from the experiences that led to totemism. The question whether it was the ego or the id that experienced and acquired these things soon comes to nothing. Reflection at once shows us that no external vicissitudes can be experienced or undergone by the id, except by way of the ego, which is the representative of the external world to the id. Nevertheless it is not possible to speak of direct inheritance in the ego. It is here that the gulf between an actual individual and the concept of a species becomes evident. Moreover, one must not take the difference between ego and id in too hard-and-fast a sense, nor forget that the ego is a specially differentiated part of the id [p. 25]. The experiences of the ego seem at first to be lost for inheritance; but, when they have been repeated often enough and with sufficient strength in many individuals in successive generations, they transform themselves, so to say, into experiences of the id, the impressions of which are preserved by heredity. Thus in the id, which is capable of being inherited, are harboured residues of the existences of countless egos; and, when the ego forms its super-ego out of the id, it may perhaps only be reviving shapes of former egos and be bringing them to resurrection.

The way in which the super-ego came into being explains how it is that the early conflicts of the ego with the object-cathexes of the id can be continued in conflicts with their heir, the super-ego. If the ego has not succeeded in properly master-ing the Oedipus complex, the energic cathexis of the latter, springing from the id, will come into operation once more in the reaction-formation of the ego ideal. The abundant com-munication between the ideal and these *Ucs.* instinctual impulses solves the puzzle of how it is that the ideal itself can to a great extent remain unconscious and inaccessible to the ego. The struggle which once raged in the deepest strata of the mind, and was not brought to an end by rapid sublimation and identification, is now continued in a higher region, like the Battle of the Huns in Kaulbach's painting.[1]

[1] [This was the battle, usually known as the Battle of Châlons, in which, in 451, Attila was defeated by the Romans and Visigoths. Wilhelm von Kaulbach (1805–1874) made it the subject of one of his mural decorations, originally painted for the Neues Museum in Berlin. In this the dead warriors are represented as continuing their fight in the sky above the battlefield, in accordance with a legend that can be traced back to the fifth century Neo-Platonist, Damascius.]

THE TWO CLASSES OF INSTINCTS

WE have already said that, if the differentiation we have made of the mind into an id, an ego, and a super-ego represents any advance in our knowledge, it ought to enable us to understand more thoroughly the dynamic relations within the mind and to describe them more clearly. We have also already concluded [p. 25] that the ego is especially under the influence of perception, and that, speaking broadly, perceptions may be said to have the same significance for the ego as instincts have for the id. At the same time the ego is subject to the influence of the instincts, too, like the id, of which it is, as we know, only a specially modified part.

I have lately developed a view of the instincts[1] which I shall here hold to and take as the basis of my further discussions. According to this view we have to distinguish two classes of instincts, one of which, the sexual instincts or Eros, is by far the more conspicuous and accessible to study. It comprises not merely the uninhibited sexual instinct proper and the instinctual impulses of an aim-inhibited or sublimated nature derived from it, but also the self-preservative instinct, which must be assigned to the ego and which at the beginning of our analytic work we had good reason for contrasting with the sexual object-instincts. The second class of instincts was not so easy to point to; in the end we came to recognize sadism as its representative. On the basis of theoretical considerations, supported by biology, we put forward the hypothesis of a death instinct, the task of which is to lead organic life back into the inanimate state; on the other hand, we supposed that Eros, by bringing about a more and more far-reaching combination of the particles into which living substance is dispersed, aims at complicating life and at the same time, of course, at preserving it. Acting in this way, both the instincts would be conservative in the strictest sense of the word, since both would be endeavouring to re-establish a state of things that was disturbed by the emergence of life. The emergence of life would thus be

Beyond the Pleasure Principle [1920g].

the cause of the continuance of life and also at the same time of the striving towards death; and life itself would be a conflict and compromise between these two trends. The problem of the origin of life would remain a cosmological one; and the problem of the goal and purpose of life would be answered dualistically.[1]

On this view, a special physiological process (of anabolism or catabolism) would be associated with each of the two classes of instincts; both kinds of instinct would be active in every particle of living substance, though in unequal proportions, so that some one substance might be the principal representative of Eros.

This hypothesis throws no light whatever upon the manner in which the two classes of instincts are fused, blended, and alloyed with each other; but that this takes place regularly and very extensively is an assumption indispensable to our conception. It appears that, as a result of the combination of unicellular organisms into multicellular forms of life, the death instinct of the single cell can successfully be neutralized and the destructive impulses be diverted on to the external world through the instrumentality of a special organ. This special organ would seem to be the muscular apparatus; and the death instinct would thus seem to express itself—though probably only in part—as an instinct of destruction directed against the external world and other organisms.[2]

Once we have admitted the idea of a fusion of the two classes of instincts with each other, the possibility of a—more or less complete—'defusion' of them forces itself upon us.[3] The sadistic component of the sexual instinct would be a classical example of a serviceable instinctual fusion; and the sadism which has made itself independent as a perversion would be typical of a defusion, though not of one carried to extremes. From this point we obtain a view of a great domain of facts which has not before been considered in this light. We perceive that for purposes of discharge the instinct of destruction is habitually brought into the service of Eros; we suspect that the epileptic fit is a product and indication of an instinctual defusion;[4] and we come to

[1] [Cf. footnote 2, p. 46 below.]
[2] [Freud returns to this in 'The Economic Problem of Masochism', p. 163 below.]
[3] [Cf. above, p. 30. What follows in regard to sadism is hinted at in *Beyond the Pleasure Principle*, Standard Ed., **18**, 54.]
[4] [Cf. Freud's later paper on Dostoevsky's fits (1928b).]

understand that instinctual defusion and the marked emergence of the death instinct call for particular consideration among the effects of some severe neuroses—for instance, the obsessional neuroses. Making a swift generalization, we might conjecture that the essence of a regression of libido (e.g. from the genital to the sadistic-anal phase) lies in a defusion of instincts, just as, conversely, the advance from the earlier phase to the definitive genital one would be conditioned by an accession of erotic components.[1] The question also arises whether ordinary ambivalence, which is so often unusually strong in the constitutional disposition to neurosis, should not be regarded as the product of a defusion; ambivalence, however, is such a fundamental phenomenon that it more probably represents an instinctual fusion that has not been completed.

It is natural that we should turn with interest to enquire whether there may not be instructive connections to be traced between the structures we have assumed to exist—the ego, the super-ego and the id—on the one hand and the two classes of instincts on the other; and, further, whether the pleasure principle which dominates mental processes can be shown to have any constant relation both to the two classes of instincts and to these differentiations which we have drawn in the mind. But before we discuss this, we must clear away a doubt which arises concerning the terms in which the problem itself is stated. There is, it is true, no doubt about the pleasure principle, and the differentiation within the ego has good clinical justification; but the distinction between the two classes of instincts does not seem sufficiently assured and it is possible that facts of clinical analysis may be found which will do away with its pretension.

One such fact there appears to be. For the opposition between the two classes of instincts we may put the polarity of love and hate.[2] There is no difficulty in finding a representative of Eros; but we must be grateful that we can find a representative of the elusive death instinct in the instinct of destruction, to which hate points the way. Now, clinical observation shows

[1] [Freud recurs to this point in *Inhibitions, Symptoms and Anxiety* (1926d), *Standard Ed.*, **20**, 114.]

[2] [For what follows, see the earlier discussion of the relation between love and hate in 'Instincts and their Vicissitudes' (1915c), *Standard Ed.*, **14**, 136–40, as well as the later one in Chapters V and VI of *Civilization and its Discontents* (1930a).]

not only that love is with unexpected regularity accompanied by hate (ambivalence), and not only that in human relationships hate is frequently a forerunner of love, but also that in a number of circumstances hate changes into love and love into hate. If this change is more than a mere succession in time—if, that is, one of them actually turns into the other—then clearly the ground is cut away from under a distinction so fundamental as that between erotic instincts and death instincts, one which presupposes physiological processes running in opposite directions.

Now the case in which someone first loves and then hates the same person (or the reverse) because that person has given him cause for doing so, has obviously nothing to do with our problem. Nor has the other case, in which feelings of love that have not yet become manifest express themselves to begin with by hostility and aggressive tendencies; for it may be that here the destructive component in the object-cathexis has hurried on ahead and is only later on joined by the erotic one. But we know of several instances in the psychology of the neuroses in which it is more plausible to suppose that a transformation does take place. In persecutory paranoia the patient fends off an excessively strong homosexual attachment to some particular person in a special way; and as a result this person whom he loved most becomes a persecutor, against whom the patient directs an often dangerous aggressiveness. Here we have a right to interpolate a previous phase which has transformed the love into hate. In the case of the origin of homosexuality, and of desexualized social feelings as well, analytic investigation has only recently taught us to recognize that violent feelings of rivalry are present which lead to aggressive inclinations, and that it is only after these have been surmounted that the formerly hated object becomes the loved one or gives rise to an identification.[1] The question arises whether in these instances we are to assume a direct transformation of hate into love. It is clear that here the changes are purely internal and an alteration in the behaviour of the object plays no part in them.

There is another possible mechanism, however, which we have come to know of by analytic investigation of the processes concerned in the change in paranoia. An ambivalent attitude is present from the outset and the transformation is effected by

[1] [See footnote 3, p. 37.]

means of a reactive displacement of cathexis, energy being withdrawn from the erotic impulse and added to the hostile one.

Not quite the same thing but something like it happens when the hostile rivalry leading to homosexuality is overcome. The hostile attitude has no prospect of satisfaction; consequently—for economic reasons, that is—it is replaced by a loving attitude for which there is more prospect of satisfaction—that is, possibility of discharge. So we see that we are not obliged in any of these cases to assume a direct transformation of hate into love, which would be incompatible with the qualitative distinction between the two classes of instincts.

It will be noticed, however, that by introducing this other mechanism of changing love into hate, we have tacitly made another assumption which deserves to be stated explicitly. We have reckoned as though there existed in the mind—whether in the ego or in the id—a displaceable energy, which, neutral in itself, can be added to a qualitatively differentiated erotic or destructive impulse, and augment its total cathexis. Without assuming the existence of a displaceable energy of this kind we can make no headway. The only question is where it comes from, what it belongs to, and what it signifies.

The problem of the quality of instinctual impulses and of its persistence throughout their various vicissitudes is still very obscure and has hardly been attacked up to the present. In the sexual component instincts, which are especially accessible to observation, it is possible to perceive a few processes which are in the same category as what we are discussing. We see, for instance, that some degree of communication exists between the component instincts, that an instinct deriving from one particular erotogenic source can make over its intensity to reinforce another component instinct originating from another source, that the satisfaction of one instinct can take the place of the satisfaction of another, and more facts of the same nature—which must encourage us to venture upon certain hypotheses.

In the present discussion, moreover, I am only putting forward a hypothesis; I have no proof to offer. It seems a plausible view that this displaceable and neutral energy, which is no doubt active both in the ego and in the id, proceeds from the narcissistic store of libido—that it is desexualized Eros. (The erotic instincts appear to be altogether more plastic, more readily diverted and displaced than the destructive instincts.) From this we can easily go on to assume that this displaceable libido is employed in the service of the pleasure principle to obviate blockages and to facilitate discharge. In this connection it is easy to observe a certain indifference as to the path along which the discharge takes place, so long as it takes place somehow. We know this trait; it is characteristic of the cathectic processes in the id. It is found in erotic cathexes, where a peculiar indifference in regard to the object displays itself; and it is especially evident in the transferences arising in analysis, which develop inevitably, irrespective of the persons who are their object. Not long ago Rank [1913] published some good examples of the way in which neurotic acts of revenge can be directed against the wrong people. Such behaviour on the part of the unconscious reminds one of the comic story of the three village tailors, one of whom had to be hanged because the only village blacksmith had committed a capital offence.[1] Punishment must be exacted even if it does not fall upon the guilty. It was in studying the dream-work that we first came upon this kind of looseness in the displacements brought about by the primary process. In that case it was the objects that were thus relegated to a position of no more than secondary importance, just as in the case we are now discussing it is the paths of discharge. It would be characteristic of the ego to be more particular about the choice both of an object and of a path of discharge.

If this displaceable energy is desexualized libido, it may also be described as *sublimated* energy; for it would still retain the main purpose of Eros—that of uniting and binding—in so far as it helps towards establishing the unity, or tendency to unity, which is particularly characteristic of the ego. If thought-processes in the wider sense are to be included among these displacements, then the activity of thinking is also supplied from the sublimation of erotic motive forces.

Here we arrive again at the possibility which has already been discussed [p. 30] that sublimation may take place regularly through the mediation of the ego. The other case will be recollected, in which the ego deals with the first object-cathexes of the id (and certainly with later ones too) by taking over the libido from them into itself and binding it to the alteration of

[1] [The story was told by Freud in the last chapter of his book on jokes (1905c), *Standard Ed.*, 8, 206.]

the ego produced by means of identification. The transformation [of erotic libido] into ego-libido of course involves an abandonment of sexual aims, a desexualization. In any case this throws light upon an important function of the ego in its relation to Eros. By thus getting hold of the libido from the object-cathexes, setting itself up as sole love-object, and desexualizing or sublimating the libido of the id, the ego is working in opposition to the purposes of Eros and placing itself at the service of the opposing instinctual impulses. It has to acquiesce in some of the other object-cathexes of the id; it has, so to speak, to participate in them. We shall come back later to another possible consequence of this activity of the ego [p. 54].

This would seem to imply an important amplification of the theory of narcissism. At the very beginning, all the libido is accumulated in the id, while the ego is still in process of formation or is still feeble. The id sends part of this libido out into erotic object-cathexes, whereupon the ego, now grown stronger, tries to get hold of this object-libido and to force itself on the id as a love-object. The narcissism of the ego is thus a secondary one, which has been withdrawn from objects.[1]

Over and over again we find, when we are able to trace instinctual impulses back, that they reveal themselves as derivatives of Eros. If it were not for the considerations put forward in *Beyond the Pleasure Principle*, and ultimately for the sadistic constituents which have attached themselves to Eros, we should have difficulty in holding to our fundamental dualistic point of view.[2] But since we cannot escape that view, we are driven to conclude that the death instincts are by their nature mute and that the clamour of life proceeds for the most part from Eros.[3]

And from the struggle against Eros! It can hardly be doubted that the pleasure principle serves the id as a compass in its struggle against the libido—the force that introduces disturb-

---

[1] [See Appendix B (p. 63) for a discussion of this.]

[2] [The consistency with which Freud held to a dualistic classification of the instincts will be seen from his long footnote at the end of Chapter VI of *Beyond the Pleasure Principle* (1920g), *Standard Ed.*, 18, 60–1, and from the historical sketch in the Editor's Note to 'Instincts and their Vicissitudes' (1915c), *Standard Ed.*, 14, 113–16.]

[3] In fact, on our view it is through the agency of Eros that the destructive instincts that are directed towards the external world have been diverted from the self.

ances into the process of life. If it is true that Fechner's principle of constancy[1] governs life, which thus consists of a continuous descent towards death, it is the claims of Eros, of the sexual instincts, which, in the form of instinctual needs, hold up the falling level and introduce fresh tensions. The id, guided by the pleasure principle—that is, by the perception of unpleasure—fends off these tensions in various ways. It does so in the first place by complying as swiftly as possible with the demands of the non-desexualized libido—by striving for the satisfaction of the directly sexual trends. But it does so in a far more comprehensive fashion in relation to one particular form of satisfaction in which all component demands converge—by discharge of the sexual substances, which are saturated vehicles, so to speak, of the erotic tensions.[2] The ejection of the sexual substances in the sexual act corresponds in a sense to the separation of soma and germ-plasm. This accounts for the likeness of the condition that follows complete sexual satisfaction to dying, and for the fact that death coincides with the act of copulation in some of the lower animals. These creatures die in the act of reproduction because, after Eros has been eliminated through the process of satisfaction, the death instinct has a free hand for accomplishing its purposes. Finally, as we have seen, the ego, by sublimating some of the libido for itself and its purposes, assists the id in its work of mastering the tensions.

[1] [Cf. *Beyond the Pleasure Principle*, Standard Ed., 18, 8–10.]

[2] [Freud's views on the part played by the 'sexual substances' will be found in Section 2 of the third of his *Three Essays* (1905*d*), *Standard Ed.*, 7, 212–16.]

THE DEPENDENT RELATIONSHIPS
OF THE EGO

THE complexity of our subject-matter must be an excuse for
the fact that none of the chapter-headings of this book quite
correspond to their contents, and that in turning to new aspects
of the topic we are constantly harking back to matters that have
already been dealt with.

Thus we have said repeatedly that the ego is formed to a
great extent out of identifications which take the place of
abandoned cathexes by the id; that the first of these identifications always behave as a special agency in the ego and stand
apart from the ego in the form of a super-ego, while later on,
as it grows stronger, the ego may become more resistant to the
influences of such identifications. The super-ego owes its
special position in the ego, or in relation to the ego, to a factor
which must be considered from two sides: on the one hand it
was the first identification and one which took place while the
ego was still feeble, and on the other hand it is the heir to the
Oedipus complex and has thus introduced the most momentous
objects into the ego. The super-ego's relation to the later altera-
tions of the ego is roughly similar to that of the primary
sexual phase of childhood to later sexual life after puberty.
Although it is accessible to all later influences, it nevertheless
preserves throughout life the character given to it by its derivation from the father-complex—namely, the capacity to stand
apart from the ego and to master it. It is a memorial of the
former weakness and dependence of the ego, and the mature
ego remains subject to its domination. As the child was once
under a compulsion to obey its parents, so the ego submits to
the categorical imperative of its super-ego.

But the derivation of the super-ego from the first object-
cathexes of the id, from the Oedipus complex, signifies even
more for it. This derivation, as we have already shown [p. 36 ff.],
brings it into relation with the phylogenetic acquisitions of the
id and makes it a reincarnation of former ego-structures which
have left their precipitates behind in the id. Thus the super-ego

is always close to the id and can act as its representative *vis-à-vis* the ego. It reaches deep down into the id and for that reason is farther from consciousness than the ego is.[1]

We shall best appreciate these relations by turning to certain clinical facts, which have long since lost their novelty but which still await theoretical discussion.

There are certain people who behave in a quite peculiar fashion during the work of analysis. When one speaks hopefully to them or expresses satisfaction with the progress of the treatment, they show signs of discontent and their condition invariably becomes worse. One begins by regarding this as defiance and as an attempt to prove their superiority to the physician, but later one comes to take a deeper and juster view. One becomes convinced, not only that such people cannot endure any praise or appreciation, but that they react inversely to the progress of the treatment. Every partial solution that ought to result, and in other people does result, in an improvement or a temporary suspension of symptoms produces in them for the time being an exacerbation of their illness; they get worse during the treatment instead of getting better. They exhibit what is known as a 'negative therapeutic reaction'.

There is no doubt that there is something in these people that sets itself against their recovery, and its approach is dreaded as though it were a danger. We are accustomed to say that the need for illness has got the upper hand in them over the desire for recovery. If we analyse this resistance in the usual way— then, even after allowance has been made for an attitude of defiance towards the physician and for fixation to the various forms of gain from illness, the greater part of it is still left over; and this reveals itself as the most powerful of all obstacles to recovery, more powerful than the familiar ones of narcissistic inaccessibility, a negative attitude towards the physician and clinging to the gain from illness.

In the end we come to see that we are dealing with what may be called a 'moral' factor, a sense of guilt, which is finding its satisfaction in the illness and refuses to give up the punishment of suffering. We shall be right in regarding this disheartening explanation as final. But as far as the patient is concerned this

[1] It may be said that the psycho-analytic or metapsychological ego stands on its head no less than the anatomical ego—the 'cortical homunculus' [p. 26].

sense of guilt is dumb; it does not tell him he is guilty; he does not feel guilty, he feels ill. This sense of guilt expresses itself only as a resistance to recovery which it is extremely difficult to overcome. It is also particularly difficult to convince the patient that this motive lies behind his continuing to be ill; he holds fast to the more obvious explanation that treatment by analysis is not the right remedy for his case.[1]

The description we have given applies to the most extreme instances of this state of affairs, but in a lesser measure this factor has to be reckoned with in very many cases, perhaps in all comparatively severe cases of neurosis. In fact it may be precisely this element in the situation, the attitude of the ego ideal, that determines the severity of a neurotic illness. We shall not hesitate, therefore, to discuss rather more fully the way in which the sense of guilt expresses itself under different conditions.

An interpretation of the normal, conscious sense of guilt

[1] The battle with the obstacle of an unconscious sense of guilt is not made easy for the analyst. Nothing can be done against it directly, and nothing indirectly but the slow procedure of unmasking its unconscious repressed roots, and of thus gradually changing it into a *conscious* sense of guilt. One has a special opportunity for influencing it when this *Ucs.* sense of guilt is a 'borrowed' one—when it is the product of an identification with some other person who was once the object of an erotic cathexis. A sense of guilt that has been adopted in this way is often the sole remaining trace of the abandoned love-relation and not at all easy to recognize as such. (The likeness between this process and what happens in melancholia is unmistakable.) If one can unmask this former object-cathexis behind the *Ucs.* sense of guilt, the therapeutic success is often brilliant, but otherwise the outcome of one's efforts is by no means certain. It depends principally on the intensity of the sense of guilt; there is often no counteracting force of a similar order of strength which the treatment can oppose to it. Perhaps it may depend, too, on whether the personality of the analyst allows of the patient's putting him in the place of his ego ideal, and this involves a temptation for the analyst to play the part of prophet, saviour and redeemer to the patient. Since the rules of analysis are diametrically opposed to the physician's making use of his personality in any such manner, it must be honestly confessed that here we have another limitation to the effectiveness of analysis; after all, analysis does not set out to make pathological reactions impossible, but to give the patient's ego *freedom* to decide one way or the other.—[Freud returned to this topic in his paper on 'The Economic Problem of Masochism' (1924c), p. 166 below, where he discussed the distinction between the unconscious sense of guilt and moral masochism. See also Chapters VII and VIII of *Civilization and its Discontents* (1930a).]

(conscience) presents no difficulties; it is based on the tension between the ego and the ego ideal and is the expression of a condemnation of the ego by its critical agency. The feelings of inferiority so well known in neurotics are presumably not far removed from it. In two very familiar maladies the sense of guilt is over-strongly conscious; in them the ego ideal displays particular severity and often rages against the ego in a cruel fashion. The attitude of the ego ideal in these two conditions, obsessional neurosis and melancholia, presents, alongside of this similarity, differences that are no less significant.

In certain forms of obsessional neurosis the sense of guilt is over-noisy but cannot justify itself to the ego. Consequently the patient's ego rebels against the imputation of guilt and seeks the physician's support in repudiating it. It would be folly to acquiesce in this, for to do so would have no effect. Analysis eventually shows that the super-ego is being influenced by processes that have remained unknown to the ego. It is possible to discover the repressed impulses which are really at the bottom of the sense of guilt. Thus in this case the super-ego knew more than the ego about the unconscious id.

In melancholia the impression that the super-ego has obtained a hold upon consciousness is even stronger. But here the ego ventures no objection; it admits its guilt and submits to the punishment. We understand the difference. In obsessional neurosis what were in question were objectionable impulses which remained outside the ego, while in melancholia the object to which the super-ego's wrath applies has been taken into the ego through identification.

It is certainly not clear why the sense of guilt reaches such an extraordinary strength in these two neurotic disorders; but the main problem presented in this state of affairs lies in another direction. We shall postpone discussion of it until we have dealt with the other cases in which the sense of guilt remains unconscious. [See p. 53.]

It is essentially in hysteria and in states of a hysterical type that this is found. Here the mechanism by which the sense of guilt remains unconscious is easy to discover. The hysterical ego fends off a distressing perception with which the criticisms of its super-ego threaten it, in the same way in which it is in the habit of fending off an unendurable object-cathexis—by an act of repression. It is the ego, therefore, that is responsible for the sense of guilt remaining unconscious. We know that as a rule the ego carries out repressions in the service and at the behest of its super-ego; but this is a case in which it has turned the same weapon against its harsh taskmaster. In obsessional neurosis, as we know, the phenomena of reaction-formation predominate; but here [in hysteria] the ego succeeds only in keeping at a distance the material to which the sense of guilt refers.

One may go further and venture the hypothesis that a great part of the sense of guilt must normally remain unconscious, because the origin of conscience is intimately connected with the Oedipus complex, which belongs to the unconscious. If anyone were inclined to put forward the paradoxical proposition that the normal man is not only far more immoral than he believes but also far more moral than he knows, psycho-analysis, on whose findings the first half of the assertion rests, would have no objection to raise against the second half.[1]

It was a surprise to find that an increase in this *Ucs.* sense of guilt can turn people into criminals. But it is undoubtedly a fact. In many criminals, especially youthful ones, it is possible to detect a very powerful sense of guilt which existed before the crime, and is therefore not its result but its motive. It is as if it was a relief to be able to fasten this unconscious sense of guilt on to something real and immediate.[2]

In all these situations the super-ego displays its independence of the conscious ego and its intimate relations with the unconscious id. Having regard, now, to the importance we have ascribed to preconscious verbal residues in the ego [p. 20 f.], the question arises whether it can be the case that the super-ego, in so far as it is *Ucs.*, consists in such word-presentations and, if it does not, what else it consists in. Our tentative answer will be that it is as impossible for the super-ego as for the ego to disclaim its origin from things heard; for it is a part of the ego and remains accessible to consciousness by way of these word-presentations (concepts, abstractions). But the *cathectic energy* does not reach these contents of the super-ego from

[1] This proposition is only apparently a paradox; it simply states that human nature has a far greater extent, both for good and for evil, than it thinks it has—i.e. than its ego is aware of through conscious perception.

[2] [A full discussion of this (together with some other references) will be found in Part III of Freud's paper on 'Some Character Types' (1916*d*), *Standard Ed.*, 14, 332–3.]

auditory perception (instruction or reading) but from sources
in the id.

The question which we put off answering [see p. 51] runs
as follows: How is it that the super-ego manifests itself essentially
as a sense of guilt (or rather, as criticism—for the sense of
guilt is the perception in the ego answering to this criticism)
and moreover develops such extraordinary harshness and
severity towards the ego? If we turn to melancholia first, we
find that the excessively strong super-ego which has obtained
a hold upon consciousness rages against the ego with merciless
violence, as if it had taken possession of the whole of the sadism
available in the person concerned. Following our view of sadism,
we should say that the destructive component had entrenched
itself in the super-ego and turned against the ego. What is now
holding sway in the super-ego is, as it were, a pure culture of the
death instinct, and in fact it often enough succeeds in driving
the ego into death, if the latter does not fend off its tyrant in
time by the change round into mania.

The reproaches of conscience in certain forms of obsessional
neurosis are as distressing and tormenting, but here the situation
is less perspicuous. It is noteworthy that the obsessional neurotic,
in contrast to the melancholic, never in fact takes the step of
self-destruction; it is as though he were immune against the
danger of suicide, and he is far better protected from it than the
hysteric. We can see that what guarantees the safety of the ego
is the fact that the object has been retained. In obsessional
neurosis it has become possible, through a regression to the pregenital organization, for the love-impulses to transform themselves into impulses of aggression against the object. Here again
the instinct of destruction has been set free and it seeks to destroy
the object, or at least it appears to have that intention. These
purposes have not been adopted by the ego and it struggles
against them with reaction-formations and precautionary
measures; they remain in the id. The super-ego, however, behaves as if the ego were responsible for them and shows at the
same time by the seriousness with which it chastises these destructive intentions that they are no mere semblance evoked by
regression but an actual substitution of hate for love. Helpless in
both directions, the ego defends itself vainly, alike against the
instigations of the murderous id and against the reproaches of
the punishing conscience. It succeeds in holding in check at

least the most brutal actions of both sides; the first outcome is interminable self-torment, and eventually there follows a systematic torturing of the object, in so far as it is within reach.

The dangerous death instincts are dealt with in the individual in various ways: in part they are rendered harmless by being fused with erotic components, in part they are diverted towards the external world in the form of aggression, while to a large extent they undoubtedly continue their internal work unhindered. How is it then that in melancholia the super-ego can become a kind of gathering-place for the death instincts?

From the point of view of instinctual control, of morality, it may be said of the id that it is totally non-moral, of the ego that it strives to be moral, and of the super-ego that it can be super-moral and then become as cruel as only the id can be. It is remarkable that the more a man checks his aggressiveness towards the exterior the more severe—that is aggressive—he becomes in his ego ideal. The ordinary view sees the situation the other way round: the standard set up by the ego ideal seems to be the motive for the suppression of aggressiveness. The fact remains, however, as we have stated it: the more a man controls his aggressiveness, the more intense becomes his ideal's inclination to aggressiveness against his ego.[1] It is like a displacement, a turning round upon his own ego. But even ordinary normal morality has a harshly restraining, cruelly prohibiting quality. It is from this, indeed, that the conception arises of a higher being who deals out punishment inexorably.

I cannot go further in my consideration of these questions without introducing a fresh hypothesis. The super-ego arises, as we know, from an identification with the father taken as a model. Every such identification is in the nature of a desexualization or even of a sublimation. It now seems as though when a transformation of this kind takes place, an instinctual defusion occurs at the same time [p. 30]. After sublimation the erotic component no longer has the power to bind the whole of the destructiveness that was combined with it, and this is released in the form of an inclination to aggression and

---

[1] [Freud returned to this paradox in Section B of 'Some Additional Notes on Dream-Interpretation as a Whole' (1925i), p. 134 below, and also in 'The Economic Problem of Masochism' (1924c), p. 170 below, and discussed it more fully in Chapter VII of *Civilization and its Discontents* (1930a).]

destruction. This defusion would be the source of the general character of harshness and cruelty exhibited by the ideal—its dictatorial 'Thou shalt'.

Let us again consider obsessional neurosis for a moment. The state of affairs is different here. The defusion of love into aggressiveness has not been effected by the work of the ego, but is the result of a regression which has come about in the id. But this process has extended beyond the id to the super-ego, which now increases its severity towards the innocent ego. It would seem, however, that in this case, no less than in that of melancholia, the ego, having gained control over the libido by means of identification, is punished for doing so by the super-ego through the instrumentality of the aggressiveness which was mixed with the libido.

Our ideas about the ego are beginning to clear, and its various relationships are gaining distinctness. We now see the ego in its strength and in its weaknesses. It is entrusted with important functions. By virtue of its relation to the perceptual system it gives mental processes an order in time and submits them to 'reality-testing'.[1] By interposing the processes of thinking, it secures a postponement of motor discharges and controls the access to motility.[2] This last power is, to be sure, a question more of form than of fact; in the matter of action the ego's position is like that of a constitutional monarch, without whose sanction no law can be passed but who hesitates long before imposing his veto on any measure put forward by Parliament. All the experiences of life that originate from without enrich the ego; the id, however, is its second external world, which it strives to bring into subjection to itself. It withdraws libido from the id and transforms the object-cathexes of the id into ego-structures. With the aid of the super-ego, in a manner that is still obscure to us, it draws upon the experiences of past ages stored in the id [p. 38].

There are two paths by which the contents of the id can penetrate into the ego. The one is direct, the other leads by way of the ego ideal; which of these two paths they take may, for some mental activities, be of decisive importance. The ego develops from perceiving instincts to controlling them, from

[1] [Cf. 'The Unconscious' (1915e), *Standard Ed.*, **14**, 188.]
[2] [Cf. 'Formulations on the Two Principles of Mental Functioning' (1911b), *Standard Ed.*, **12**, 221.]

obeying instincts to inhibiting them. In this achievement a large share is taken by the ego ideal, which indeed is partly a reaction-formation against the instinctual processes of the id. Psycho-analysis is an instrument to enable the ego to achieve a progressive conquest of the id.

From the other point of view, however, we see this same ego as a poor creature owing service to three masters and consequently menaced by three dangers: from the external world, from the libido of the id, and from the severity of the super-ego. Three kinds of anxiety correspond to these three dangers, since anxiety is the expression of a retreat from danger. As a frontier-creature, the ego tries to mediate between the world and the id, to make the id pliable to the world and, by means of its muscular activity, to make the world fall in with the wishes of the id. In point of fact it behaves like the physician during an analytic treatment: it offers itself, with the attention it pays to the real world, as a libidinal object to the id, and aims at attaching the id's libido to itself. It is not only a helper to the id; it is also a submissive slave who courts his master's love. Whenever possible, it tries to remain on good terms with the id; it clothes the id's *Ucs.* commands with its *Pcs.* rationalizations; it pretends that the id is showing obedience to the admonitions of reality, even when in fact it is remaining obstinate and unyielding; it disguises the id's conflicts with reality and, if possible, its conflicts with the super-ego too. In its position midway between the id and reality, it only too often yields to the temptation to become sycophantic, opportunist and lying, like a politician who sees the truth but wants to keep his place in popular favour.

Towards the two classes of instincts the ego's attitude is not impartial. Through its work of identification and sublimation it gives the death instincts in the id assistance in gaining control over the libido, but in so doing it runs the risk of becoming the object of the death instincts and of itself perishing. In order to be able to help in this way it has had itself to become filled with libido; it thus itself becomes the representative of Eros and thenceforward desires to live and to be loved.

But since the ego's work of sublimation results in a defusion of the instincts and a liberation of the aggressive instincts in the super-ego, its struggle against the libido exposes it to the danger of maltreatment and death. In suffering under the attacks of the super-ego or perhaps even succumbing to them, the ego is meeting with a fate like that of the protista which are destroyed by the products of decomposition that they themselves have created.[1] From the economic point of view the morality that functions in the super-ego seems to be a similar product of decomposition.

Among the dependent relationships in which the ego stands, that to the super-ego is perhaps the most interesting.

The ego is the actual seat of anxiety.[2] Threatened by dangers from three directions, it develops the flight-reflex by with-drawing its own cathexis from the menacing perception or from the similarly regarded process in the id, and emitting it as anxiety. This primitive reaction is later replaced by the carrying-out of protective cathexes (the mechanism of the phobias). What it is that the ego fears from the external and from the libidinal danger cannot be specified; we know that the fear is of being overwhelmed or annihilated, but it cannot be grasped analytically.[3] The ego is simply obeying the warning of the pleasure principle. On the other hand, we can tell what is hidden behind the ego's dread of the super-ego, the fear of conscience.[4] The superior being, which turned into the ego ideal, once threatened castration, and this dread of castration is probably the nucleus round which the subsequent fear of conscience has gathered; it is this dread that persists as the fear of conscience.

The high-sounding phrase, 'every fear is ultimately the fear of death', has hardly any meaning, and at any rate cannot be justified.[5] It seems to me, on the contrary, perfectly correct to

[1] [Freud had discussed these animalculae in *Beyond the Pleasure Princi-ple*, *Standard Ed.*, 18, 48. They would probably now be discribed as 'protozoa' rather than 'protista'.]

[2] [What follows on the subject of anxiety must be read in connection with Freud's revised views as stated in *Inhibitions, Symptoms and Anxiety* (1926d), where most of the points raised here are further discussed.]

[3] [The notion of the ego being 'overwhelmed' (of an '*Überwältigung*') occurs very early in Freud's writings. See, for instance, a mention of it in Part II of his first paper on 'The Neuro-Psychoses of Defence' (1894a). But it plays a prominent part in his discussion of the mechanism of the neuroses in Draft K of January 1, 1896, in the Fliess correspondence (Freud, 1950a). There is an evident connection here with the 'traumatic situation' of *Inhibitions, Symptoms and Anxiety* (1926d).]

[4] ['*Gewissensangst*.' An Editor's footnote on the use of this word will be found in Chapter VII of *Inhibitions, Symptoms and Anxiety*, *Standard Ed.*, 20, 128.]   [5] [Cf. Stekel (1908, 5).]

distinguish the fear of death from dread of an object (realistic anxiety) and from neurotic libidinal anxiety. It presents a difficult problem to psycho-analysis, for death is an abstract concept with a negative content for which no unconscious correlative can be found. It would seem that the mechanism of the fear of death can only be that the ego relinquishes its narcissistic libidinal cathexis in a very large measure—that is, that it gives up itself, just as it gives up some *external* object in other cases in which it feels anxiety. I believe that the fear of death is something that occurs between the ego and the super-ego.

We know that the fear of death makes its appearance under two conditions (which, moreover, are entirely analogous to situations in which other kinds of anxiety develop), namely, as a reaction to an external danger and as an internal process, as for instance in melancholia. Once again a neurotic manifestation may help us to understand a normal one.

The fear of death in melancholia only admits of one explanation: that the ego gives itself up because it feels itself hated and persecuted by the super-ego, instead of loved. To the ego, therefore, living means the same as being loved—being loved by the super-ego, which here again appears as the representative of the id. The super-ego fulfils the same function of protecting and saving that was fulfilled in earlier days by the father and later by Providence or Destiny. But, when the ego finds itself in an excessive real danger which it believes itself unable to overcome by its own strength, it is bound to draw the same conclusion. It sees itself deserted by all protecting forces and lets itself die. Here, moreover, is once again the same situation as that which underlay the first great anxiety-state of birth[1] and the infantile anxiety of longing—the anxiety due to separation from the protecting mother.[2]

These considerations make it possible to regard the fear of death, like the fear of conscience, as a development of the fear of castration. The great significance which the sense of guilt has in the neuroses makes it conceivable that common neurotic

---

[1] [Some discussion of the appearance of this notion here will be found in the Editor's Introduction to *Inhibitions, Symptoms and Anxiety*, *Standard Ed.*, **20**, 85–6.]

[2] [This foreshadows the 'separation anxiety' discussed in *Inhibitions, Symptoms and Anxiety* (1926d), *Standard Ed.*, **20**, 151.]

anxiety is reinforced in severe cases by the generating of anxiety between the ego and the super-ego (fear of castration, of conscience, of death).

The id, to which we finally come back, has no means of showing the ego either love or hate. It cannot say what it wants; it has achieved no unified will. Eros and the death instinct struggle within it; we have seen with what weapons the one group of instincts defends itself against the other. It would be possible to picture the id as under the domination of the mute but powerful death instincts, which desire to be at peace and (prompted by the pleasure principle) to put Eros, the mischief-maker, to rest; but perhaps that might be to undervalue the part played by Eros.

APPENDIX A

THE DESCRIPTIVE AND THE DYNAMIC UNCONSCIOUS

A CURIOUS point arises out of two sentences both of which appear on p. 15 above. The Editor's attention was drawn to it in a private communication from Dr. Ernest Jones, who had come across it in the course of examining Freud's correspondence.

On October 28, 1923, a few months after this work appeared, Ferenczi wrote to Freud in these terms: '. . . Nevertheless I venture to put a question to you . . . . since there is a passage in *The Ego and the Id* which, without your solution, I do not understand. . . . On p. 13[1] I find the following: ". . . that in the descriptive sense there are two kinds of unconscious, but in the dynamic sense only one." Since, however, you write on p. 12[1] that the latent unconscious is unconscious only descriptively, not in the dynamic sense, I had thought that it was precisely the dynamic line of approach that called for the hypothesis of there being two sorts of *Ucs.*, while description knows only *Cs.* and *Ucs.*'

To this Freud replied on October 30, 1923: '. . . Your question about the passage on p. 13 of *The Ego and the Id* has positively horrified me. What appears there gives a directly opposite sense to p. 12; and in the sentence on p. 13 "descriptive" and "dynamic" have simply been transposed.'

A little consideration of this startling affair suggests, however, that Ferenczi's criticism was based on a misunderstanding and that Freud was over-hasty in accepting it. The confusions which underlie Ferenczi's remarks are not very easily sorted out, and a rather lengthy argument is inevitable. Since, however, others besides Ferenczi may fall into the same error, it seems worth while to try to clear the matter up.

We will start off with the first half of Freud's later sentence: 'in the descriptive sense there are two kinds of unconscious.' The meaning of this seems perfectly clear: the term 'unconscious' in its descriptive sense covers two things—the latent unconscious and the repressed unconscious. Freud might, however, have expressed the idea even more clearly. Instead of

[1] Of the German edition. Both sentences are on p. 15 here.

'two kinds of unconscious [*zweierlei Unbewusstes*]' he might have said explicitly that in the descriptive sense there are 'two kinds of things that are unconscious'. And in fact Ferenczi evidently misunderstood the words: he took them to be saying that the term 'descriptively unconscious' had two different *meanings*. This, as he rightly saw, could not be so: the term unconscious, used descriptively, could only have one meaning—that the thing it was applied to was not conscious. In logical terminology, he thought Freud was speaking of the *connotation* of the term whereas he was actually speaking of its *denotation*.

We now proceed to the second half of Freud's later sentence: 'but in the dynamic sense [there is] only one [kind of unconscious]'. Here again the meaning seems perfectly clear: the term 'unconscious' in its dynamic sense covers only one thing—the repressed unconscious. This is once more a statement about the *denotation* of the term; though even if it had been about its *connotation* it would still be true—the term 'dynamic unconscious' can only have one meaning. Ferenczi, however, objects to it, on the ground that 'it was precisely the dynamic line of approach that called for the hypothesis of there being two sorts of *Ucs.*'. Ferenczi was once more misunderstanding Freud. He took him to be saying that if we consider the term 'unconscious', bearing dynamic factors in mind, we see that it has only one meaning—which would, of course, have been the opposite of everything that Freud was arguing. Whereas what Freud really meant was that all the things that are unconscious dynamically (i.e. that are repressed) fall into one class.—The position is made a little more confused by Ferenczi's using the symbol '*Ucs.*' to mean 'unconscious' in the descriptive sense—a slip which Freud himself makes by implication on p. 18.

Thus this later sentence of Freud's seems altogether immune from criticism in itself. But is it, as Ferenczi suggests and as Freud himself seems to agree, incompatible with the earlier sentence? This earlier sentence speaks of the latent unconscious as being 'unconscious only descriptively, not in the dynamic sense'. Ferenczi appears to have thought that this contradicts the later statement that 'in the descriptive sense there are two kinds of unconscious'. But the two statements do not contradict each other: the fact that the latent unconscious is only descriptively unconscious does not in the least imply that it is the only thing that is descriptively unconscious.

There is, indeed, a passage in Lecture XXXI of Freud's *New Introductory Lectures*, written some ten years later than the present work, in which the whole of this argument is repeated in very similar terms. In that passage it is explained more than once that in the descriptive sense both the preconscious and the repressed are unconscious, but that in the dynamic sense the term is restricted to the repressed.

It must be pointed out that this interchange of letters took place only a very few days after Freud had undergone an extremely severe operation. He was not yet able to write (his reply was dictated), and he was probably in no condition to weigh the argument thoroughly. It seems likely that on reflection he realized that Ferenczi's discovery was a mare's nest, for the passage was never altered in the later editions of the book.

APPENDIX B

THE GREAT RESERVOIR OF LIBIDO

THERE is considerable difficulty over this matter, which is mentioned in the first footnote on p. 30 and discussed at greater length on p. 46.

The analogy seems to have made its first appearance in a new section added to the third edition of the *Three Essays* (1905*d*), which was published in 1915 but had been prepared by Freud in the autumn of 1914. The passage runs as follows (*Standard Ed.*, 7, 218): 'Narcissistic or ego libido seems to be the great reservoir from which the object-cathexes are sent out and into which they are withdrawn once more; the narcissistic libidinal cathexis of the ego is the original state of things, realized in earliest childhood, and is merely covered by the later extrusions of libido, but in essentials persists behind them.'

The same notion had, however, been expressed earlier in another favourite analogy of Freud's, which appears sometimes as an alternative and sometimes alongside the 'great reservoir'.[1] This earlier passage is in the paper on narcissism itself (1914*c*), which was written by Freud in the early part of the same year, 1914 (*Standard Ed.*, 14, 75): 'Thus we form the idea of there being an original libidinal cathexis of the ego, from which some is later given off to objects, but which fundamentally persists and is related to the object-cathexis much as the body of an amoeba is related to the pseudopodia which it puts out.'

The two analogies appear together in a semi-popular paper written at the end of 1916 for a Hungarian periodical ('A Difficulty in the Path of Psycho-Analysis', 1917*a*, *Standard Ed.*, 17, 139): 'The ego is a great reservoir from which the libido that is destined for objects flows out and into which it flows back from those objects . . . As an illustration of this state of things we may think of an amoeba, whose viscous substance puts out pseudopodia . . .'

The amoeba appears once more in Lecture XXVI of the

---

[1] This analogy had appeared already in a rudimentary form in the third essay in *Totem and Taboo*, which was first published early in 1913. (*Standard Ed.*, 13, 89.)

Introductory Lectures (1916–17), dating from 1917, and the reservoir in *Beyond the Pleasure Principle* (1920g), *Standard Ed.*, **18**, 51: 'Psycho-analysis . . . came to the conclusion that the ego is the true and original reservoir of libido, and that it is only from that reservoir that libido is extended on to objects.'

Freud included a very similar passage in an encyclopaedia article which he wrote in the summer of 1922 (1923a, *Standard Ed.*, **18**, 257), and then almost immediately afterwards came the announcement of the id, and what appears like a drastic correction of the earlier statements: 'Now that we have distinguished between the ego and the id, we must recognize the id as the great reservoir of libido . . .' And again: 'At the very beginning, all the libido is accumulated in the id, while the ego is still in process of formation or is still feeble. The id sends part of this libido out into erotic object-cathexes, whereupon the ego, now grown stronger, tries to get hold of this object-libido and to force itself on the id as a love-object. The narcissism of the ego is thus a secondary one, which has been withdrawn from objects.' (Pp. 30n. and 46 above.)

This new position seems quite clearly intelligible, and it is therefore a little disturbing to come upon the following sentence, written only a year or so after *The Ego and the Id*, in the *Autobiographical Study* (1925d [1924]), *Standard Ed.*, **20**, 56: 'All through the subject's life his ego remains the great reservoir of his libido, from which object-cathexes are sent out and into which the libido can stream back again from the objects.' [1]

The sentence, it is true, occurs in the course of a historical sketch of the development of psycho-analytic theory; but there is no indication of the change of view announced in *The Ego and the Id*. And, finally, we find this passage in one of Freud's very last writings, in Chapter II of the *Outline of Psycho-Analysis* (1940a), written in 1938: 'It is hard to say anything of the behaviour of the libido in the id and in the super-ego. All that we know about it relates to the ego, in which at first the whole available quota of libido is stored up. We call this state the absolutely primary narcissism. It lasts till the ego begins to cathect the ideas of objects with libido, to transform narcissistic libido into object-libido. Throughout the whole of life the ego remains the great reservoir, from which libidinal cathexes are

[1] An almost identical statement is made in Lecture XXXII of the *New Introductory Lectures* (1933a).

sent out to objects and into which they are also once more withdrawn, just as an amoeba behaves with its pseudopodia.'

Do these later passages imply that Freud had retracted the opinions he expressed in the present work? It seems difficult to believe it, and there are two points that may help towards a reconciliation of the apparently conflicting views. The first is a very small one. The analogy of the 'reservoir' is from its very nature an ambiguous one: a reservoir can be regarded either as a water storage tank or as a source of water supply. There is no great difficulty in applying the image in both senses both to the ego and to the id, and it would certainly have clarified the various passages that have been quoted—and in particular the footnote on p. 30—if Freud had shown more precisely which picture was in his mind.

The second point is of greater importance. In the *New Introductory Lectures*, only a few pages after the passage referred to in the footnote above, in the course of a discussion of masochism, Freud writes: 'If it is true of the destructive instinct as well that the ego—but what we have in mind here is rather the id, the whole person—originally includes all the instinctual impulses . . .' The parenthesis points, of course, to a primitive state of things in which the id and the ego are still undifferentiated.[1] And there is a similar, but more definite, remark in the *Outline*, this time two paragraphs before the passage already quoted: 'We picture some such initial state as one in which the total available energy of Eros, which henceforward we shall speak of as "libido", is present in the still undifferentiated ego-id . . .' If we take this as being the true essence of Freud's theory, the apparent contradiction in his expression of it is diminished. This 'ego-id' was originally the 'great reservoir of libido' in the sense of being a storage tank. After differentiation had occurred, the id would continue as a storage tank but, when it began sending out cathexes (whether to objects or to the now differentiated ego) it would in addition be a source of supply. But the same would be true of the ego as well, for it would be a storage tank of narcissistic libido as well as, on one view, a source of supply for object-cathexes.

This last point leads us, however, to a further question, on which it seems inevitable to suppose that Freud held different views at different times. In *The Ego and the Id* (p. 46) 'at the

[1] This is, of course, a familiar view of Freud's.

very beginning, all the libido is accumulated in the id'; then 'the id sends part of this libido out into erotic object-cathexes', which the ego tries to get control of by forcing itself on the id as a love-object: 'the narcissism of the ego is thus a secondary one.' But in the *Outline*, 'at first the whole available quota of libido is stored up in the ego', 'we call this state the absolutely primary narcissism' and 'it lasts until the ego begins to cathect the ideas of objects with libido'. Two different processes seem to be envisaged in these two accounts. In the first the original object-cathexes are thought of as going out direct from the id, and only reaching the ego indirectly; in the second the whole of the libido is thought of as going from the id to the ego and only reaching the objects indirectly. The two processes do not seem incompatible, and it is possible that both may occur; but on this question Freud is silent.

A SEVENTEENTH-CENTURY
DEMONOLOGICAL NEUROSIS
(1923 [1922])

THE SECOND APPEARANCE OF THE DEVIL TO
CHRISTOPH HAIZMANN

EDITOR'S NOTE

EINE TEUFELSNEUROSE IM SIEBZEHNTEN JAHRHUNDERT

(a) GERMAN EDITIONS:

1923   *Imago*, **9** (1), 1–34.
1924   *G.S.*, **10**, 409–45.
1924   Leipzig, Vienna and Zurich: Internationaler Psycho-
         analytischer Verlag. Pp. 43.
1928   'Bibliophiles' limited edition, with 7 plates. Same
         publishers. Pp. 81.
1940   *G.W.*, **13**, 317–53.

(b) ENGLISH TRANSLATION:

'A Neurosis of Demoniacal Possession in the Seventeenth
                            Century'
1925   *C.P.*, **4**, 436–72. (Tr. E. Glover.)

The present translation, under a new title, is a considerably
modified version of the one published in 1925. The 'Bibliophiles' edition was produced for the 1928 Congress of German
Bibliophiles in Vienna. It contained black and white reproductions of three of the paintings (representing the first, second
and fifth appearances of the Devil) and of four folios of the
manuscript.

This was written in the last months of 1922 (Jones, 1957,
105). The origin of the paper is sufficiently explained by Freud
himself at the beginning of Section I (p. 73). Freud's interest
in witchcraft, possession and allied phenomena was of long
standing. It seems possible that it was stimulated by his studies
at the Salpêtrière in 1885–6. Charcot himself had paid much
attention to the historical aspects of neurosis, a fact referred to
at more than one point in Freud's 'Report' on his visit to Paris
(1956a [1886]). There is an account of a sixteenth-century case
of possession at the beginning of Lecture XVI in the first set of
Charcot's lectures translated by Freud (1886f) and a discussion

of the hysterical nature of mediaeval 'demonio-manias' in the seventh of the *Leçons du mardi* in the second set of Freud's translations (1892–93a). Moreover, in his obituary of Charcot (1893f), he laid especial emphasis on this side of his teacher's work.

Two letters to Fliess, of January 17 and 24, 1897 (Freud, 1950a, Letters 56 and 57), which discuss witches and their relation to the Devil, show that this interest had not diminished; in the first of them, indeed, he speaks as though the topic was one which had often been discussed between him and Fliess. There is already a suggestion that the Devil may be a father-figure, and the part played by anal material in mediaeval beliefs about witches is particularly insisted upon. Both of these points recur in a short allusion to the subject in the paper on 'Character and Anal Erotism' (1908b), *Standard Ed.*, **9**, 174. We learn from Jones (1957, 378) that on January 27, 1909, Hugo Heller, the Vienna bookseller and publisher, read a paper to the Vienna Psycho-Analytical Society, of which he was a member, on 'The History of the Devil'. The minutes of the Society have unfortunately not been made accessible to us, but, according to Jones, Freud spoke at length on the psychological composition of the belief in the Devil, evidently on much the same lines as in Section III of the present paper. In this section of the paper, too, Freud passes beyond the discussion of an individual case and of the limited demonological problem to a consideration of some of the wider questions involved in the adoption by males of a feminine attitude towards the father. And here he brings up the history of Dr. Schreber as a parallel, though he nowhere classifies the present case as one of paranoia.

A sumptuous volume has recently been brought out under the title *Schizophrenia 1677* (London, 1956: Dawson) by Dr. Ida Macalpine and Dr. R. A. Hunter. This includes a facsimile of the manuscript of the 'Trophy of Mariazell' and coloured reproductions of the nine paintings attached to it.[1] An examination of these has made it possible to make one or two additions and corrections to Freud's account of the manuscript, which was no doubt based entirely on the transcription and report of Dr. Payer-Thurn (see p. 73). It must be added that the lengthy commentaries of Dr. Macalpine and Dr. Hunter are largely

[1] Reproductions of the pictures in black and white are included in an earlier article (1954) by the same authors.

directed to criticism of Freud's views on the case; and it has unfortunately been impossible to adopt their translation of the many passages from the manuscript quoted by Freud, since at two or three important points their rendering of the original is inconsistent with Freud's.

No attempt has been made in the present translation to imitate the style of the seventeenth-century German of the manuscript.

A SEVENTEENTH-CENTURY DEMONO-
LOGICAL NEUROSIS[1]

[INTRODUCTION]

THE neuroses of childhood have taught us that a number of
things can easily be seen in them with the naked eye which at a
later age are only to be discovered after a thorough investigation. We may expect that the same will turn out to be true of
neurotic illnesses in earlier centuries, provided that we are prepared to recognize them under names other than those of our
present-day neuroses. We need not be surprised to find that,
whereas the neuroses of our unpsychological modern days take
on a hypochondriacal aspect and appear disguised as organic
illnesses, the neuroses of those early times emerge in demonological trappings. Several authors, foremost among them
Charcot,[2] have, as we know, identified the manifestations of
hysteria in the portrayals of possession and ecstasy that have
been preserved for us in the productions of art. If more attention
had been paid to the histories of such cases at the time, it would
not have been difficult to retrace in them the subject-matter of
a neurosis.

The demonological theory of those dark times has won in the
end against all the somatic views of the period of 'exact' science.
The states of possession correspond to our neuroses, for the
explanation of which we once more have recourse to psychical
powers. In our eyes, the demons are bad and reprehensible
wishes, derivatives of instinctual impulses that have been
repudiated and repressed. We merely eliminate the projection
of these mental entities into the external world which the
middle ages carried out; instead, we regard them as having
arisen in the patient's internal life, where they have their abode.

---

[1] [In the English translation of 1925 the following footnote appeared
at this point: 'The author wishes to add to the English translation two
footnotes (which appear within square brackets), and to express his
regret that they were omitted from the German version.' Actually what
was in question were *additions* to two existing footnotes, on pp. 86 and
87. They were not included in later German editions.]

[2] [Cf. Editor's Note, pp. 69–70.]

72

THE STORY OF CHRISTOPH HAIZMANN
THE PAINTER

I AM indebted to the friendly interest of Hofrat Dr. Payer-Thurn, director of the former Imperial Fideikommissbibliothek[1] of Vienna, for the opportunity of studying a seventeenth-century demonological neurosis of this kind. Payer-Thurn had discovered a manuscript in this library which originated from the shrine of Mariazell[2] and in which there was a detailed account of a miraculous redemption from a pact with the Devil through the grace of the Blessed Virgin Mary. His interest was aroused by the resemblance of this story to the legend of Faust, and has led him to undertake the exhaustive publication and editing of the material. Finding, however, that the person whose redemption was described had been subject to convulsive seizures and visions he approached me for a medical opinion on the case. We came to an agreement to publish our investigations independently and separately.[3] I should like to take this opportunity of thanking him for his original suggestion and for the many ways in which he has assisted me in the study of the manuscript.

This demonological case history leads to really valuable findings which can be brought to light without much interpretation —much as a vein of pure metal may sometimes be struck which must elsewhere be laboriously smelted from the ore.

The manuscript, an exact copy of which lies before me, falls into two quite distinct sections. One is a report, written in Latin, by a monastic scribe or compiler; the other is a fragment from the patient's diary, written in German. The first section contains a preface and a description of the actual miraculous

---

[1] [A law library for the registration of entails (somewhat akin to the library of the Record Office in London), now included in the National Library of Austria.]

[2] [A well-known place of pilgrimage, some eighty miles south-west of Vienna.]

[3] [Payer-Thurn's paper was published the year after Freud's.]

cure. The second can scarcely have been of any significance for the reverend Fathers but so much the more is it of value for us. It serves in large part to confirm our judgement of the case, which might otherwise have been hesitant, and we have good cause to be grateful to the clergy for having preserved the document although it added nothing to support the tenor of their views and, indeed, may rather have weakened it.

But before going further into the composition of this little manuscript brochure, which bears the title *Trophaeum Mariano-Cellense*, I must relate a part of its contents, which I take from the preface.

On September 5, 1677, the painter Christoph Haizmann,[1] a Bavarian, was brought to Mariazell, with a letter of introduction from the village priest of Pottenbrunn (in lower Austria) not far away.[2] The letter states that the man had been staying in Pottenbrunn for some months, pursuing his occupation of painting. On August 29, while in the church there, he had been seized with frightful convulsions. As these convulsions recurred during the following days, he had been examined by the *Praefectus Dominii Pottenbrunnensis*[3] with a view to discovering what it was that was oppressing him and whether perhaps he had entered into illicit traffic with the Evil Spirit.[4] Upon this, the man had admitted that nine years before, when he was in a state of despondency about his art and doubtful whether he could support himself, he had yielded to the Devil, who had tempted him nine times, and that he had given him his bond in writing to belong to him in body and soul after a period of nine years. This period would expire on the twenty-fourth day of the current month.[5] The letter went on to say that the

---

[1] [This is the spelling of the name used throughout in the original manuscript, with one possible exception. The German editions of Freud's paper adopt the form 'Haitzmann'.]

[2] No mention is anywhere made of the painter's age. The context suggests that he was a man of between thirty and forty, probably nearer the lower figure. He died, as we shall see [p. 78], in 1700.

[3] [Prefect of the Domain of Pottenbrunn.]

[4] We will merely note in passing the possibility that this interrogation inspired in the sufferer—'suggested' to him—the phantasy of his pact with the Devil.

[5] *Quorum et finis 24 mensis hujus futurus appropinquat.* [This refers to September, at the beginning of which the letter of introduction was written.]

unfortunate man had repented and was convinced that only the grace of the Mother of God at Mariazell could save him, by compelling the Evil One to deliver up the bond, which had been written in blood. For this reason the village priest ventured to recommend *miserum hunc hominem omni auxilio destitutum*[1] to the benevolence of the Fathers of Mariazell.

So far the narrative of Leopoldus Braun, the village priest of Pottenbrunn, dated September 1, 1677.

We can now proceed with the analysis of the manuscript It consists of three parts:

(1) A coloured title-page representing the scene of the signing of the pact and the scene of the redemption in the chapel of Mariazell. On the next sheet[2] are eight pictures, also coloured, representing the subsequent appearances of the Devil, with a short legend in German attached to each. These pictures are not the originals; they are copies—faithful copies, we are solemnly assured—of the original paintings by Christoph Haizmann.

(2) The actual *Trophaeum Mariano-Cellense* (in Latin), the work of a clerical compiler who signs himself at the foot 'P.A.E.' and appends to these initials four lines of verse containing his biography. The *Trophaeum* ends with a deposition by the Abbot Kilian of St. Lambert,[3] dated September 12, 1729, which is in a different handwriting from that of the compiler. It testifies to the exact correspondence of the manuscript and the pictures with the originals preserved in the archives. There is no mention of the year in which the *Trophaeum* was compiled. We are free to assume that it was done in the same year in which the Abbot Kilian made his deposition—that is, in 1729;

[1] ['This wretched man, who was bereft of all help.']

[2] [This does not seem to fit in with the account given by Macalpine and Hunter (1956, 55, see p. 70 above): 'The manuscript is made up of twenty foolscap folios measuring 307 × 196 mm. Five folios are devoted to paintings of the Devil in the various shapes and guises in which the painter saw him during his illness; and a triptych showing his first meeting with the Devil, the centre piece of which depicts the return of one of the pacts in the Shrine at Mariazell.' The distribution of the pictures is not explicitly described in this account, but presumably one of the five folios was occupied by the triptych (Freud's 'title-page') and each of the remaining four contained two of the smaller pictures.]

[3] [The monks of the Convent of St. Lambert were in charge of the shrine.]

or, since the last date mentioned in the text is 1714, we may put the compiler's work somewhere between the years 1714 and 1729. The miracle which was to be preserved from oblivion by this manuscript occurred in 1677—that is to say, between thirty-seven and fifty-two years earlier.

(3) The painter's diary, written in German and covering the period from his redemption in the chapel till January 13 of the following year, 1678. It is inserted in the text of the *Trophaeum* near the end.

The core of the actual *Trophaeum* consists of two pieces of writing: the letter of introduction, mentioned above [p. 74], from the village priest, Leopold Braun of Pottenbrunn, dated September 1, 1677, and the report by the Abbot Franciscus of Mariazell and St. Lambert, describing the miraculous cure. This is dated September 12, 1677, that is to say, only a few days later. The activity of the editor or compiler, P.A.E., has provided a preface which as it were fuses the contents of these two documents; he has also added some connecting passages of little importance, and, at the end, an account of the subsequent vicissitudes of the painter, based on enquiries made in the year 1714.[1]

The painter's previous history is thus told three times over in the *Trophaeum*: (1) in the village priest of Pottenbrunn's letter of introduction, (2) in the formal report by the Abbot Franciscus and (3) in the editor's preface. A comparison of these three sources discloses certain discrepancies which it will be not unimportant for us to follow up.

I can now continue with the painter's story. After he had undergone a prolonged period of penance and prayer at Mariazell, the Devil appeared to him in the sacred Chapel at midnight, on September 8, the Nativity of the Virgin, in the form of a winged dragon, and gave him back the pact, which was written in blood. We shall learn later, to our surprise, that *two* bonds with the Devil appear in Christoph Haizmann's story—an earlier one, written in black ink, and a later one, written in blood. The one referred to in the description of the scene of exorcism, as can also be seen from the picture on the title-page, is the one written in blood—that is, the later one.

---

[1] This would seem to suggest that the *Trophaeum*, too, dates from 1714.

At this point a doubt as to the credibility of the clerical reporters may well arise in our minds and warn us not to waste our labours on a product of monastic superstition. We are told that several clerics, mentioned by name, assisted at the exorcism and were present in the Chapel when the Devil appeared. If it had been asserted that they, too, saw the Devil appear in the form of a dragon and offer the painter the paper written in red (*Schedam sibi porrigentem conspexisset*),[1] we should be faced by several unpleasant possibilities, among which that of a collective hallucination would be the mildest. But the Abbot Franciscus's testimony dispels this doubt. Far from asserting that the assisting clerics saw the Devil too, he only states in straightforward and sober words that the painter suddenly tore himself away from the Fathers who were holding him, rushed into the corner of the Chapel where he saw the apparition, and then returned with the paper in his hand.[2]

The miracle was great, and the victory of the Holy Mother over Satan without question; but unfortunately the cure was not a lasting one. It is once more to the credit of the clergy that they have not concealed this. After a short time the painter left Mariazell in the best of health and went to Vienna, where he lived with a married sister. On October 11 fresh attacks began, some of them very severe, and these are reported in the diary until January 13 [1678]. They consisted in visions and '*absences*', in which he saw and experienced every kind of thing, in convulsive seizures accompanied by the most painful sensations, on one occasion in paralysis of the legs, and so on. This time, however, it was not the Devil who tormented him; it was by sacred figures that he was vexed—by Christ and by the Blessed Virgin herself. It is remarkable that he suffered no less through these heavenly manifestations and the punishments they inflicted on him than he had formerly through his traffic with the Devil. In his diary, indeed, he included these fresh experiences too as manifestations of the Devil; and when, in

[1] [See next footnote.]

[2] '. . . [*poenitens*] *ipsumque Daemonem ad Aram Sac. Cellae per fenestrellam in cornu Epistolae, Schedam sibi porrigentem conspexisset, eo advolans e Religiosorum manibus, qui eum tenebant, ipsam Schedam ad manum obtinuit. . . .*'

['. . . (the penitent) saw the Demon himself by the sacred altar of Zell through the little window on the Epistle side, offering him the paper; he rushed to the place from the hands of the Fathers who were holding him, and seized the same paper. . . .']

May, 1678, he returned to Mariazell, he complained of *maligni Spiritûs manifestationes* ['manifestations of the Evil Spirit'].[1]

He told the reverend Fathers that his reason for returning was that he had to require the Devil to give him back another, earlier bond, which had been written in ink.[2] This time once more the Blessed Virgin and the pious Fathers helped him to obtain the fulfilment of his request. As to how this came about, however, the report is silent. It merely states shortly: *quâ iuxta votum redditâ* ['when this had been returned in accordance with his prayer']—he prayed once again and received the pact back. After this he felt quite free and entered the Order of the Brothers Hospitallers.

We have occasion yet again to acknowledge that in spite of the obvious purpose of his efforts, the compiler has not been tempted into departing from the veracity required of a case history. For he does not conceal the outcome of the enquiry that was made in 1714 from the Superior of the Monastery of the Brothers Hospitallers [in Vienna] concerning the painter's later history. The Reverend Pater Provincialis reported that Brother Chrysostomus had again been repeatedly tempted by the Evil Spirit, who tried to seduce him into making a fresh pact (though this only happened 'when he had drunk somewhat too much wine').[3] But by the grace of God, it had always been possible to repel these attempts. Brother Chrysostomus had died of a hectic fever 'peacefully and of good comfort'[4] in the year 1700 in the Monastery of the Order, at Neustatt on the Moldau.

---

[1] [The manuscript reads: '*de* . . . *maligni Spiritûs infestatione* (of . . . molestation by the Evil Spirit)'.]

[2] This bond had been signed in September, 1668, and by May, 1678, nine and a half years later, it would long since have fallen due.

[3] ['Wenn er etwas mehrers von Wein getrunken.']

[4] ['Sanft und trostreich.']

II

THE MOTIVE FOR THE PACT WITH
THE DEVIL

IF we look at this bond with the Devil as if it were the case history of a neurotic, our interest will turn in the first instance to the question of its motivation, which is, of course, intimately connected with its exciting cause. Why does anyone sign a bond with the Devil? Faust, it is true, asked contemptuously: 'Was willst du armer Teufel geben?' ['What hast thou to give, poor Devil?']¹ But he was wrong. In return for an immortal soul, the Devil has many things to offer which are highly prized by men: wealth, security from danger, power over mankind and the forces of nature, even magical arts, and, above all else, enjoyment—the enjoyment of beautiful women. These services performed or undertakings made by the Devil are usually mentioned specifically in the agreement made with him.² What, then, was the motive which induced Christoph Haizmann to make his pact?

Curiously enough, it was none of these very natural wishes. To put the matter beyond doubt, one has only to read the short remarks attached by the painter to his illustrations of the apparitions of the Devil. For example, the caption to the third vision runs: 'On the third occasion within a year and a half, he appeared to me in this loathsome shape, with a book in his hand which was full of magic and black arts . . .'³ But from

---

¹ [*Faust*, Part I, Scene 4.]

² Cf. *Faust*, Part I, Scene 4:

> Ich will mich *hier* zu deinem Dienst verbinden,
> Auf deinem Wink nicht rasten und nicht ruhn;
> Wenn wir uns *drüben* wieder finden,
> So sollst du mir das Gleiche thun.

> [*Here*, an unwearied slave, I'll wear thy tether,
> And to thine every nod obedient be:
> When *There* again we come together,
> Then thou shalt do the same for me.
>
> (Bayard Taylor's translation.)]

³ ['Zum driten ist er mir in anderthalb Jahren in diser abscheühlichen Gestalt erschinen, mit einen Buuch in der Handt, darin lauter Zauberey und schwarze Kunst war begrüffen . . .']

79

the legend attached to a later apparition we learn that the Devil reproached him violently for having 'burnt his before-mentioned book',[1] and threatened to tear him to pieces if he did not give it back.

At his fourth appearance the Devil showed him a large yellow money-bag and a great ducat and promised him to give him as many of these as he wanted at any time. But the painter is able to boast that he 'had taken nothing whatever of the kind'.[2]

Another time the Devil asked him to turn to enjoyment and entertainment,[3] and the painter remarks that 'this indeed came to pass at his desire; but I did not continue for more than three days and it was then brought to an end'.[4]

Since he rejected magical arts, money and pleasures when they were offered him by the Devil, and still less made them conditions of the pact, it becomes really imperative to know what the painter in fact wanted from the Devil when he signed a bond with him. *Some* motive he must have had for his dealings with the Devil.

On this point, too, the *Trophaeum* provides us with reliable information. He had become low-spirited, was unable or un-willing to work properly and was worried about making a livelihood; that is to say, he was suffering from melancholic depression, with an inhibition in his work and (justified) fears about his future. We can see that what we are dealing with really is a case history. We learn, too, the exciting cause of the illness, which the painter himself, in the caption to one of his pictures of the Devil, actually calls a melancholia ('that I should seek diversion and banish melancholy'[5]). The first of our three sources of information, the village priest's letter of introduction, speaks, it is true, only of the state of depression ('*dum artis suae progressum emolumentumque secuturum* pusillanimis *perpenderet*'[6]), but the second source, the Abbot Franciscus's report, tells us the cause of this despondency or depression as

---

[1] ['. . . sein vorgemeldtes Buuch verbrennt.']

[2] ['. . . aber ich solliches gar nit angenomben.']

[3] [There is some indication in the illustration to the original manu-script that this has a sexual meaning.]

[4] ['. . . welliches zwar auch auf sein begehren geschehen aber ich yber drey Tag nit continuirt, vnd gleich widerumb aufgelöst worden.']

[5] ['. . . solte mich darmit belustigen und meläncoley vertreiben.']

[6] ['. . . when he was feeling despondent about the progress of his art and his future earnings . . .']

well. He says: '*acceptâ aliquâ pusillanimitate* ex morte parentis';[1] and in the compiler's preface the same words are used, though in a reversed order: ('*ex morte parentis acceptâ aliquâ pusillanimitate*'). His father, then, had died and he had in consequence fallen into a state of melancholia; whereupon the Devil had approached him and asked him why he was so downcast and sad, and had promised 'to help him in every way and to give him support'.[2]

Here was a person, therefore, who signed a bond with the Devil in order to be freed from a state of depression. Undoubtedly an excellent motive, as anyone will agree who can have an understanding sense of the torments of such a state and who knows as well how little medicine can do to alleviate this ailment. Yet no one who has followed the story so far as this would be able to guess what the wording of this bond (or rather, of these two bonds)[3] with the Devil actually was.

These bonds bring us two great surprises. In the first place, they mention no *undertaking* given by the Devil in return for whose fulfilment the painter pledges his eternal bliss, but only a *demand* made by the Devil which the painter must satisfy. It strikes us as quite illogical and absurd that this man should give up his soul, not for something he is to *get* from the Devil but for something he is to *do* for him. But the undertaking given by the *painter* seems even stranger.

The first 'syngrapha' [bond], written in ink, runs as follows: 'Ich Christoph Haizmann vndterschreibe mich disen Herrn sein leibeigener Sohn auff 9. Jahr. 1669 Jahr.'[4] The second, written in blood, runs:—

'Anno 1669.

'Christoph Haizmann. Ich verschreibe mich disen Satan ich

---

[1] ['. . . having become somewhat despondent owing to the death of his parent . . .']

[2] ['. . . auf alle Weiss zu helfen und an die Handt zu gehen.']—The first picture on the title-page and its caption represent the Devil in the form of an 'honest citizen' ['ersamer Bürger'. He is also so represented in the first of the eight separate pictures (cf. p. 85 and the frontispiece).]

[3] Since there were two of them—the first written in ink, and the second written about a year later in blood—both said still to be in the treasury of Mariazell and to be transcribed in the *Trophaeum*.

[4] ['I, Christoph Haizmann, subscribe myself to this Lord as his bounden son till the ninth year. Year 1669.']

sein leibeigner Sohn zu sein, und in 9. Jahr ihm mein Leib und Seel zuzugeheren.'[1]

All our astonishment vanishes, however, if we read the text of the bonds in the sense that what is represented in them as a demand made by the Devil is, on the contrary, a service performed by him—that is to say, it is a demand made by the *painter*. The incomprehensible pact would in that case have a straightforward meaning and could be paraphrased thus. The Devil undertakes to replace the painter's lost father for nine years. At the end of that time the painter becomes the property, body and soul, of the Devil, as was the usual custom in such bargains. The train of thought which motivated the painter in making the pact seems to have been this: his father's death had made him lose his spirits and his capacity to work; if he could only obtain a father-substitute he might hope to regain what he had lost.

A man who has fallen into a melancholia on account of his father's death must really have been fond of him. But, if so, it is very strange that such a man should have hit upon the idea of taking the Devil as a substitute for the father whom he loved.

---

[1] ['Christoph Haizmann. I sign a bond with this Satan, to be his bounden son and in the ninth year to belong to him body and soul.']

THE DEVIL AS A FATHER-SUBSTITUTE

I FEAR that sober critics will not be prepared to admit that this fresh interpretation has made the meaning of this pact with the Devil clear. They will have two objections to make to it.

In the first place they will say that it is not necessary to regard the bond as a contract in which the undertakings of both parties have been set out. On the contrary, they will argue, it contains only the painter's undertaking; the Devil's is omitted from the text, and is, as it were, *sousentendu*: the painter gives *two* undertakings—firstly to be the Devil's son for nine years, and secondly to belong to him entirely after death. In this way one of the premisses on which our conclusion is built would be disposed of.

The second objection will be that we are not justified in attaching any special importance to the expression 'the Devil's bounden son'; that this is no more than a common figure of speech, which anyone could interpret in the same way as the reverend Fathers may have done. For in their Latin translation they did not mention the relationship of son promised in the bonds, but merely say that the painter '*mancipavit*' himself—made himself a bondslave—to the Evil One and had undertaken to lead a sinful life and to deny God and the Holy Trinity. Why depart from this obvious and natural view of the matter?[1] The position would simply be that a man, in the torment and perplexity of a melancholic depression, signs a bond with the Devil, to whom he ascribes the greatest therapeutic power. That the depression was occasioned by his father's death would then be irrelevant; the occasion might quite as well have been something else.

All this sounds convincing and reasonable. Psycho-analysis has once more to meet the reproach that it makes hair-splitting complications in the simplest things and sees mysteries and

---

[1] In point of fact, when we come to consider later [p. 96 ff.] at what time and for whom these bonds were drawn up, we shall realize that their text had to be expressed in unobtrusive and generally comprehensible terms. It is enough for us, however, that it contains an ambiguity which we can take as the starting-point of our discussion.

problems where none exist, and that it does this by laying undue stress on insignificant and irrelevant details, such as occur everywhere, and making them the basis of the most far-reaching and strangest conclusions. It would be useless for us to point out that this rejection of our interpretation would do away with many striking analogies and break a number of subtle connections which we are able to demonstrate in this case. Our opponents will say that those analogies and connections do not in fact exist, but have been imported into the case by us with quite uncalled-for ingenuity.

I will not preface my reply with the words, 'to be honest' or 'to be candid', for one must always be able to be these things without any special preliminaries. I will instead say quite simply that I know very well that no reader who does not already believe in the justifiability of the psycho-analytic mode of thought will acquire that belief from the case of the seventeenth-century painter, Christoph Haizmann. Nor is it my intention to make use of this case as evidence of the validity of psycho-analysis. On the contrary, I presuppose its validity and am employing it to throw light on the painter's demonological illness. My justification for doing so lies in the success of our investigations into the nature of the neuroses in general. We may say in all modesty that to-day even the more obtuse among our colleagues and contemporaries are beginning to realize that no understanding of neurotic states can be reached without the help of psycho-analysis.

'These shafts can conquer Troy, these shafts alone'

as Odysseus confesses in the *Philoctetes* of Sophocles.

If we are right in regarding our painter's bond with the Devil as a neurotic phantasy, there is no need for any further apology for considering it psycho-analytically. Even small indications have a meaning and importance, and quite specially when they are related to the conditions under which a neurosis originates. To be sure, it is as possible to overvalue as to undervalue them, and it is a matter of judgement how far one should go in exploiting them. But anyone who does not believe in psycho-analysis—or, for the matter of that, even in the Devil—must be left to make what he can of the painter's case, whether he is able to furnish an explanation of his own or whether he sees nothing in it that needs explaining.

We therefore come back to our hypothesis that the Devil with whom the painter signed the bond was a direct substitute for his father. And this is borne out by the shape in which the Devil first appeared to him—as an honest elderly citizen with a brown beard, dressed in a red cloak and leaning with his right hand on a stick, with a black dog beside him[1] (cf. the first picture). Later on his appearance grows more and more terrifying—more mythological, one might say. He is equipped with horns, eagle's claws and bat's wings. Finally he appears in the chapel as a flying dragon. We shall have to come back later to a particular detail of his bodily shape.

It does indeed sound strange that the Devil should be chosen as a substitute for a loved father. But this is only so at first sight, for we know a good many things which lessen our surprise. To begin with, we know that God is a father-substitute; or, more correctly, that he is an exalted father; or, yet again, that he is a copy of a father as he is seen and experienced in childhood—by individuals in their own childhood and by mankind in its prehistory as the father of the primitive and primal horde. Later on in life the individual sees his father as something different and lesser. But the ideational image belonging to his childhood is preserved and becomes merged with the inherited memory-traces of the primal father to form the individual's idea of God. We also know, from the secret life of the individual which analysis uncovers, that his relation to his father was perhaps ambivalent from the outset, or, at any rate, soon became so. That is to say, it contained two sets of emotional impulses that were opposed to each other: it contained not only impulses of an affectionate and submissive nature, but also hostile and defiant ones. It is our view that the same ambivalence governs the relations of mankind to its Deity. The unresolved conflict between, on the one hand, a longing for the father and, on the other, a fear of him and a son's defiance of him, has furnished us with an explanation of important characteristics of religion and decisive vicissitudes in it.[2]

Concerning the Evil Demon, we know that he is regarded as the antithesis of God and yet is very close to him in his nature. His history has not been so well studied as that of God; not all

---

[1] [Cf. the frontispiece to this volume.] In Goethe [*Faust*, Part I, Scenes 2 and 3], a black dog like this turns into the Devil himself.

[2] Cf. *Totem and Taboo* (1912–13) and Reik (1919).

religions have adopted the Evil Spirit, the opponent of God, and his prototype in the life of the individual has so far remained obscure. One thing, however, is certain: gods can turn into evil demons when new gods oust them. When one people has been conquered by another, their fallen gods not seldom turn into demons in the eyes of the conquerors. The evil demon of the Christian faith—the Devil of the Middle Ages—was, according to Christian mythology, himself a fallen angel and of a godlike nature. It does not need much analytic perspicacity to guess that God and the Devil were originally identical—were a single figure which was later split into two figures with opposite attributes.[1] In the earliest ages of religion God himself still possessed all the terrifying features which were afterwards combined to form a counterpart of him.

We have here an example of the process, with which we are familiar, by which an idea that has a contradictory—an ambivalent—content becomes divided into two sharply contrasted opposites. The contradictions in the original nature of God are, however, a reflection of the ambivalence which governs the relation of the individual to his personal father. If the benevolent and righteous God is a substitute for his father, it is not to be wondered at that his hostile attitude to his father, too, which is one of hating and fearing him and of making complaints against him, should have come to expression in the creation of Satan. Thus the father, it seems, is the individual prototype of both God and the Devil. But we should expect religions to bear ineffaceable marks of the fact that the primitive primal father was a being of unlimited evil—a being less like God than the Devil.

It is true that it is by no means easy to demonstrate the traces of this satanic view of the father in the mental life of the individual. When a boy draws grotesque faces and caricatures, we may no doubt be able to show that he is jeering at his father in them; and when a person of either sex is afraid of robbers and burglars at night, it is not hard to recognize these as split-off portions of the father.[2] The animals, too, which appear in

[1] Cf. Reik, 1923, Chapter VII [quoting Ernest Jones, 1912. (See footnote 1, p. 72.)]

[2] In the familiar fairy tale of 'The Seven Little Goats', the Father Wolf appears as a burglar. [This fairy tale figures prominently in the 'Wolf Man' case history (1918b).]

children's animal phobias are most often father-substitutes, as were the totem animals of primaeval times. But that the Devil is a duplicate of the father and can act as a substitute for him has not been shown so clearly elsewhere as in the demonological neurosis of this seventeenth-century painter. That is why, at the beginning of this paper [p. 73], I foretold that a demonological case history of this kind would yield in the form of pure metal material which, in the neuroses of a later epoch (no longer superstitious but hypochrondriacal instead) has to be laboriously extracted by analytic work from the ore of free associations and symptoms.[1] A deeper penetration into the analysis of our painter's illness will probably bring stronger conviction. It is no unusual thing for a man to acquire a melancholic depression and an inhibition in his work as a result of his father's death. When this happens, we conclude that the man had been attached to his father with an especially strong love, and we remember how often a severe melancholia appears as a neurotic form of mourning.[2]

In this we are undoubtedly right. But we are not right if we conclude further that this relation has been merely one of love. On the contrary, his mourning over the loss of his father is the more likely to turn into melancholia, the more his attitude to him bore the stamp of ambivalence. This emphasis on ambivalence, however, prepares us for the possibility of the father being subjected to a debasement, as we see happening in the painter's demonological neurosis. If we were able to learn as much about Christoph Haizmann as about a patient undergoing an analysis with us, it would be an easy matter to elicit this ambivalence,

[1] The fact that in our analyses we so seldom succeed in finding the Devil as a father-substitute may be an indication that for those who come to us for analysis this figure from mediaeval mythology has long since played out its part. For the pious Christian of earlier centuries belief in the Devil was no less a duty than belief in God. In point of fact, he needed the Devil in order to be able to keep hold of God. The later decrease in faith has, for various reasons, first and foremost affected the figure of the Devil.

If we are bold enough to apply this idea of the Devil as a father-substitute to cultural history, we may also be able to see the witch-trials of the Middle Ages in a new light [as has already been shown by Ernest Jones in his chapter on witches in his book on the nightmare (1912). (See footnote 1, p. 72.)—Cf. also Editor's Note, pp. 69–70 above.]

[2] [For this and the following paragraph see 'Mourning and Melancholia' (1917e).]

to get him to remember when and under what provocations he
was given cause to fear and hate his father; and, above all, to
discover what were the accidental factors that were added to
the typical motives for a hatred of the father which are necessarily inherent in the natural relationship of son to father.
Perhaps we might then find a special explanation for the
painter's inhibition in work. It is possible that his father
had opposed his wish to become a painter. If that was so, his
inability to practise his art after his father's death would on the
one hand be an expression of the familiar phenomenon of
'deferred obedience'[1]; and. on the other hand, by making him
incapable of earning a livelihood, it would be bound to increase
his longing for his father as a protector from the cares of life.
In its aspect as deferred obedience it would also be an expression of remorse and a successful self-punishment.

Since, however, we cannot carry out an analysis of this sort
with Christoph Haizmann, who died in the year 1700, we must
content ourselves with bringing out those features of his case
history which may point to the typical exciting causes of a
negative attitude to the father. There are only a few such
features, nor are they very striking, but they are of great
interest.

Let us first consider the part played by the number nine. The
pact with the Evil One was for nine years. On this point the
unquestionably trustworthy report by the village priest of
Pottenbrunn is quite clear: *pro novem annis Syngraphen scriptam
tradidit.*[2] This letter of introduction, dated September 1, 1677,
is also able to inform us that the appointed time was about to
expire in a few days: *quorum et finis 24 mensis hujus futurus
appropinquat.*[3] The pact would therefore have been signed on
September 24, 1668.[4] In the same report, indeed, yet another
use is made of the number nine. The painter claims to have
withstood the temptations of the Evil One nine times—'*nonies*'
—before he yielded to him. This detail is no longer mentioned

---

[1] [An example of this will be found in the analysis of 'little Hans'
(1909*b*), *Standard Ed.*, **10**, 35.]

[2] ['He handed over a pact signed for nine years.']

[3] ['. . . the end of which is about to approach on the twenty-fourth of
this month.']

[4] The contradictory fact that both the pacts as transcribed bear the
date 1669 will be considered later [p. 93 ff.].

in the later reports. In the Abbot's deposition the phrase '*post annos novem* [after nine years]' is used, and the compiler repeats '*ad novem annos* [for nine years]' in his summary—a proof that this number was not regarded as indifferent.

The number nine is well known to us from neurotic phantasies. It is the number of the months of pregnancy, and wherever it appears it directs our attention to a phantasy of pregnancy. In our painter's case, to be sure, the number refers to years, not months; and it will be objected that nine is a significant number in other ways as well. But who knows whether it may not in general owe a good deal of its sanctity to the part it plays in pregnancy? Nor need we be disconcerted by the change from nine months to nine years. We know from dreams[1] what liberties 'unconscious mental activity' takes with numbers. If, for instance, the number five occurs in a dream, this can invariably be traced back to a five that is important in waking life; but whereas in waking life the five was a five years' difference in age or a company of five people, it appeared in the dream as five bank-notes or five fruits. That is to say, the number is kept, but its denominator is changed according to the requirements of condensation and displacement. Nine years in a dream could thus easily correspond to nine months in real life. The dream-work plays about with the numbers of waking life in another way, too, for it shows a sovereign disregard for noughts and does not treat them as numbers at all. Five dollars in a dream can stand for fifty or five hundred or five thousand dollars in reality.[2]

Another detail in the painter's relations to the Devil has once more a sexual reference. On the first occasion, as I have mentioned, he saw the Evil One in the shape of an honest citizen. But already on the second occasion the Devil was naked and misshapen, and had two pairs of female breasts.[3] In none of his subsequent apparitions are the breasts absent, either as a single or a double pair. Only in one of them does the Devil exhibit, in addition to the breasts, a large penis ending in a snake. This stressing of the female sexual character by introducing large pendulous breasts (there is never any indication of the

---

[1] [Cf. *The Interpretation of Dreams* (1900a), Chapter VI, Section F, *Standard Ed.*, **5**, 414-18.]

[2] [Cf. an example of this in 'Dreams and Folklore' (1957a [1911]), *Standard Ed.*, **12**, 186.]   [3] [Cf. plate facing p. 69.]

female genitals) is bound to appear to us as a striking contradiction of our hypothesis that the Devil had the meaning of a father-substitute for the painter. And, indeed, such a way of representing the Devil is in itself unusual. Where 'devil' is thought of in a generic sense, and devils appear in numbers, there is nothing strange about depicting female devils; but that *the* Devil, who is a great individuality, the Lord of Hell and the Adversary of God, should be represented otherwise than as a male, and, indeed, as a super-male, with horns, tail and a big penis-snake—this, I believe, is never found.

These two slight indications give us an idea of what the typical factor is which determines the negative side of the painter's relation to his father. What he is rebelling against is his feminine attitude to him which culminates in a phantasy of bearing him a child (the nine years). We have an accurate knowledge of this resistance from our analyses, where it takes on very strange forms in the transference and gives us a great deal of trouble. With the painter's mourning for his lost father, and the heightening of his longing for him, there also comes about in him a re-activation of his long-since repressed phantasy of pregnancy, and he is obliged to defend himself against it by a neurosis and by debasing his father.

But why should his father, after being reduced to the status of a Devil, bear this physical mark of a woman? The feature seems at first hard to interpret; but soon we find two explanations which compete with each other without being mutually exclusive. A boy's feminine attitude to his father undergoes repression as soon as he understands that his rivalry with a woman for his father's love has as a precondition the loss of his own male genitals—in other words, castration. Repudiation of the feminine attitude is thus the result of a revolt against castration. It regularly finds its strongest expression in the converse phantasy of castrating the father, of turning *him* into a woman. Thus the Devil's breasts would correspond to a projection of the subject's own femininity on to the father-substitute. The second explanation of these female additions to the Devil's body no longer has a hostile meaning but an affectionate one. It sees in the adoption of this shape an indication that the child's tender feelings towards his mother have been displaced on to his father; and this suggests that there has previously been a strong fixation on the mother, which, in its turn, is responsible for part of the child's hostility towards his father. Large breasts are the positive sexual characteristics of the mother even at a time when the negative characteristic of the female—her lack of a penis—is as yet unknown to the child.[1]

If our painter's repugnance to accepting castration made it impossible for him to appease his longing for his father, it is perfectly understandable that he should have turned for help and salvation to the image of his mother. This is why he declared that only the Holy Mother of God of Mariazell could release him from his pact with the Devil and why he obtained his freedom once more on the day of the Mother's Nativity (September 8). Whether the day on which the pact was made— September 24—was not also determined in some similar way, we shall of course never know.

Among the observations made by psycho-analysis of the mental life of children there is scarcely one which sounds so repugnant and unbelievable to a normal adult as that of a boy's feminine attitude to his father and the phantasy of pregnancy that arises from it. It is only since Senatspräsident Daniel Paul Schreber, a judge presiding over a division of the Appeal Court of Saxony, published the history of his psychotic illness and his extensive recovery from it,[2] that we can discuss the subject without trepidation or apology. We learn from this invaluable book that, somewhere about the age of fifty, the Senatspräsident became firmly convinced that God—who, incidentally, ex-hibited distinct traits of his father, the worthy physician, Dr. Schreber—had decided to emasculate him, to use him as a woman, and to beget from him 'a new race of men born from the spirit of Schreber'.[3] (His own marriage was childless.) In his revolt against this intention of God's, which seemed to him highly unjust and 'contrary to the Order of Things', he fell ill with symptoms of paranoia, which, however, underwent a process of involution in the course of years, leaving only a small residue behind. The gifted author of his own case history could not have guessed that in it he had uncovered a typical pathogenic factor.

This revolt against castration or a feminine attitude has been torn out of its organic context by Alfred Adler. He has linked

---

[1] Cf. *Leonardo da Vinci and a Memory of his Childhood* (1910c).

[2] *Denkwürdigkeiten eines Nervenkranken*, 1903. See my analysis of his case (1911c).   [3] [*Standard Ed.*, **12**, 48 and 58.]

it superficially or falsely with the longing for power, and has postulated it as an independent 'masculine protest'. Since a neurosis can only arise from a conflict between two trends, it is as justifiable to see the cause of 'every' neurosis in the masculine protest as it is to see it in the feminine attitude against which the protest is being made. It is quite true that this masculine protest plays a regular part in the formation of character—in some types of people a very large part—and that we meet it in the analysis of neurotic men as a vigorous resistance. Psycho-analysis has attached due importance to the masculine protest in connection with the castration complex, without being able to accept its omnipotence or its omnipresence in neuroses. The most marked case of a masculine protest with all its manifest reactions and character-traits that I have met with in analysis was that of a patient who came to me for treatment on account of an obsessional neurosis in whose symptoms the unresolved conflict between a masculine and a feminine attitude (fear of castration and desire for castration) found clear expression. In addition, the patient had developed masochistic phantasies which were wholly derived from a wish to accept castration; and he had even gone beyond these phantasies to real satisfaction in perverse situations. The whole of his state rested—like Adler's theory itself—on the repression and denial of early infantile fixations of love.[1]

Senatspräsident Schreber found the way to recovery when he decided to give up his resistance to castration and to accommodate himself to the feminine role cast for him by God. After this, he became lucid and calm, was able to put through his own discharge from the asylum and led a normal life—with the one exception that he devoted some hours every day to the cultivation of his femaleness, of whose gradual advance towards the goal determined by God he remained convinced.

[1] [Freud had discussed Adler's 'masculine protest' at greater length a few years earlier in ' "A Child is Being Beaten" ' (1919e), Standard Ed., 17, 200 ff.]

THE TWO BONDS

A REMARKABLE detail in our painter's story is the statement that he signed two different bonds with the Devil.

The first, written in black ink, ran as follows:[1]

'I, Chr. H., subscribe myself to this Lord as his bounden son till the ninth year.'

The second, written in blood, ran:

'Chr. H. I sign a bond with this Satan, to be his bounden son, and in the ninth year to belong to him body and soul.'

The originals of both are said to have been in the archives at Mariazell when the *Trophaeum* was compiled, and both bear the same date—1669.

I have already made a number of references to the two bonds; and I now propose to deal with them in greater detail, although it is precisely here that the danger of overvaluing trifles seems especially great.

It is unusual for anyone to sign a bond with the Devil twice, in such a way that the first document is replaced by the second, but without losing its own validity. Perhaps this occurrence is less surprising to other people, who are more at home with demonological material. For my part, I could only look on it as a special peculiarity of our case, and my suspicions were aroused when I found that the reports were at variance precisely on this point. Examination of these discrepancies will afford us, unexpectedly, a deeper understanding of the case history.

The village priest of Pottenbrunn's letter of introduction describes a very simple and clear situation. In it mention is only made of one bond, which was written in blood by the painter nine years before and which was due to expire in a few days' time—on September 24 [1677]. It must therefore have been drawn up on September 24, 1668; unfortunately this date, although it can be inferred with certainty, is not explicitly stated.

The Abbot Franciscus's deposition, which was dated, as we

[1] [The German versions will be found above on pp. 81-2.]

know, a few days later (September 12, 1677), already describes
a more complicated state of affairs. It is plausible to assume that
the painter had given more precise information in the interval.
The deposition relates that the painter had signed two bonds:
one in the year 1668 (a date which should also be the correct
one according to the letter of introduction), written in black
ink, and the other *'sequenti anno* [in the following year] *1669'*,
written in blood. The bond that he received back on the day of
the Nativity of the Virgin [September 8] was the one written
in blood—viz. the later bond, which had been signed in 1669.
This does not emerge from the Abbot's deposition, for there it
merely says later *'schedam redderet* [should give back the paper]'
and *'schedam sibi porrigentem conspexisset* [saw him offering him the
paper]' as if there could only be a single document in question.
But it does follow from the subsequent course of the story, and
also from the coloured title-page of the *Trophaeum*, where what
is clearly a *red* script can be seen on the paper which the demon
dragon is holding. The further course of the story is, as I have
already related, that the painter returned to Mariazell in May,
1678, after he had experienced further temptations from the
Evil One in Vienna; and that he begged that, through a further
act of Grace on the part of the Holy Mother, the first document,
written in ink, might also be given back to him. In what way
this came about is not so fully described as on the first occasion.
We are merely told: *'quâ juxta votum redditâ* [when this had been
returned in accordance with his prayer]'; and in another
passage the compiler says that this particular bond was thrown
to the painter by the Devil 'crumpled up and torn into four
pieces' [1] on May 9, 1678, at about nine o'clock in the evening.

Both bonds, however, bear the date of the same year—1669.

This incompatibility is either of no significance or may put us
on the following track.

If we take as a starting-point the Abbot's account, as being
the more detailed one, we are confronted with a number of
difficulties. When Christoph Haizmann confessed to the village
priest of Pottenbrunn that he was hard pressed by the Devil and
that the time-limit would soon run out, he could only (in 1677)
have been thinking of the bond which he had signed in 1668—
namely, the first one, written in black (which is referred to in
the letter of introduction as the only one, but is described there

---

[1] [. . . *'in globum convolutam et in quatuor partes dilaceratam . . .'*]

as being written in blood). But a few days later, at Mariazell, he was only concerned to get back the later bond, in blood, which was not nearly due to expire then (1669–77), and allowed the first one to become overdue. This latter was not reclaimed till 1678—that is, when it had run into its tenth year. Furthermore, why are both the bonds dated in the same year (1669), when one of them is explicitly attributed to the following year ('*anno subsequenti*' [1])?

The compiler must have noticed these difficulties, for he made an attempt to remove them. In his preface he adopted the Abbot's version, but he modified it in one particular. The painter, he says, signed a bond with the Devil in 1669 in ink, but afterwards ('*deinde vero*') in blood. He thus overrode the express statement of both reports that one bond was signed in 1668, and he ignored the Abbot's remark in his deposition to the effect that there was a difference in the year-number between the two bonds. This he did in order to keep in harmony with the dating of the two documents that were given back by the Devil.

In the Abbot's deposition a passage appears in brackets after the words '*sequenti vero anno* [but in the following year] *1669*'. It runs: '*sumitur hic alter annus pro nondum completo, uti saepe in loquendo fieri solet, nam eundem annum indicant syngraphae, quarum atramento scripta ante praesentem attestationem nondum habita fuit.*'[2] This passage is clearly an interpolation by the compiler; for the Abbot, who had only seen one bond, could not have stated that both bore the same date. The placing of the passage in brackets, moreover, must have been intended to show that it was an addition to the text of the deposition.[3] It represents another attempt on the compiler's part to reconcile the incompatible evidence. He agrees that the first bond was signed in 1668; but he thinks that, since the year was already far advanced (it was September), the painter had post-dated it by a year so that both bonds were able to show the same year. His invoking the fact that people often do the same sort of thing in conversation

---

[1] [This is derived from the compiler's preface. The 'sequenti anno' quoted above (p. 94) and again below is from the Abbot's deposition.]

[2] ['Here the second (later) year is taken instead of the one that was not yet completed, as is often done in conversation; for the same year is indicated by (both) syngraphae (bonds), of which the one written in ink had not yet been received back before the present deposition.']

[3] [It is also written in very much smaller script than the rest of the Abbot's deposition.]

seems to me to stamp his whole attempt at an explanation as no more than a feeble evasion.

I cannot tell whether my presentation of the case has made any impression on the reader and whether it has put him in a position to take an interest in these minute details. I myself have found it impossible to arrive with any certainty at the true state of affairs; but, in studying this confused business, I hit upon a notion which has the advantage of giving the most natural picture of the course of events, even though once more the written evidence does not entirely fit in with it.

My view is that when the painter first came to Mariazell he spoke only of *one* bond, written in the regular way in blood, which was about to fall due and which had therefore been signed in September, 1668—all exactly as described in the village priest's letter of introduction. In Mariazell, too, he presented this bond in blood as the one which the Demon had given back to him under compulsion from the Holy Mother. We know what happened subsequently. The painter left the shrine soon afterwards and went to Vienna, where he felt free till the middle of October. Then, however, he began once more to be subjected to sufferings and apparitions, in which he saw the work of the Evil Spirit. He again felt in need of redemption, but was faced with the difficulty of explaining why the exorcism in the holy Chapel had not brought him a lasting deliverance. He would certainly not have been welcome at Mariazell if he had returned there uncured and relapsed. In this quandary, he invented an earlier, first bond, which, however, was to be written in ink, so that its supersession in favour of a later bond, written in blood, should seem more plausible. Having returned to Mariazell, he had this alleged first bond given back to him too. After this he was left in peace by the Evil One; but at the same time he did something else, which will show us what lay in the background of his neurosis.

The drawings he made were undoubtedly executed during his second stay at Mariazell: the title-page, which is a single composition, contains a representation of both the bond scenes. The attempt to make his new story tally with his earlier one may well have caused him embarrassment. It was unfortunate for him that his additional invention could only be of an earlier bond and not of a later one. Thus he could not avoid the awkward result that he had redeemed one—the blood bond—

too soon (in the eighth year), and the other—the black bond—
too late (in the tenth year). And he betrayed the double editing
of the story by making a mistake in the dating of the bonds and
attributing the earlier one as well as the later to the year 1669.
This mistake has the significance of a piece of unintentional
honesty: it enables us to guess that the supposedly earlier bond
was fabricated at the later date. The compiler, who certainly
did not begin revising the material before 1714, and perhaps not
till 1729, had to do his best to resolve its not inconsiderable
contradictions. Finding that both the bonds before him were
dated 1669, he had recourse to the evasion which he interpolated in the Abbot's deposition.

It is easy to see where the weak spot lies in this otherwise
attractive reconstruction. Reference is already made to the
existence of two bonds, one in black and one in blood, in the
Abbot's deposition. I therefore have the choice between accus-
ing the compiler of having also made an alteration in the
deposition, an alteration closely related to his interpolation, or
confessing that I am unable to unravel the tangle.[1]

---

[1] The compiler, it seems to me, was between two fires. On the one
hand, he found, in the village priest's letter of introduction as well as in
the Abbot's deposition, the statement that the bond (or at any rate the
first bond) had been signed in 1668; on the other hand, both bonds,
which had been preserved in the archives, bore the date 1669. As he had
two bonds before him, it seemed certain to him that two bonds had been
signed. If, as I believe, the Abbot's deposition mentioned only one bond,
he was obliged to insert in the deposition a reference to the other and
then remove the contradiction by the hypothesis of the post-dating. The
textual alteration which he made occurs immediately before the interpolation, which can only have been written by him. He was obliged to
link the interpolation to the alteration with the words '*sequenti vero anno*
[but in the following year] 1669', since the painter had expressly
written in his (very much damaged) caption to the title-page:

'A year after He
... terrible threatenings in
... shape No. 2, was forced
... to sign a bond in blood.'
['*Nach einem Jahr würdt Er*
... *schrökhliche betrohungen in ab-*
... *gestalt Nr. 2 bezwungen sich*
... *n Bluot zu verschreiben.*']

The painter's blunder [*Verschreiben*] in writing his *Syngraphae*—a
blunder which I have been obliged to assume in my attempted explanation—appears to me to be no less interesting than are the actual

The reader will long ago have judged this whole discussion superfluous and the details concerned in it too unimportant. But the matter gains a new interest if it is pursued in a certain direction.

I have just expressed the view that, when the painter was disagreeably surprised by the course taken by his illness, he invented an earlier bond (the one in ink) in order to be able to maintain his position with the reverend Fathers at Mariazell. Now I am writing for readers who, although they believe in psycho-analysis, do not believe in the Devil; and they might object that it was absurd for me to bring such an accusation against the poor wretch—*hunc miserum*, as he is called in the letter of introduction. For, they will say, the bond in blood was just as much a product of his phantasy as the allegedly earlier one in ink. In reality, no Devil appeared to him at all, and the whole business of pacts with the Devil only existed in his imagination. I quite realize this: the poor man cannot be denied the right to supplement his original phantasy with a new one, if altered circumstances seem to require it.

But here, too, the matter goes further. After all, the two bonds were not phantasies like the visions of the Devil. They were documents, preserved, according to the assurances of the copyist and the deposition of the later Abbot Kilian, in the archives of Mariazell, for all to see and touch. We are therefore in a dilemma. Either we must assume that both the papers which were supposed to have been given back to the painter through divine Grace were written by him at the time when he needed them; or else, despite all the solemn assurances, the confirmatory evidence of witnesses, signed and sealed, and so on, we shall be obliged to deny the credibility of the reverend Fathers of Mariazell and St. Lambert. I must admit that I am unwilling to cast doubts on the Fathers. I am inclined to think, it is true, that the compiler, in the interests of consistency, has falsified some things in the deposition made by the first Abbot; but a 'secondary revision' such as this does not go much beyond what is carried out even by modern lay historians, and

bonds. [There is a pun here on the word '*Verschreiben*', which means 'making a mistake in writing' as well as 'signing a bond'.—At the beginning of Chapter X of *The Psychopathology of Everyday Life* (1901*b*), *Standard Ed.*, **6**, 220, Freud points out that an accidental slip often reveals a deliberate falsification.]

at all events it was done in good faith. In another respect, the reverend Fathers have established a good claim to our confidence. As I have said already [pp. 77 and 78] there was nothing to prevent them from suppressing the accounts of the incompleteness of the cure and the continuance of the temptations. And even the description of the scene of exorcism in the Chapel, which one might have viewed with some apprehension, is soberly written and inspires belief. So there is nothing for it but to lay the blame on the painter. No doubt he had the red bond with him when he went to penitential prayer in the Chapel, and he produced it afterwards as he came back to his spiritual assistants from his meeting with the Demon. Nor need it have been the same paper which was later preserved in the archives, and, according to our construction, it may have borne the date 1668 (nine years before the exorcism).

THE FURTHER COURSE OF THE NEUROSIS

But if this is so, we should be dealing not with a neurosis but with a deception, and the painter would be a malingerer and forger instead of a sick man suffering from possession. But the transitional stages between neurosis and malingering are, as we know, very fluid. Nor do I see any difficulty in supposing that the painter wrote this paper and the later one, and took them with him, in a peculiar state, similar to the one in which he had his visions. Indeed there was no other course open to him if he wished to carry into effect his phantasy of his pact with the Devil and of his redemption.

On the other hand, the diary written in Vienna, which he gave to the clerics on his second visit to Mariazell, bears the stamp of veracity. It undoubtedly affords us a deep insight into the motivation—or let us rather say, the exploitation—of the neurosis.

The entries extend from the time of the successful exorcism till January 13[1] of the following year, 1678.

Until October 11 he felt very well in Vienna, where he lived with a married sister; but after that he had fresh attacks, with visions, convulsions, loss of consciousness and painful sensations, and these finally led to his return to Mariazell in May, 1678.

The story of his fresh illness falls into three phases. First, temptation appeared in the form of a finely dressed cavalier, who tried to persuade him to throw away the document attesting his admission to the Brotherhood of the Holy Rosary.[2] He resisted this temptation, whereupon the same thing happened next day; only this time the scene was laid in a magnificently decorated hall in which grand gentlemen were dancing with beautiful ladies. The same cavalier who had tempted him before made a proposal to him connected with painting[3] and promised to give him a handsome sum of money in return. After he had made this vision disappear by prayer, it was repeated once more a few days later, in a still more pressing form. This

---

[1] [In all the German editions except the first this is misprinted '15'.]

[2] [A religious order to which he had been admitted on his arrival in Vienna.]   [3] This passage is unintelligible to me.

time the cavalier sent one of the most beautiful of the ladies who sat at the banqueting table to him to persuade him to join their company, and he had difficulty in defending himself from the temptress. Most terrifying of all, moreover, was the vision which occurred soon after this. He saw a still more magnificent hall, in which there was a 'throne built up of gold pieces'. Cavaliers were standing about awaiting the arrival of their King. The same person who had so often made proposals to him now approached him and summoned him to ascend the throne, for they 'wanted to have him for their King and to honour him for ever'. This extravagant phantasy concluded the first, perfectly transparent, phase of the story of his temptation.

There was bound to be a revulsion against this. An ascetic reaction reared its head. On October 20 a great light appeared, and a voice came from it, making itself known as Christ, and commanded him to forswear this wicked world and serve God in the wilderness for six years. The painter clearly suffered more from these holy apparitions than from the earlier demoniacal ones; it was only after two and a half hours that he awoke from this attack. In the next attack the holy figure surrounded by light was much more unfriendly. He issued threats against him for not having obeyed the divine behest and led him down into Hell so that he might be terrified by the fate of the damned. Evidently, however, this failed in its effect, for the apparitions of the figure surrounded by light, which purported to be Christ, were repeated several more times. Each time the painter underwent an *absence* and an ecstasy lasting for hours. In the grandest of these ecstasies the figure surrounded by light took him first into a town in whose streets people were perpetrating all the acts of darkness; and then, in contrast, took him to a lovely meadow in which anchorites were leading a godly life and were receiving tangible evidence of God's grace and care. There then appeared, instead of Christ, the Holy Mother herself, who, reminding him of what she had already done on his behalf, called on him to obey the command of her dear Son. 'Since he could not truly resolve so to do', Christ appeared to him again the next day and upbraided him soundly with threats and promises. At last he gave way and made up his mind to leave the world and to do what was required of him. With this decision, the second phase ended. The painter states that from this time onwards he had no more visions and no more temptations.

Nevertheless, his resolution cannot have been firm enough or he must have delayed its execution too long; for while he was in the midst of his devotions, on December 26, in St. Stephen's [Cathedral], catching sight of a strapping young woman accompanied by a smartly dressed gentleman, he could not fend off the thought that he might himself be in this gentleman's place. This called for punishment, and that very evening it overtook him like a thunderbolt. He saw himself in bright flames and sank down in a swoon. Attempts were made to rouse him but he rolled about in the room till blood flowed from his mouth and nose. He felt that he was surrounded by heat and noisome smells, and he heard a voice say that he had been condemned to this state as a punishment for his vain and idle thoughts. Later he was scourged with ropes by Evil Spirits, and was told that he would be tormented like this every day until he had decided to enter the Order of Anchorites. These experiences continued up to the last entry in his diary (January 13).

We see how our unfortunate painter's phantasies of temptation were succeeded by ascetic ones and finally by phantasies of punishment. The end of his tale of suffering we know already. In May he went to Mariazell, told his story of an earlier bond written in black ink, to which he explicitly attributed his continued torment by the Devil, received this bond back, too, and was cured.

During his second stay there he painted the pictures which are copied in the *Trophaeum*. Then he took a step which was in keeping with the demands of the ascetic phase of his diary. He did not, it is true, go into the wilderness to become an anchorite, but he joined the Order of the Brothers Hospitallers: *religiosus factus est*.

Reading the diary, we gain insight into another part of the story. It will be remembered that the painter signed a bond with the Devil because after his father's death, feeling depressed and unable to work, he was worried about making a livelihood. These factors of depression, inhibition in his work and mourning for his father are somehow connected with one another, whether in a simple or a complicated way. Perhaps the reason why the apparitions of the Devil were so over-generously furnished with breasts was that the Evil One was meant to become his foster-father. This hope was not fulfilled, and the painter continued to be in a bad state. He could not work properly, or he was out of luck and could not find enough employment. The village priest's letter of introduction speaks of him as '*hunc miserum omni auxilio destitutum*' [p. 75]. He was thus not only in moral straits but was suffering material want. In the account [in his diary] of his later visions, we find remarks here and there indicating—as do the contents of the scenes described—that even after the successful first exorcism, nothing had been changed in his situation. We come to know him as a man who fails in everything and who is therefore trusted by no one. In his first vision the cavalier asked him 'what he is going to do, since he has no one to stand by him'. The first series of visions in Vienna tallied completely with the wishful phantasies of a poor man, who had come down in the world and who hungered for enjoyment: magnificent halls, high living, a silver dinner-service and beautiful women. Here we find what was missing in his relations with the Devil made good. At that time he had been in a melancholia which made him unable to enjoy anything and obliged him to reject the most attractive offers. After the exorcism the melancholia seems to have been overcome and all his worldly-minded desires had once more become active.

In one of the ascetic visions he complained to his guide (Christ) that nobody had any faith in him, so that he was unable to carry out the commands laid upon him. The reply he was given is, unfortunately, obscure to us: 'Although they will not believe me, yet I know well what has happened, but I am not able to declare it.' Especially illuminating, however, are the experiences which his heavenly Guide made him have among the anchorites. He came to a cave in which an old man had been sitting for the last sixty years, and in answer to a question he learnt that this old man had been fed every day by God's angels. And then he saw for himself how an angel brought the old man food: 'Three dishes with food, a loaf, a dumpling and some drink.' After the anchorite had eaten, the angel collected everything and carried it away. We can see what the temptation was which the pious visions offered the painter: they were meant to induce him to adopt a mode of existence in which he need no longer worry about sustenance. The utterances of Christ in the last vision are also worthy of note. After threatening that, if he did not prove amenable, something would happen which would oblige him and the people to believe [in it[1]], Christ gave him a

[1] ['*Daran*', in square brackets in the German.]

direct warning that 'I should not heed the people; even if they were to persecute me or give me no help, God would not abandon me'.

Christoph Haizmann was enough of an artist and a child of the world to find it difficult to renounce this sinful world. Nevertheless, in view of his helpless position, he did so in the end. He entered a Holy Order. With this, both his internal struggle and his material need came to an end. In his neurosis, this outcome was reflected in the fact of his seizures and visions being brought to an end by the return of an alleged first bond. Actually, both portions of his demonological illness had the same meaning. He wanted all along simply to make his life secure. He tried first to achieve this with the help of the Devil at the cost of his salvation; and when this failed and had to be given up, he tried to achieve it with the help of the clergy at the cost of his freedom and most of the possibilities of enjoyment in life. Perhaps he himself was only a poor devil who simply had no luck; perhaps he was too ineffective or too untalented to make a living, and was one of those types of people who are known as 'eternal sucklings'—who cannot tear themselves away from the blissful situation at the mother's breast, and who, all through their lives, persist in a demand to be nourished by someone else.— And so it was that, in this history of his illness, he followed the path which led from his father, by way of the Devil as a father-substitute, to the pious Fathers of the Church.

To superficial observation Haizmann's neurosis appears to be a masquerade which overlays a part of the serious, if commonplace, struggle for existence. This is not always the case, but it is not infrequently so. Analysts often discover how unprofitable it is to treat a business man who 'though otherwise in good health, has for some time shown signs of a neurosis'. The business catastrophe with which he feels himself threatened throws up the neurosis as a by-product; and this gives him the advantage of being able to conceal his worries about his real life behind his symptoms. But apart from this the neurosis serves no useful purpose whatever, since it uses up forces which would have been more profitably employed in dealing rationally with the dangerous situation.

In a far greater number of cases the neurosis is more autonomous and more independent of the interests of self-preservation and self-maintenance. In the conflict which creates the neurosis, what are at stake are either solely libidinal interests or libidinal interests in intimate connections with self-preservative ones. In all three instances the dynamics of the neurosis are the same. A dammed-up libido which cannot be satisfied in reality succeeds, with the help of a regression to old fixations, in finding discharge through the repressed unconscious. The sick man's ego, in so far as it can extract a 'gain from illness' out of this process, countenances the neurosis, although there can be no doubt of its injuriousness in its economic aspect.

Nor would our painter's wretched situation in life have provoked a demonological neurosis in him if his material need had not intensified his longing for his father. After his melancholia and the Devil had been disposed of, however, he still had to face a struggle between his libidinal enjoyment of life and his realization that the interests of self-preservation called imperatively for renunciation and asceticism. It is interesting to see that the painter was very well aware of the unity of the two portions of his illness, for he attributed both to the bonds which he had signed with the Devil. On the other hand, he made no sharp distinction between the operations of the Evil Spirit and those of the Divine Powers. He had only one description for both: they were manifestations of the Devil.

REMARKS ON THE THEORY AND PRACTICE
OF DREAM-INTERPRETATION
(1923 [1922])

BEMERKUNGEN ZUR THEORIE UND PRAXIS DER TRAUMDEUTUNG

(*a*) GERMAN EDITIONS:

1923   *Int. Z. Psychoanal.*, **9** (1), 1–11.

1925   *G.S.*, **3**, 305–18.

1925   *Traumlehre*, 49–62.

1931   *Sexualtheorie und Traumlehre*, 354–68.

1940   *G.W.*, **13**, 301–14.

(*b*) ENGLISH TRANSLATION:
'Remarks upon the Theory and Practice of
Dream-Interpretation'

1943   *Int. J. Psycho-Anal.*, **24** (1–2), 66–71. (Tr. James
Strachey.)

1945   *Yb. Psychoan.*, **1**, 13–30. (Reprint of above.)

1950   *C.P.*, **5**, 136–49. (Revised reprint of above.)

The present translation is a corrected version, with additional notes, of the one published in 1950.

The contents of this paper were communicated by Freud to his companions during a walking-tour in the Harz mountains in September, 1921 (Jones, 1957, 86), the same tour in which he read them two other papers, 1941*d* and 1922*b* (*Standard Ed.*, **18**, 175 and 223). The present paper, however, was not actually written until a year later, in July, 1922, at Gastein (Jones, ibid., 93). (The date of the year of writing is wrongly given as '1923' in Jones, 1955, 269.) It will be seen that Sections VIII and X reflect Freud's interest in the 'compulsion to repeat' and in the demonstration of an 'ego ideal', as discussed in his contemporary works, *Beyond the Pleasure Principle* (1920*g*) and *Group Psychology* (1921*c*) respectively.

REMARKS ON THE THEORY AND PRACTICE
OF DREAM-INTERPRETATION

THE accidental circumstance that the last editions of my
Interpretation of Dreams (1900a)[1] have been printed from stereo-
type plates has led me to issue the following remarks in an
independent form, instead of introducing them into the text as
modifications or additions.

I

In interpreting a dream during an analysis a choice lies open
to one between several technical procedures.[2]

One can (*a*) proceed chronologically and get the dreamer to
bring up his associations to the elements of the dream in the
order in which those elements occurred in his account of the
dream. This is the original, classical method, which I still
regard as the best if one is analysing one's own dreams.

Or one can (*b*) start the work of interpretation from some one
particular element of the dream which one picks out from the
middle of it. For instance, one can choose the most striking
piece of it, or the piece which shows the greatest clarity or sensory intensity; or, again, one can start off from some spoken
words in the dream, in the expectation that they will lead to the
recollection of some spoken words in waking life.

Or one can (*c*) begin by entirely disregarding the manifest
content and instead ask the dreamer what events of the previous
day are associated in his mind with the dream he has just
described.

Finally, one can (*d*), if the dreamer is already familiar with
the technique of interpretation, avoid giving him any instructions and leave it to him to decide with which associations to the
dream he shall begin.

I cannot lay it down that one or the other of these techniques
is preferable or in general yields better results.

---

[1] [The sixth and seventh editions, published in 1921 and 1922.]
[2] [Cf. the similar discussion near the beginning of Lecture XXIX of
the *New Introductory Lectures* (1933a).]

II

What is of far greater importance is the question of whether the work of interpretation proceeds under a *pressure of resistance* which is *high* or *low*—a point on which the analyst never remains long in doubt. If the pressure is high, one may perhaps succeed in discovering what the things are with which the dream is concerned, but one cannot make out what it says about these things. It is as though one were trying to listen to a conversation taking place at a distance or in a very low voice. In that case, one can feel confident that there is not much prospect of collaborating with the dreamer, one decides not to bother too much about it and not to give him much help, and one is content to put before him a few translations of symbols that seem probable.

The majority of dreams in a difficult analysis are of this kind; so that one cannot learn much from them about the nature and mechanism of dream-formation. Least of all can one learn anything from them upon the recurring question of where the dream's wish-fulfilment may lie hidden. When the pressure of resistance is quite extremely high, one meets with the phenomenon of the dreamer's associations broadening instead of deepening. In place of the desired associations to the dream that has already been narrated, there appear a constant succession of new fragments of dream, which in their turn remain without associations.

It is only when the resistance is kept within moderate limits that the familiar picture of the work of interpretation comes into view: the dreamer's associations begin by *diverging* widely from the manifest elements, so that a great number of subjects and ranges of ideas are touched on, after which, a second series of associations quickly *converge* from these on to the dream-thoughts that are being looked for. When this is so, collaboration between the analyst and the dreamer becomes possible; whereas under a high pressure of resistance it would not even be of any advantage.

A number of dreams which occur during analyses are untranslatable even though they do not actually make much show of the resistance that is there. They represent free renderings of the latent dream-thoughts behind them and are comparable to successful creative writings which have been artistically worked over and in which the basic themes are still recognizable though they have been subjected to any amount of re-arrangement and transformation. Dreams of this kind serve in the treatment as an introduction to thoughts and memories of the dreamer without their own actual content coming into account.

III

It is possible to distinguish between dreams *from above* and dreams *from below*, provided the distinction is not made too sharply. Dreams from below are those which are provoked by the strength of an unconscious (repressed) wish which has found a means of being represented in some of the day's residues. They may be regarded as inroads of the repressed into waking life. Dreams from above correspond to thoughts or intentions of the day before which have contrived during the night to obtain reinforcement from repressed material that is debarred from the ego.[1] When this is so, analysis as a rule disregards this unconscious ally and succeeds in inserting the latent dream-thoughts into the texture of waking thought. This distinction calls for no modification in the theory of dreams.

IV

In some analyses, or in some periods of an analysis, a divorce may become apparent between dream-life and waking life, like the divorce between the activity of phantasy and waking life which is found in the 'continued story' (a novel in day-dreams). In that case one dream leads off from another, taking as its central point some element which was lightly touched upon in its predecessor, and so on. But we find far more frequently that dreams are not attached to one another but are interpolated into a successive series of portions of waking thought.

V

The interpretation of a dream falls into two phases: the phase

[1] [Freud makes some further remarks on 'dreams from above' in his letter to Maxime Leroy on some dreams of Descartes (1929*b*). He had already noticed the existence of such dreams in *The Interpretation of Dreams* (1900*a*), *Standard Ed.*, 5, 560.]

in which it is translated and the phase in which it is judged or
has its value assessed. During the first phase one must not allow
oneself to be influenced by any consideration whatever for the
second phase. It is as though one had before one a chapter from
some work in a foreign language—by Livy, for instance. The
first thing one wants to know is what Livy says in the chapter;
and it is only after this that the discussion arises of whether
what one has read is a historical narrative or a legend or a
digression on the part of the author.

What conclusions can one draw from a correctly translated
dream? I have an impression that analytic practice has not
always avoided errors and over-estimations on this point, partly
owing to an exaggerated respect for the 'mysterious unconscious'. It is only too easy to forget that a dream is as a rule
merely a thought like any other, made possible by a relaxation
of the censorship and by unconscious reinforcement, and distorted by the operation of the censorship and by unconscious
revision.[1]

Let us take as an example the so-called dreams of recovery. If
a patient has had a dream of this kind, in which he seems to
abandon the restrictions of his neurosis—if, for instance, he
overcomes some phobia or gives up some emotional attachment
—we are inclined to think that he has made a great step forward, that he is ready to take his place in a new state of life, that
he has begun to reckon on his recovery, etc. This may often be
true, but quite as often such dreams of recovery only have the
value of dreams of convenience:[2] they signify a wish to be well
at last, in order to avoid another portion of the work of analysis
which is felt to lie ahead. In this sense, dreams of recovery very
frequently occur, for instance, when the patient is about to
enter upon a new and disagreeable phase of the transference.
He is behaving in this just like some neurotics who after a few

---

[1] [The fact that dreams are merely 'a form of thinking' is often
insisted on by Freud. See, for instance, his 'History of the Psycho-
Analytic Movement' (1914d), *Standard Ed.*, 14, 65, 'Some Neurotic
Mechanisms' (1922b), ibid., 18, 229 and a long footnote added to *The
Interpretation of Dreams* in 1925, ibid., 5, 506–7.]

[2] [See *The Interpretation of Dreams*, ibid., 4, 123 ff. For examples and
a discussion of these dreams and of the 'corroborative' dreams in Section VII below, see Section III of the case of female homosexuality
(1920a), ibid., 18, 164–6.]

hours of analysis declare they have been cured—because they want to escape all the unpleasantness that is bound to come up for discussion in the analysis. Sufferers from war neuroses, too, who gave up their symptoms because the therapy adopted by the army doctors succeeded in making being ill even more uncomfortable than serving at the front—these sufferers, too, were following the same economic laws and in both cases alike the cures have proved to be only temporary.[1]

VI

It is by no means easy to arrive at general conclusions upon the value of correctly translated dreams. If a conflict due to ambivalence is taking place in a patient, then the emergence in him of a hostile thought certainly does not imply a permanent overcoming of his affectionate impulse—that is to say, a resolution of the conflict: neither does any such implication follow from a *dream* with a similarly hostile content. During a conflict such as this arising from ambivalence, there are often two dreams every night, each of them representing an opposite attitude. In that case the progress lies in the fact that a complete isolation of the two contrasted impulses has been achieved and that each of them, with the help of its unconscious reinforcements, can be followed and understood to its extreme limits. And if it sometimes happens that one of the two ambivalent dreams has been forgotten, one must not be deceived into assuming that a decision has been made in favour of the one side. The fact that one of the dreams has been forgotten shows, it is true, that for the moment one tendency is in the ascendant, but that is true only of the one day, and may be changed. The next night may perhaps bring the opposite expression into the foreground. The true state of the conflict can only be determined by taking into account all the other indications, including those of waking life.

VII

The question of the value to be assigned to dreams is intimately related to the other question of their susceptibility to

[1] [Cf. Freud's memorandum on the treatment of war neuroses (1955c [1920]), *Standard Ed.*, 17, 213–14.]

influence from 'suggestion' by the physician. Analysts may at first be alarmed at the mention of this possibility.[1] But on further reflection this alarm will give place to the realization that the influencing of the patient's dreams is no more a blunder on the part of the analyst or disgrace to him than the guiding of the patient's conscious thoughts.

The fact that the manifest content of dreams is influenced by the analytic treatment stands in no need of proof. It follows from our knowledge that dreams take their start from waking life and work over material derived from it. Occurrences during analytic treatment are of course among the impressions of waking life and soon become some of the most powerful of these. So it is not to be wondered at that patients should dream of things which the analyst has discussed with them and of which he has aroused expectations in them. At least it is no more to be wondered at than what is implied in the familiar fact of 'experimental' dreams.[2]

But from here our interest proceeds to the question whether the latent dream-thoughts that have to be arrived at by interpretation can also be influenced or suggested by the analyst. And to this the answer must once more be that they obviously can be. For a portion of these latent dream-thoughts correspond to preconscious thought-formations, perfectly capable of being conscious, with which the dreamer might quite well have reacted to the physician's remarks in his waking state too—whether the patient's reactions were in harmony with those remarks or in opposition to them. In fact, if we replace the dream by the dream-thoughts which it contains, the question of how far one can suggest dreams coincides with the more general question of how far a patient in analysis is accessible to suggestion.

On the mechanism of dream-formation itself, on the dream-work in the strict sense of the word, one never exercises any influence: of that one may be quite sure.

Besides that portion of the dream which we have already discussed—the preconscious dream-thoughts—every true dream contains indications of the repressed wishful impulses to which it owes the possibility of its formation. The doubter will reply that they appear in the dream because the dreamer knows that

[1] [Cf. paragraph '4', near the end of Lecture XV of the *Introductory Lectures* (1916–17).]

[2] [See *The Interpretation of Dreams*, ibid., 4, 181 n. and 5, 384.]

he ought to produce them—that they are expected by the analyst. The analyst himself will rightly think otherwise.

If a dream brings up situations that can be interpreted as referring to scenes from the dreamer's past, it seems especially important to ask whether the physician's influence can also play a part in such contents of the dream as these. And this question is most urgent of all in the case of what are called 'corroborative' dreams, dreams which, as it were, 'tag along behind' the analysis.[1] With some patients these are the only dreams that one obtains. Such patients reproduce the forgotten experiences of their childhood only after one has constructed them from their symptoms, associations and other signs and has propounded these constructions to them.[2] Then follow the corroborative dreams, concerning which, however, the doubt arises whether they may not be entirely without evidential value, since they may have been imagined in compliance with the physician's words instead of having been brought to light from the dreamer's unconscious. This ambiguous position cannot be escaped in the analysis, since with these patients unless one interprets, constructs and propounds, one never obtains access to what is repressed in them.

The situation takes a favourable turn if the analysis of a corroborative dream of this sort, which 'tags along behind', is immediately followed by feelings of remembering what has hitherto been forgotten. But even then the sceptic can fall back upon an assertion that the recollections are illusory. Moreover, such feelings are for the most part absent. The repressed material is only allowed through bit by bit; and every lack of completeness inhibits or delays the forming of a sense of conviction. Furthermore, what we are dealing with may not be the reproduction of a real and forgotten event but the bringing forward of an unconscious phantasy, about which no feeling of memory is ever to be expected, though the possibility may sometimes remain of a sense of subjective conviction.

Is it possible, then, that corroborative dreams are really the result of suggestion, that they are 'obliging' dreams? The patients who produce only corroborative dreams are the same patients in whom doubt plays the principal part in resistance.

[1] [See the technical paper on dream-interpretation (1911*e*), *Standard Ed.*, 12, 96.]

[2] [See Freud's late paper 'Constructions in Analysis' (1937*d*).]

One makes no attempt at shouting down this doubt by means of one's authority or at reducing it by arguments. It must persist until it is brought to an end in the further course of the analysis. The analyst, too, may himself retain a doubt of the same kind in some particular instances. What makes him certain in the end is precisely the complication of the problem before him, which is like the solution of a jig-saw puzzle. A coloured picture, pasted upon a thin sheet of wood and fitting exactly into a wooden frame, is cut into a large number of pieces of the most irregular and crooked shapes. If one succeeds in arranging the confused heap of fragments, each of which bears upon it an unintelligible piece of drawing, so that the picture acquires a meaning, so that there is no gap anywhere in the design and so that the whole fits into the frame—if all these conditions are fulfilled, then one knows that one has solved the puzzle and that there is no alternative solution.

An analogy of this kind can of course have no meaning for a patient while the work of analysis is still uncompleted. At this point I recall a discussion which I was led into with a patient whose exceptionally ambivalent attitude was expressed in the most intense compulsive doubt. He did not dispute my interpretations of his dreams and was very much struck by their agreement with the hypotheses which I put forward. But he asked whether these corroborative dreams might not be an expression of his compliance towards me. I pointed out that the dreams had also brought up a quantity of details of which I could have had no suspicion and that his behaviour in the treatment apart from this had not been precisely characterized by compliance. Whereupon he switched over to another theory and asked whether his narcissistic wish to be cured might not have caused him to produce these dreams, since, after all, I had held out to him a prospect of recovery if he were able to accept my constructions. I could only reply that I had not yet come across any such mechanism of dream-formation. But a decision was reached by another road. He recollected some dreams which he had had before starting analysis and indeed before he had known anything about it; and the analysis of these dreams, which were free from all suspicion of suggestion, led to the same interpretations as the later ones. It is true that his obsession for contradiction once more found a way out in the idea that the earlier dreams had been less clear than those that occurred during the treatment; but I was satisfied with their similarity. I think that in general it is a good plan occasionally to bear in mind the fact that people were in the habit of dreaming before there was such a thing as psycho-analysis.

VIII

It may well be that dreams during psycho-analysis succeed in bringing to light what is repressed to a greater extent than dreams outside that situation. But it cannot be proved, since the two situations are not comparable; the employment of dreams in analysis is something very remote from their original purpose. On the other hand, it cannot be doubted that within an analysis far more of the repressed is brought to light in connection with dreams than by any other method. In order to account for this, there must be some motive power, some unconscious force, which is better able to lend support to the purposes of analysis during the state of sleep than at other times. What is here in question cannot well be any factor other than the patient's compliance towards the analyst which is derived from his parental complex—in other words, the positive portion of what we call the transference; and in fact, in many dreams which recall what has been forgotten and repressed, it is impossible to discover any other unconscious wish to which the motive force for the formation of the dream can be attributed. So that if anyone wishes to maintain that most of the dreams that can be made use of in analysis are obliging dreams and owe their origin to suggestion, nothing can be said against that opinion from the point of view of analytic theory. In that case I need only add a reference to what I have said in my *Introductory Lectures* [(1916–17) Lecture XXVIII], where I have dealt with the relation between transference and suggestion and shown how little the trustworthiness of our results is affected by a recognition of the operation of suggestion in our sense.

In *Beyond the Pleasure Principle* (1920g) [*Standard Ed.*, **18**, 18 ff.] I have dealt with the economic problem of how what are in every respect distressing experiences of the early infantile sexual period can succeed in forcing their way through to some kind of reproduction. I was obliged to ascribe to them an extraordinarily strong upward drive in the shape of the 'compulsion to repeat'—a force able to overcome the repression which, in obedience to the pleasure principle, weighs down upon them—though not until 'the work of treatment has gone half-way to meet it and has loosened the repression'. Here we may add that it is the positive transference that gives this assistance to the compulsion to repeat. Thus an alliance has been made between the treatment and the compulsion to repeat, an alliance which is directed in the first instance against the pleasure principle but of which the ultimate purpose is the establishment of the dominion of the reality principle. As I have shown in the passage to which I am referring, it happens only too often that the compulsion to repeat throws over its obligations under this alliance and is not content with the return of the repressed merely in the form of dream-pictures.

IX

So far as I can at present see, dreams that occur in a traumatic neurosis are the only *genuine* exceptions [ibid., **18**, 32 f.], and punishment dreams are the only *apparent* exceptions [ibid., **5**, 557 f.], to the rule that dreams are directed towards wish-fulfilment. In the latter class of dreams we are met by the remarkable fact that actually nothing belonging to the latent dream-thoughts is taken up into the manifest content of the dream. Something quite different appears instead, which must be described as a reaction-formation against the dream-thoughts, a rejection and complete contradiction of them. Such offensive action as this against the dream can only be ascribed to the critical agency of the ego and it must therefore be assumed that the latter, provoked by the unconscious wish-fulfilment, has been temporarily re-established even during the sleeping state. It might have reacted to the undesirable content of the dream by waking up; but it has found a means, by the construction of the punishment dream, of avoiding an interruption of sleep.

For instance, in the case of the well-known dreams of the poet Rosegger which I discussed in *The Interpretation of Dreams* [ibid., **5**, 473–7], we must suspect the existence of a suppressed version with an arrogant and boastful text, whereas the actual dream said to him: 'You are an incompetent journeyman tailor.' It would, of course, be useless to look for a repressed wishful impulse as the motive power for a manifest dream such as this;

one must be content with the fulfilment of the wish for self-criticism.

A dream-structure of this kind will excite less astonishment if one considers how frequently dream-distortion, acting in the service of the censorship, replaces a particular element by something that is in some sense or other its opposite or contrary. It is only a short step from there to the replacement of a characteristic portion of the content of the dream by a defensive contradiction, and one further step will lead to the whole objectionable dream-content being replaced by the punishment dream. I should like to give a couple of characteristic examples of the intermediate phase in the falsification of the manifest content.

Here is an extract from the dream of a girl with a strong fixation to her father, who had difficulty in talking during the analysis. She was sitting in a room with a girl friend, and dressed only in a kimono. A gentleman came in and she felt embarrassed. But the gentleman said: 'Why, this is the girl we saw once before dressed so nicely!'—The gentleman stood for me, and, further back, for her father. But we can make nothing of the dream unless we make up our mind to replace the most important element in the gentleman's speech by its contrary: 'This is the girl I saw once before *undressed* and who looked so nice then!' When she was a child of three or four she had for some time slept in the same room as her father and everything goes to suggest that she used then to throw back her clothes in her sleep to please her father. The subsequent repression of her pleasure in exhibiting herself was the motive for her secretiveness in the treatment, her dislike of showing herself openly.

And here is another scene from the same dream. She was reading her own case history, which she had before her in print. In it was a statement that 'a young man murdered his *fiancée*—cocoa—that comes under anal erotism.' This last phrase was a thought that she had in the dream at the mention of cocoa.[1]— The interpretation of this piece of the dream was even more difficult than the former one. It emerged at last that before going to sleep she had been reading my 'History of an Infantile Neurosis' (1918*b*), the central point of which is the

[1] [The German word '*Kakao*' suggests '*Kaka*', the nursery expression for 'faeces'. Cf. an example of the same connection in a footnote to 'Character and Anal Erotism' (1908*b*), *Standard Ed.*, 9, 172.]

real or imagined observation by a patient of his parents copulating. She had already once before related this case history to her own, and this was not the only indication that in her case as well there was a question of an observation of the same kind. The young man murdering his fiancée was a clear reference to a sadistic view of the scene of copulation. But the next element, the cocoa, was very remote from it. Her only association to cocoa was that her mother used to say that cocoa gave one a headache, and she maintained that she had heard the same thing from other women. Moreover, she had at one time identified herself with her mother by means of headaches like hers. Now I could find no link between the two elements of the dream except by supposing that she wanted to make a diversion from the consequences of the observation of coitus. No, she was saying, coitus had nothing to do with the procreation of children; children came from something one ate (as they do in fairy tales); and the mention of anal erotism, which looks like an attempt in the dream at interpretation, supplemented the infantile theory which she had called to her help, by adding anal birth to it.

X

Astonishment is sometimes expressed at the fact that the dreamer's ego can appear two or more times in the manifest dream, once as himself and again disguised behind the figures of other people.[1] During the course of the construction of the dream, the secondary revision has evidently sought to obliterate this multiplicity of the ego, which cannot fit in with any possible scenic situation; but it is re-established by the work of interpretation. In itself this multiplicity is no more remarkable than the multiple appearance of the ego in a waking thought, especially when the ego divides itself into subject and object, puts one part of itself as an observing and critical agency in contrast to the other, or compares its present nature with its recollected past, which was also ego once; for instance, in such sentences as 'When *I* think what *I*'ve done to this man' or 'When *I* think that *I* too was a child once'. But I should reject as a meaningless and unjustifiable piece of speculation the notion that *all* figures that appear in a dream are to be regarded as frag-

[1] [See *The Interpretation of Dreams*, ibid., 4, 323. In 1925 Freud added a sentence to the original passage, giving the gist of what follows here.]

mentations and representatives of the dreamer's own ego. It is enough that we should keep firmly to the fact that the separation of the ego from an observing, critical, punishing agency (an ego ideal) must be taken into account in the interpretation of dreams as well.

SOME ADDITIONAL NOTES ON DREAM-INTERPRETATION AS A WHOLE

(1925)

EDITOR'S NOTE

EINIGE NACHTRÄGE ZUM GANZEN DER TRAUMDEUTUNG

(*a*) GERMAN EDITIONS:
1925 *G.S.*, **3**, 172–84.
1925 *Traumlehre*, 63–76.
1931 *Sexualtheorie und Traumlehre*, 369–81 (Omitting Part III).
1952 *G.W.*, **1**, 559–73.

(*b*) ENGLISH TRANSLATION:
'Some Additional Notes upon Dream-Interpretation
as a Whole'
1943 *Int. J. Psycho-Anal.*, **24** (1–2), 71–5. (Tr. James Strachey.)
1950 *C.P.*, **5**, 150–62. (Revised reprint of above.)

Volume III of the *Gesammelte Schriften*, in which this first appeared, was published in the autumn of 1925. At about the same time (September, 1925) the third only of these essays was included in *Almanach 1926* (pp. 27–31) and was also printed in *Imago*, **11** (3) (1925) 234–8. A reprint of the English translation of the third essay only was included in *Psychoanalysis and the Occult*, New York, 1953, International Universities Press, 87–90, edited by George Devereux. The present translation is a slightly modified version, with additional notes, of the one published in 1950.

These three short essays have had a somewhat chequered bibliographical history. As was explained in the Editor's Introduction to *The Interpretation of Dreams (Standard Ed.*, **4**, xii), when the first collected edition of Freud's works (the *Gesammelte Schriften*) was brought out, it was decided to devote the second volume to an exact reprint of the first edition of *Die Traumdeutung* and to collect in the third volume all the alterations and additions to that work which had been made in its later editions. Among this additional material were three whole '*Zusatzkapiteln* (Supplementary Chapters)'. The first two of these (dealing with symbols and secondary revision respectively) consisted almost entirely of old material which had been added to the book from the second edition onwards. But *Zusatzkapitel* C (the present group of papers) was entirely new and had never appeared in any previous edition. There can be little doubt, however, that Freud intended to include it in all later editions of *Die Traumdeutung*, for the place at which it was to appear—at the very end of the book—was indicated clearly in the reprint of the first edition in the *Gesammelte Schriften* (**2**, 538).[1]

This was in 1925. The next normal, one-volume, edition of *Die Traumdeutung* (the 8th) appeared in 1930. It included all the new material from the 1925 edition, with the single exception of Supplementary Chapter C. One immediate consequence of this was its absence also from the revised English (Brill) translation of 1932. Nor is it included in the edition of *Die Traumdeutung* which occupies the double volume **2–3** of the *Gesammelte Werke* (1942). Indeed,[2] it seemed dogged by misfortunes, for it was accidentally overlooked when its turn came for inclusion at the correct chronological point in *G.W.*, **14** (published in 1948) and room had finally to be found for it at the end of *G.W.*, **1**, the last volume of the series to appear, in 1952. The German text had thus been lost sight of for over twenty years.

There is a possible explanation of the earliest of these events —the omission of the chapter from the 8th edition of *Die Traumdeutung*. Freud's more than half-acceptance of the genuineness of telepathy in the last of these essays had, on its first appearance, provoked some strong protests from Ernest Jones on the ground that it would damage the cause of psychoanalysis in scientific circles, particularly in England. The account given of the episode by Jones (1957, 422 ff.) shows that Freud seemed unmoved by the protests; but it is conceivable that he nevertheless yielded to them to the extent of not including the essay in the canon of the most famous of all his works.

---

[1] In the course of these essays, moreover, Freud speaks of 'this book' and 'these pages' with obvious reference to *The Interpretation of Dreams* (pp. 131 and 132 below).

[2] The first two essays only were reprinted in 1931 in the collective volume of Freud's shorter writings on dreams. The absence of the third essay goes to confirm the hypothesis in the last paragraph of this note.

SOME ADDITIONAL NOTES ON DREAM-INTERPRETATION AS A WHOLE

(A) THE LIMITS TO THE POSSIBILITY OF INTERPRETATION[1]

It may be asked whether it is possible to give a complete and assured translation into the language of waking life (that is, an interpretation) of every product of dream-life. This question will not be treated here in the abstract but with reference to the conditions under which one works at interpreting dreams.

Our mental activities pursue either a useful aim or an immediate yield of pleasure. In the former case what we are dealing with are intellectual judgements, preparations for action or the conveyance of information to other people. In the latter case we describe these activities as play or phantasy. What is useful is itself (as is well known) only a circuitous path to pleasurable satisfaction. Now, dreaming is an activity of the second kind, which is indeed, from the point of view of evolution, the earlier one. It is misleading to say that dreams are concerned with the tasks of life before us or seek to find a solution for the problems of our daily work. That is the business of preconscious thought. Useful work of this kind is as remote from dreams as is any intention of conveying information to another person. When a dream deals with a problem of actual life, it solves it in the manner of an irrational wish and not in the manner of a reasonable reflection. There is only one useful task, only one function, that can be ascribed to a dream, and that is the guarding of sleep from interruption. A dream may be described as a piece of phantasy working on behalf of the maintenance of sleep.

It follows from this that it is on the whole a matter of indifference to the sleeping ego what may be dreamt during the

---

[1] [Freud had touched on this question more briefly in several earlier passages: in *The Interpretation of Dreams* itself (1900*a*), *Standard Ed.*, 5, 524–5, in *The Psychopathology of Everyday Life* (1901*b*), Chapter XII (E), ibid., 6, 269, and in the technical paper on dream-analysis (1911*e*), ibid., 12, 93–4.]

night so long as the dream performs its task, and that those dreams best fulfil their function about which one knows nothing after waking. If it so often happens otherwise, if we remember dreams—even after years and decades—it always means that there has been an irruption of the repressed unconscious into the normal ego. Without this concession to it the repressed would not have consented to lend its help to the removal of the threat of disturbance to sleep. We know that it is the fact of this irruption that gives dreams their importance for psychopathology. If we can uncover a dream's motivating force, we shall obtain unsuspected information about the repressed impulses in the unconscious; and on the other hand, if we can undo its distortions, we shall overhear preconscious thought taking place in states of internal reflection which would not have attracted consciousness to themselves during the day-time.

No one can practise the interpretation of dreams as an isolated activity: it remains a part of the work of analysis. In analysis we direct our interest according to necessity, now to the preconscious content of the dream and now to the unconscious contribution to its formation; and we often neglect the one element in favour of the other. Nor would it be of any avail for anyone to endeavour to interpret dreams outside analysis. He would not succeed in escaping the conditions of the analytic situation; and if he worked at his own dreams, he would be undertaking a self-analysis. This comment would not apply to someone who did without the dreamer's collaboration and sought to interpret dreams by intuitive insight. But dream-interpretation of such a kind, without reference to the dreamer's associations, would in the most favourable case remain a piece of unscientific virtuosity of very doubtful value.

If one practises dream-interpretation according to the sole justifiable technical procedure, one soon notices that success depends entirely upon the tension of resistance between the awakened ego and the repressed unconscious. Work under a 'high pressure of resistance' demands (as I have explained elsewhere [p. 110 above]) a different attitude on the part of the analyst from work under a low pressure. In analysis one has for long periods at a time to deal with strong resistances which are still unknown to one and which it will in any case be impossible to overcome so long as they remain unknown. It is therefore not to be wondered at that only a certain portion of a patient's dream-products can be translated and made use of, and, even at that, most often incompletely. Even if, owing to one's own experience, one is in a position to understand many dreams to the interpretation of which the dreamer has contributed little, one must always remember that the certainty of such interpretations remains in doubt and one hesitates to press one's conjectures upon the patient.

Critical voices will now be raised. It will be objected that, since it is not possible to interpret every dream that is dealt with, one should cease asserting more than one can establish and should be content to say that *some* dreams can be shown by interpretation to have a meaning but that as to the rest we are in ignorance. But the very fact that success in interpretation depends upon the resistance absolves the analyst from the necessity for such modesty. He may have the experience of a dream that was at first unintelligible becoming clear during the very same hour after some fortunate remark has got rid of one of the dreamer's resistances. A portion of the dream which the patient had hitherto forgotten may suddenly occur to him and may bring the key to the interpretation; or a new association may emerge which may throw light upon the darkness. It sometimes happens, too, that, after months or years of analytic labour, one returns to a dream which at the beginning of the treatment seemed meaningless and incomprehensible but which is now, in the light of knowledge obtained in the meantime, completely elucidated.[1] And if one further takes into consideration the argument from the theory of dreams that the model dream-products of children invariably have a clear meaning and are easy to interpret,[2] then it will be justifiable to assert that dreams are quite generally mental structures that are capable of interpretation, though the situation may not always allow of an interpretation being reached.

When the interpretation of a dream has been discovered, it is not always easy to decide whether it is a 'complete' one— that is, whether further preconscious thoughts may not also have found expression in the same dream.[3] In that case we

[1] [Cf. a remark by Freud on the length of time required for the interpretation of the 'Wolf Man's' dream (1918*b*), *Standard Ed.*, **17**, 33.]

[2] [See, however, the qualifying remark added in 1925 to *The Interpretation of Dreams*, ibid., **4**, 127, footnote 1.]

[3] [Cf. ibid., **4**, 279 and **5**, 523.]

must consider the meaning proved which is based on the
dreamer's associations and our estimate of the situation, without on that account feeling bound to reject the other meaning.
It remains possible, though unproven; one must become accustomed to a dream being thus capable of having many meanings.
Moreover, the blame for this is not always to be laid upon incompleteness of the work of interpretation; it may just as well
be inherent in the latent dream-thoughts themselves. Indeed
it may happen in waking life, quite apart from the situation of
dream-interpretation, that one is uncertain whether some remark that one has heard or some piece of information that one
has received is open to construction this way or that, or whether
it is hinting at something else beyond its obvious meaning.

One interesting occurrence which has been insufficiently in-
vestigated is to be seen where the same manifest dream-content
gives simultaneous expression to a set of concrete ideas and to
an abstract line of thought based upon them. It is of course
difficult for the dream-work to find a means for representing
abstract thoughts.[1]

[1] [See a footnote to the metapsychological paper on dreams (1917d),
ibid., 14, 228, and a passage added to *The Interpretation of Dreams* in 1919,
ibid.. 5, 523–4.]

(B) MORAL RESPONSIBILITY FOR THE CONTENT OF DREAMS

In the introductory chapter of this book [*The Interpretation of Dreams*] (which discusses 'The Scientific Literature Dealing with the Problem of Dreams')[1] I have shown the way in which writers have reacted to what is felt as the distressing fact that the unbridled content of dreams is so often at odds with the moral sense of the dreamer. (I deliberately avoid speaking of 'criminal' dreams, as such a description, which would overstep the limits of psychological interest, seems to me quite uncalled-for.) The immoral character of dreams has naturally provided a fresh motive for denying them any psychical value: if dreams are the meaningless product of disordered mental activity, then there can be no ground for assuming responsibility for their apparent content.

The problem of responsibility for the manifest content of dreams has been fundamentally shifted and indeed disposed of by the explanations given in my *Interpretation of Dreams*.

We know now that the manifest content is a deception, a *façade*. It is not worth while to submit it to an ethical examination or to take its breaches of morality any more seriously than its breaches of logic or mathematics. When the 'content' of the dream is spoken of, what must be referred to can only be the content of the preconscious thoughts and of the repressed wishful impulse which are revealed behind the *façade* of the dream by the work of interpretation. Nevertheless, this immoral *façade* has a question to put to us. We have heard that the latent dream-thoughts have to submit to a severe censorship before they are allowed access to the manifest content. How can it happen, then, that this censorship, which makes difficulties over more trivial things, breaks down so completely over these manifestly immoral dreams?

The answer is not easy to come by and may perhaps not seem completely satisfying. If, in the first place, one submits these dreams to interpretation, one finds that some of them have given no offence to the censorship because *au fond* they

[1] [See Section F of that chapter, 'The Moral Sense in Dreams', *Standard Ed.*, 4, 66–74. See also ibid., 5, 619–21.]

have no bad meaning. They are innocent boastings or identifications that put up a mask of pretence; they have not been
censored because they do not tell the truth.[1] But others of
them—and, it must be admitted, the majority—really mean
what they say and have undergone no distortion from the
censorship. They are an expression of immoral, incestuous and
perverse impulses or of murderous and sadistic lusts. The
dreamer reacts to many of these dreams by waking up in a
fright, in which case the situation is no longer obscure to us.
The censorship has neglected its task, this has been noticed too
late, and the generation of anxiety is a substitute for the distortion that has been omitted. In still other instances of such
dreams, even that expression of affect is absent. The objectionable matter is carried along by the height of the sexual excite-
ment that has been reached during sleep, or it is viewed with
the same tolerance with which even a waking person can regard
a fit of rage, an angry mood or the indulgence in cruel
phantasies.

But our interest in the genesis of these *manifestly* immoral
dreams is greatly reduced when we find from analysis that the
majority of dreams—innocent dreams, dreams without affect
and anxiety-dreams—are revealed, when the distortions of the
censorship have been undone, as the fulfilments of immoral
—egoistic, sadistic, perverse or incestuous—wishful impulses.
As in the world of waking life, these masked criminals are far
commoner than those with their vizors raised. The straightforward dream of sexual relations with one's mother, which
Jocasta alludes to in the *Oedipus Rex*,[2] is a rarity in comparison
with all the multiplicity of dreams which psycho-analysis must
interpret in the same sense.

I have dealt so exhaustively in these pages [i.e., of *The
Interpretation of Dreams*] with this characteristic of dreams, which
indeed provides the motive for their distortion, that I can pass
at once from this topic to the problem that lies before us: Must
one assume responsibility for the content of one's dreams? For
the sake of completeness, it should, however, be added that
dreams do not always offer immoral wish-fulfilments, but often
energetic reactions against them in the form of 'punishment
dreams'. In other words, the dream-censorship can not only
express itself in distortions and the generation of anxiety, but

[1] [Cf. ibid., 5, 437.]   [2] [Cf. ibid., 4, 264.]

can go so far as to blot out the immoral subject-matter completely and replace it by something else that serves as an
atonement, though it allows one to see what lies behind.[1] But
the problem of responsibility for the immoral content of dreams
no longer exists for us as it formerly did for writers who knew
nothing of latent dream-thoughts and the repressed part of our
mental life. Obviously one must hold oneself responsible for
the evil impulses of one's dreams. What else is one to do with
them? Unless the content of the dream (rightly understood) is
inspired by alien spirits, it is a part of my own being. If I seek
to classify the impulses that are present in me according to
social standards into good and bad, I must assume responsibility for both sorts; and if, in defence, I say that what is unknown, unconscious and repressed in me is not my 'ego',[2] then
I shall not be basing my position upon psycho-analysis, I shall
not have accepted its conclusions—and I shall perhaps be
taught better by the criticisms of my fellow-men, by the disturbances in my actions and the confusion of my feelings. I
shall perhaps learn that what I am disavowing not only 'is' in
me but sometimes 'acts' from out of me as well.

It is true that in the metapsychological sense this bad repressed content does not belong to my 'ego'—that is, assuming
that I am a morally blameless individual—but to an 'id' upon
which my ego is seated. But this ego developed out of the id, it
forms with it a single biological unit, it is only a specially modified peripheral portion of it, and it is subject to the influences
and obeys the suggestions that arise from the id. For any vital
purpose, a separation of the ego from the id would be a hopeless
undertaking.

Moreover, if I were to give way to my moral pride and tried
to decree that for purposes of moral valuation I might disregard the evil in the id and need not make my ego responsible
for it, what use would that be to me? Experience shows me that
I nevertheless *do* take that responsibility, that I am somehow
compelled to do so. Psycho-analysis has made us familiar with
a pathological condition, obsessional neurosis, in which the

[1] [See pp. 118–19 above.]

[2] [As Freud himself points out in the next paragraph, the German
'*Ich*' here stands for something more like the English 'self'. This ambiguity in the German usage is discussed in the Editor's Introduction to
The Ego and the Id (1923*b*), pp. 7–8 above.]

poor ego feels itself responsible for all sorts of evil impulses of which it knows nothing, impulses which are brought up against it in consciousness but which it is unable to acknowledge. Something of this is present in every normal person. It is a remarkable fact that the more moral he is the more sensitive is his 'conscience'.[1] It is just as though we could say that the healthier a man is, the more liable he is to contagions and to the effects of injuries. This is no doubt because conscience is itself a reaction-formation against the evil that is perceived in the id. The more strongly the latter is suppressed, the more active is the conscience.

The ethical narcissism of humanity should rest content with the knowledge that the fact of distortion in dreams, as well as the existence of anxiety-dreams and punishment-dreams, afford just as clear evidence of his *moral* nature as dream-interpretation gives of the existence and strength of his *evil* nature. If anyone is dissatisfied with this and would like to be 'better' than he was created, let him see whether he can attain anything more in life than hypocrisy or inhibition.

The physician will leave it to the jurist to construct for social purposes a responsibility that is artificially limited to the meta-psychological ego. It is notorious that the greatest difficulties are encountered by the attempts to derive from such a construction practical consequences which are not in contradiction to human feelings.

[1] [This paradox had been mentioned in *The Ego and the Id* (1923*b*), p. 54 above, and is further discussed in 'The Economic Problem of Masochism' (1924*c*), p. 170 below. It is considered at greater length in Chapter VII of *Civilization and its Discontents* (1930*a*).]

(C) THE OCCULT SIGNIFICANCE OF DREAMS[1]

There seems to be no end to the problems of dream-life. But this can only be surprising if we forget that all the problems of mental life recur in dreams with the addition of a few new ones arising from the special nature of dreams. Many of the things that we study in dreams, because we meet with them there, have nevertheless little or nothing to do with the psychological peculiarity of dreams. Thus, for instance, symbolism is not a dream-problem, but a topic connected with our archaic thinking—our 'basic language', as it was aptly called by the paranoic Schreber.[2] It dominates myths and religious ritual no less than dreams, and dream-symbolism can scarcely even claim that it is peculiar in that it conceals more particularly things that are important sexually. Again, it is not to be expected that the explanation of anxiety-dreams will be found in the theory of dreams. Anxiety is a problem rather of neurosis, and all that remains to be discussed is how it comes about that anxiety can arise under dream conditions.[3]

The position is just the same, I think, in the matter of the relation of dreams to the alleged facts of the occult world. But, since dreams themselves have always been mysterious things, they have been brought into intimate connection with the other unknown mysteries. No doubt, too, they have a historic claim to that position, since in primaeval ages, when our mythology was being formed, dream-images may have played a part in the origin of ideas about spirits.

There would seem to be two categories of dreams with a claim to being reckoned as occult phenomena: prophetic dreams and telepathic ones. A countless multitude of witnesses speak in favour of both of them, while against both of them there is the obstinate aversion, or maybe prejudice, of science

There can, indeed, be no doubt that there are such things

[1] [This subject and much of this actual material were dealt with by Freud at greater length in a posthumously published paper 'Psycho-Analysis and Telepathy' (1941d [1921]), as well as in 'Dreams and Telepathy' (1922a) and in Lecture XXX ('Dreams and Occultism') of his *New Introductory Lectures* (1933a).]

[2] [Cf. the Schreber analysis (1911c), *Standard Ed.*, 12, 23.]

[3] [Cf. *The Interpretation of Dreams* (1900a) *Standard Ed.*, 5, 582 and footnote 2.]

as prophetic dreams, in the sense that their content gives some sort of picture of the future; the only question is whether these predictions coincide to any noticeable extent with what really happens subsequently. I must confess that upon this point my resolution in favour of impartiality deserts me. The notion that there is any mental power, apart from acute calculation, which can foresee future events in detail is on the one hand too much in contradiction to all the expectations and presumptions of science and on the other hand corresponds too closely to certain ancient and familiar human desires which criticism must reject as unjustifiable pretensions. I am therefore of opinion that after one has taken into account the untrustworthiness, credulity and unconvincingness of most of these reports, together with the possibility of falsifications of memory facilitated by emotional causes and the inevitability of a few lucky shots, it may be anticipated that the spectre of veridical prophetic dreams will disappear into nothing. Personally, I have never experienced anything or learnt of anything that could encourage a more favourable presumption.[1]

It is otherwise with telepathic dreams. But at this point it must be made quite clear that no one has yet maintained that telepathic phenomena—the reception of a mental process by one person from another by means other than sensory perception—are exclusively related to dreams. Thus once again telepathy is not a dream-problem: our judgement upon whether it exists or not need not be based on a study of telepathic dreams.

If reports of telepathic occurrences (or, to speak less exactly, of thought-transference) are submitted to the same criticism as stories of other occult events, there remains a considerable amount of material which cannot be so easily neglected. Further, it is much more possible to collect observations and experiences of one's own in this field which justify a favourable attitude to the problem of telepathy, even though they may not be enough to carry an assured conviction. One arrives at a provisional opinion that it may well be that telepathy really exists and that it provides the kernel of truth in many other hypotheses that would otherwise be incredible.

[1] [Cf. the posthumously published analysis of an allegedly prophetic dream (1941c [1899]). This is printed as Appendix A to *The Interpretation of Dreams, Standard Ed.*, **5**, 623 and also summarized in *The Psychopathology of Everyday Life* (1901b), ibid., **6**, 262-3.]

It is certainly right in what concerns telepathy to adhere obstinately to the same sceptical position and only to yield grudgingly to the force of evidence. I believe I have found a class of material which is exempt from the doubts which are otherwise justified—namely, unfulfilled prophecies made by professional fortune-tellers. Unluckily, I have but few such observations at my disposal; but two among these have made a powerful impression on me. I am not in a position to describe them in such detail as would produce a similar effect upon other people, and I must restrict myself to bringing out a few essential points.

A prediction had been made, then, to the enquirers (at a strange place and by a strange fortune-teller, who was at the same time carrying out some, presumably irrelevant, ritual) that something would happen to them at a particular time, which in fact did *not* come true. The date at which the prophecy should have been fulfilled was long past. It was striking that those concerned reported their experience not with derision or disappointment but with obvious satisfaction. Included among what had been told them there were certain quite definite details which seemed capricious and unintelligible and would only have been justified if they had hit the mark. Thus, for instance, the palmist told a woman who was twenty-seven (though she looked much younger) and who had taken off her wedding-ring, that she would be married and have two children before she was thirty-two.[1] The woman was forty-three when, now seriously ill, she told me the story in her analysis: she had remained childless. If one knew her private history (of which the 'Professor' in the lounge of the Paris hotel was certainly ignorant) one could understand the two numbers included in the prophecy. The girl had married after an unusually intense attachment to her father and had then had a passionate longing for children, so as to be able to put her husband in the place of her father. After years of disappointment, when she was on the brink of a neurosis, she obtained the prophecy, which promised her—the lot of her mother. For it was a fact that the latter had had two children by the time she was thirty-two. Thus it was only by the help of psycho-analysis that it was possible to give a significant interpretation of the peculiarities of this pretended

[1] [This story is told more fully in Lecture XXX of Freud, 1933a and more fully still in Freud, 1941d [1921], *Standard Ed.*, 18, 185 ff.]

message from without. But there was then no better explanation of the whole, unequivocally determined chain of events than to suppose that a strong wish on the part of the questioner—the strongest unconscious wish, in fact, of her whole emotional life and the motive force of her impending neurosis—had made itself manifest to the fortune-teller by being directly transferred to him while his attention was being distracted by the performances he was going through.[1]

I have often had an impression, in the course of experiments in my private circle, that strongly emotionally coloured recollections can be successfully transferred without much difficulty. If one has the courage to subject to an analytic examination the associations of the person to whom the thoughts are supposed to be transferred, correspondences often come to light which would otherwise have remained undiscovered. On the basis of a number of experiences I am inclined to draw the conclusion that thought-transference of this kind comes about particularly easily at the moment at which an idea emerges from the unconscious, or, in theoretical terms, as it passes over from the 'primary process' to the 'secondary process'.

In spite of the caution which is prescribed by the importance, novelty and obscurity of the subject, I feel that I should not be justified in holding back any longer these considerations upon the problem of telepathy. All of this has only this much to do with dreams: if there are such things as telepathic messages, the possibility cannot be dismissed of their reaching someone during sleep and coming to his knowledge in a dream. Indeed, on the analogy of other perceptual and intellectual material, the further possibility arises that telepathic messages received in the course of the day may only be dealt with during a dream of the following night.[2] There would then be nothing contradictory in the material that had been telepathically communicated being modified and transformed in the dream like any other material. It would be satisfactory if with the help of psycho-analysis we could obtain further and better authenticated knowledge of telepathy.

---

[1] [The significance of this distraction of the fortune-teller's attention is considered in 'Psycho-Analysis and Telepathy' (1941d), ibid., 18, 184.]

[2] [Similarly in 'Dreams and Telepathy' (1922a), *Standard Ed.*, 18, 220.]

THE INFANTILE GENITAL
ORGANIZATION
(AN INTERPOLATION INTO THE
THEORY OF SEXUALITY)
(1923)

DIE INFANTILE GENITALORGANISATION
(EINE EINSCHALTUNG IN DIE SEXUALTHEORIE)

(a) GERMAN EDITIONS:
1923   *Int. Z. Psychoanal.*, **9** (2), 168–71.
1924   *G.S.*, **5**, 232–7.
1926   *Psychoanalyse der Neurosen*, 140–6.
1931   *Sexualtheorie und Traumlehre*, 188–93.
1940   *G.W.*, **13**, 291–8.

(b) ENGLISH TRANSLATION:
    'The Infantile Genital Organization of the Libido:
        A Supplement to the Theory of Sexuality.'
1924   *Int. J. Psycho-Anal.*, **5**, 125–9. (Tr. Joan Riviere.)
1924   *C.P.*, **2**, 244–9. (Reprint of above.)

The present translation, with a modified title, is based on the
one published in 1924.

This paper was written in February, 1923 (Jones 1957, 106).
It is essentially, as its sub-title implies, an addition to Freud's
Three Essays on the Theory of Sexuality (1905*d*); and in fact a new
footnote giving the gist of what is put forward here was added
to the edition of that work which appeared in the following
year (1924), *Standard Ed.*, **7**, 199–200. The starting-point of this
paper is mainly from Sections 5 and 6 of the *Three Essays*, ibid.,
194–9, both of which date only from 1915. But it also takes
up ideas that will be found in the last pages of the paper on
'The Disposition to Obsessional Neurosis' (1913*i*), ibid., **12**,
324–6, as well as many that go back still earlier, to 'The Sexual
Theories of Children' (1908*c*), ibid., **9**, 215–20.

THE INFANTILE GENITAL ORGANIZATION

(AN INTERPOLATION INTO THE
THEORY OF SEXUALITY)

THE difficulty of the work of research in psycho-analysis is clearly shown by the fact of its being possible, in spite of whole decades of unremitting observation, to overlook features that are of general occurrence and situations that are characteristic, until at last they confront one in an unmistakable form. The remarks that follow are intended to make good a neglect of this sort in the field of infantile sexual development.

Readers of my *Three Essays on the Theory of Sexuality* (1905*d*) will be aware that I have never undertaken any thorough re-modelling of that work in its later editions, but have retained the original arrangement and have kept abreast of the advances made in our knowledge by means of interpolations and altera-tions in the text.[1] In doing this, it may often have happened that what was old and what was more recent did not admit of being merged into an entirely uncontradictory whole. Origin-ally, as we know, the accent was on a portrayal of the funda-mental difference between the sexual life of children and of adults; later, the *pregenital organizations* of the libido made their way into the foreground, and also the remarkable and momen-tous fact of the *diphasic onset* of sexual development. Finally, our interest was engaged by the *sexual researches* of children; and from this we were able to recognize the far-reaching *approximation of the final outcome of sexuality in childhood* (in about the fifth year) to the definitive form taken by it in the adult. This is the point at which I left things in the last (1922) edition of my *Three Essays*.

On p. 63 of that volume[2] I wrote that 'the choice of an object, such as we have shown to be characteristic of the pubertal phase of development, has already frequently or habitually been effected during the years of childhood: that is to say, the whole of the sexual currents have become directed

[1] [Cf. *Standard Ed.*, **7**, 126.]

[2] [This corresponds to *Standard Ed.*, **7**, 199, where there will also be found a footnote, added in 1924, which briefly summarizes the findings in the present paper. The whole section of the book from which this passage is quoted had itself only been added to the work in 1915.]

towards a single person in relation to whom they seek to achieve their aims. This then is the closest approximation possible in childhood to the final form taken by sexual life after puberty. The only difference lies in the fact that in childhood the combination of the component instincts and their subordination under the primacy of the genitals have been effected only very incompletely or not at all. Thus the establishment of that primacy in the service of reproduction is the last phase through which the organization of sexuality passes.'

To-day I should no longer be satisfied with the statement that in the early period of childhood the primacy of the genitals has been effected only very incompletely or not at all. The approximation of the child's sexual life to that of the adult goes much further and is not limited solely to the coming into being of the choice of an object. Even if a proper combination of the component instincts under the primacy of the genitals is not effected, nevertheless, at the height of the course of development of infantile sexuality, interest in the genitals and in their activity acquires a dominating significance which falls little short of that reached in maturity. At the same time, the main characteristic of this 'infantile genital organization' is its *difference* from the final genital organization of the adult. This consists in the fact that, for both sexes, only one genital, namely the male one, comes into account. What is present, therefore, is not a primacy of the genitals, but a primacy of the *phallus*.

Unfortunately we can describe this state of things only as it affects the male child; the corresponding processes in the little girl are not known to us. The small boy undoubtedly perceives the distinction between men and women, but to begin with he has no occasion to connect it with a difference in their genitals. It is natural for him to assume that all other living beings, humans and animals, possess a genital like his own; indeed, we know that he looks for an organ analogous to his own in inanimate things as well.[1] This part of the body, which is easily excitable, prone to changes and so rich in sensations, occupies the boy's interest to a high degree and is constantly setting new

[1] [Cf. the analysis of 'Little Hans' (1909*b*), *Standard Ed.*, **10**, 9.]—It is, incidentally, remarkable what a small degree of attention the other part of the male genitals, the little sac with its contents, attracts in children. From all one hears in analyses, one would not guess that the male genitals consisted of anything more than the penis.

tasks to his instinct for research. He wants to see it in other people as well, so as to compare it with his own; and he behaves as though he had a vague idea that this organ could and should be bigger. The driving force which this male portion of the body will develop later at puberty expresses itself at this period of life mainly as an urge to investigate, as sexual curiosity. Many of the acts of exhibitionism and aggression which children commit, and which in later years would be judged without hesitation to be expressions of lust, prove in analysis to be experiments undertaken in the service of sexual research.

In the course of these researches the child arrives at the discovery that the penis is not a possession which is common to all creatures that are like himself. An accidental sight of the genitals of a little sister or playmate provides the occasion for this discovery. In unusually intelligent children, the observation of girls urinating will even earlier have aroused a suspicion that there is something different here. For they will have seen a different posture and heard a different sound, and will have made attempts to repeat their observations so as to obtain enlightenment. We know how children react to their first impressions of the absence of a penis. They disavow the fact[1]

[1] [From now on, the concept of 'disavowal' comes to occupy a more and more important place in Freud's writings. In the present passage the German word used is *'leugnen'*, but its place is later almost invariably taken by the allied form *'verleugnen'*. It appears in a somewhat different connection in the paper on 'The Loss of Reality in Neurosis and Psychosis' (1924*e*), p. 184 below; but usually, as here, the topic concerned is the castration complex. See, for instance, the papers on masochism (1924*c*), p. 165 below and on the distinction between the sexes (1925*j*), p. 252 below. In his later paper on fetishism (1927*e*), Freud differentiates between the correct use of the words *'Verdrängung'* (repression)' and *'Verleugnung'* (disavowal)'. There, and in the unfinished posthumous paper on 'Splitting of the Ego' (1940*e* [1938]) and in Chapter VIII of the (also unfinished) *Outline* (1940*a* [1938]), the term serves as a basis for an addition to metapsychological theory. Actually, the notion had been hinted at very much earlier—at the end of a long footnote to the paper on 'The Two Principles of Mental Functioning' (1911*b*), *Standard Ed.*, 12, 220*n*.—The word *Verleugnung* has in the past often been translated 'denial' and the associated verb by 'to deny'. These are, however, ambiguous words and it has been thought better to choose 'to disavow' in order to avoid confusion with the German *'verneinen'*, used, for instance, in the paper on 'Negation' (1925*h*), p. 235 below. This latter German word is, once more in order to avoid ambiguity, there translated by 'to negate'.]

and believe that they *do* see a penis, all the same. They gloss over the contradiction between observation and preconception by telling themselves that the penis is still small and will grow bigger presently;[1] and they then slowly come to the emotionally significant conclusion that after all the penis had at least been there before and been taken away afterwards. The lack of a penis is regarded as a result of castration, and so now the child is faced with the task of coming to terms with castration in relation to himself. The further developments are too well known generally to make it necessary to recapitulate them here. But it seems to me that *the significance of the castration complex can only be rightly appreciated if its origin in the phase of phallic primacy is also taken into account.*[2]

We know, too, to what a degree depreciation of women, horror of women, and a disposition to homosexuality are derived from the final conviction that women have no penis. Ferenczi (1923) has recently, with complete justice, traced back the mythological symbol of horror—Medusa's head—to the impression of the female genitals devoid of a penis.[3]

It should not be supposed, however, that the child quickly and readily makes a generalization from his observation that some women have no penis. He is in any case debarred from doing so by his assumption that the lack of a penis is the result of having been castrated as a punishment. On the contrary, the child believes that it is only unworthy female persons that have lost their genitals—females who, in all probability, were guilty of inadmissible impulses similar to his own. Women

---

[1] [Cf. the 'Little Hans' analysis, *Standard Ed.*, **10**, 11.]

[2] It has been quite correctly pointed out that a child gets the idea of a narcissistic injury through a bodily loss from the experience of losing his mother's breast after sucking, from the daily surrender of his faeces and, indeed, even from his separation from the womb at birth. Nevertheless, one ought not to speak of a castration complex until this idea of a loss has become connected with the male genitals. [This point is treated at greater length in a footnote added in 1923 to the 'Little Hans' analysis, *Standard Ed.*, **10**, 8. It is also mentioned in 'The Dissolution of the Oedipus Complex' (1924*d*), p. 175 below.]

[3] I should like to add that what is indicated in the myth is the *mother's* genitals. Athene, who carries Medusa's head on her armour, becomes in consequence the unapproachable woman, the sight of whom extinguishes all thought of a sexual approach.—[Freud had himself drafted a short paper on this subject a year earlier, which was published posthumously (1940*c* [1922]).]

whom he respects, like his mother, retain a penis for a long time. For him, being a woman is not yet synonymous with being without a penis.[1] It is not till later, when the child takes up the problems of the origin and birth of babies, and when he guesses that only women can give birth to them—it is only then that the mother, too, loses her penis. And, along with this, quite complicated theories are built up to explain the exchange of the penis for a baby. In all this, the female genitals never seem to be discovered. The baby, we know, is supposed to live inside the mother's body (in her bowel) and to be born through the intestinal outlet. These last theories carry us beyond the stretch of time covered by the infantile sexual period.

It is not unimportant to bear in mind what transformations are undergone, during the sexual development of childhood, by the polarity of sex with which we are familiar. A first antithesis is introduced with the choice of object, which, of course, presupposes a subject and an object. At the stage of the pregenital sadistic-anal organization, there is as yet no question of male and female; the antithesis between *active* and *passive* is the dominant one.[2] At the following stage of infantile genital organization, which we now know about, *maleness* exists, but not femaleness. The antithesis here is between having *a male genital* and being *castrated*. It is not until development has reached its completion at puberty that the sexual polarity coincides with *male* and *female*. Maleness combines [the factors of] subject, activity and possession of the penis; femaleness takes over [those of] object and passivity. The vagina is now valued as a place of shelter for the penis; it enters into the heritage of the womb.

---

[1] I learnt from the analysis of a young married woman who had no father but several aunts that she clung, until quite far on in the latency period, to the belief that her mother and her aunts had a penis. One of her aunts, however, was feeble-minded; and she regarded this aunt as castrated, as she felt herself to be. [Cf. a footnote to *The Ego and the Id*, p. 31, *n.* 1 above.]

[2] Cf. [a passage added in 1915 to] *Three Essays on the Theory of Sexuality*, (1905d) *Standard Ed.*, 7, 198. [See further a footnote also added to the same work in 1915, ibid., 219–20.]

NEUROSIS AND PSYCHOSIS
(1924 [1923])

NEUROSE UND PSYCHOSE

(a) GERMAN EDITIONS:
1924   Int. Z. Psychoanal., **10** (1), 1–5.
1924   G.S., **5**, 418–22.
1926   Psychoanalyse der Neurosen, 163–8.
1931   Neurosenlehre und Technik, 186–91.
1940   G.W., **13**, 387–91.

(b) ENGLISH TRANSLATION:
                'Neurosis and Psychosis'
1924   C.P., **2**, 250–4. (Tr. Joan Riviere.)

The present translation is based on that of 1924.

This was written during the late autumn of 1923. It is an application of the new hypotheses put forward in *The Ego and the Id* to the particular question of the genetic difference between neuroses and psychoses. This same discussion was carried further in another paper, written a few months after the present one, 'The Loss of Reality in Neurosis and Psychosis' (1924e), p. 183 below. The roots of the matter were already under discussion by Freud in Section III of his first paper on 'The Neuro-Psychoses of Defence' (1894a).

In the second paragraph of this paper, Freud speaks of its having been stimulated by 'a train of thought raised in other quarters'. It seems likely that what he was referring to was a work on the psycho-analysis of general paralysis by Hollós and Ferenczi (1922), which had just appeared and to which a theoretical section was contributed by Ferenczi.

NEUROSIS AND PSYCHOSIS

In my recently published work, *The Ego and the Id* (1923*b*), I have proposed a differentiation of the mental apparatus, on the basis of which a number of relationships can be represented in a simple and perspicuous manner. As regards other points—for instance, in what concerns the origin and role of the super-ego —enough remains obscure and unelucidated. Now one may reasonably expect that a hypothesis of this kind should prove useful and helpful in other directions as well, if only to enable us to see what we already know from another angle, to group it differently and to describe it more convincingly. Such an application of the hypothesis might also bring with it a profitable return from grey theory to the perpetual green of experience.[1]

In the work I have mentioned I described the numerous dependent relationships of the ego, its intermediate position between the external world and the id and its efforts to humour all its masters at once. In connection with a train of thought raised in other quarters, which was concerned with the origin and prevention of the psychoses, a simple formula has now occurred to me which deals with what is perhaps the most important genetic difference between a neurosis and a psychosis: *neurosis is the result of a conflict between the ego and its id, whereas psychosis is the analogous outcome of a similar disturbance in the relations between the ego and the external world.*

There are certainly good grounds for being suspicious of such simple solutions of a problem. Moreover, the most that we may expect is that this formula will turn out to be correct in the roughest outline. But even that would be something. One recalls at once, too, a whole number of discoveries and findings which seem to support our thesis. All our analyses go to show that the transference neuroses originate from the ego's refusing to accept

[1] [Grau, teurer Freund, ist alle Theorie,
Und grün des Lebens goldner Baum.

My worthy friend, gray is all theory,
And green alone Life's golden tree.
(Trans. Bayard Taylor, emended.)
Mephistopheles in *Faust*, Part I, Scene 4.]

149

a powerful instinctual impulse in the id or to help it to find a motor outlet, or from the ego's forbidding that impulse the object at which it is aiming. In such a case the ego defends itself against the instinctual impulse by the mechanism of repression. The repressed material struggles against this fate. It creates for itself, along paths over which the ego has no power, a substitutive representation (which forces itself upon the ego by way of a compromise)—the symptom. The ego finds its unity threatened and impaired by this intruder, and it continues to struggle against the symptom, just as it fended off the original instinctual impulse. All this produces the picture of a neurosis. It is no contradiction to this that, in undertaking the repression, the ego is at bottom following the commands of its super-ego—commands which, in their turn, originate from influences in the external world that have found representation in the super-ego. The fact remains that the ego *has* taken sides with those powers, that in it their demands have more strength than the instinctual demands of the id, and that the ego is the power which sets the repression in motion against the portion of the id concerned and which fortifies the repression by means of the anticathexis of resistance. The ego has come into conflict with the id in the service of the super-ego and of reality; and this is the state of affairs in every transference neurosis.

On the other side, it is equally easy, from the knowledge we have so far gained of the mechanism of the psychoses, to adduce examples which point to a disturbance in the relationship between the ego and the external world. In Meynert's amentia —an acute hallucinatory confusion which is perhaps the most extreme and striking form of psychosis—either the external world is not perceived at all, or the perception of it has no effect whatever.[1] Normally, the external world governs the ego in two ways: firstly, by current, present perceptions which are always renewable, and secondly, by the store of memories o earlier perceptions which, in the shape of an 'internal world', form a possession of the ego and a constituent part of it. In amentia, not only is the acceptance of new perceptions refused, but the internal world, too, which, as a copy of the external

[1] [A passage in Chapter VIII of Freud's posthumous *Outline of Psycho-Analysis* (1940*a* [1938]) qualifies this statement. Cf. footnote 1, p. 153 below.]

world, has up till now represented it, loses its significance (its cathexis). The ego creates, autocratically, a new external and internal world; and there can be no doubt of two facts—that this new world is constructed in accordance with the id's wishful impulses, and that the motive of this dissociation from the external world is some very serious frustration by reality of a wish—a frustration which seems intolerable. The close affinity of this psychosis to normal dreams is unmistakable. A precondition of dreaming, moreover, is a state of sleep, and one of the features of sleep is a complete turning away from perception and the external world.[1]

We know that other forms of psychosis, the schizophrenias, are inclined to end in affective hebetude—that is, in a loss of all participation in the external world. In regard to the genesis of delusions, a fair number of analyses have taught us that the delusion is found applied like a patch over the place where originally a rent had appeared in the ego's relation to the external world. If this precondition of a conflict with the external world is not much more noticeable to us than it now is, that is because, in the clinical picture of the psychosis, the manifestations of the pathogenic process are often overlaid by manifestations of an attempt at a cure or a reconstruction.[2]

The aetiology common to the onset of a psychoneurosis and of a psychosis always remains the same. It consists in a frustration, a non-fulfilment, of one of those childhood wishes which are for ever undefeated and which are so deeply rooted in our phylogenetically determined organization. This frustration is in the last resort always an external one;[3] but in the individual case it may proceed from the internal agency (in the super-ego) which has taken over the representation of the demands of reality. The pathogenic effect depends on whether, in a conflictual tension of this kind, the ego remains true to its dependence on the external world and attempts to silence the id, or whether it lets itself be overcome by the id and thus torn away from reality. A complication is introduced into this apparently simple situation, however, by the existence of the super-ego, which, through a link that is not yet clear to us, unites in itself

[1] [Cf. the metapsychological paper on dreams (1917d).]
[2] [Cf. the Schreber analysis (1911c), *Standard Ed.*, **12**, 71.]
[3] [See some remarks in the discussion of frustration in 'Types of Onset of Neurosis' (1912c), *Standard Ed.*, **12**, 234.]

influences coming from the id as well as from the external world, and is to some extent an ideal model of what the whole endeavour of the ego is aiming at—a reconciliation between its various dependent relationships.[1] The attitude of the super-ego should be taken into account—which has not hitherto been done —in every form of psychical illness. We may provisionally assume that there must also be illnesses which are based on a conflict between the ego and the super-ego. Analysis gives us a right to suppose that melancholia is a typical example of this group; and we would set aside the name of 'narcissistic psycho-neuroses' for disorders of that kind. Nor will it clash with our impressions if we find reasons for separating states like melancholia from the other psychoses. We now see that we have been able to make our simple genetic formula more complete, without dropping it. Transference neuroses correspond to a conflict between the ego and the id; narcissistic neuroses, to a conflict between the ego and the super-ego; and psychoses, to one between the ego and the external world. It is true that we cannot tell at once whether we have really gained any new knowledge by this, or have only enriched our store of formulas; but I think that this possible application of the proposed differentiation of the mental apparatus into an ego, a super-ego and an id cannot fail to give us courage to keep that hypothesis steadily in view.

The thesis that neuroses and psychoses originate in the ego's conflicts with its various ruling agencies—that is, therefore, that they reflect a failure in the functioning of the ego, which is at pains to reconcile all the various demands made on it—this thesis needs to be supplemented in one further point. One would like to know in what circumstances and by what means the ego can succeed in emerging from such conflicts, which are certainly always present, without falling ill. This is a new field of research, in which no doubt the most varied factors will come up for examination. Two of them, however, can be stressed at once. In the first place, the outcome of all such situations will undoubtedly depend on economic considerations—on the relative magnitudes of the trends which are struggling with one another. In the second place, it will be possible for the ego to avoid a rupture in any direction by deforming itself, by submitting to encroachments on its own unity and even perhaps

[1] [Cf. 'The Economic Problem of Masochism' (1924c), p. 167 below.]

by effecting a cleavage or division of itself.[1] In this way the inconsistencies, eccentricities and follies of men would appear in a similar light to their sexual perversions, through the acceptance of which they spare themselves repressions.

In conclusion, there remains to be considered the question of what the mechanism, analogous to repression, can be by means of which the ego detaches itself from the external world. This cannot, I think, be answered without fresh investigations; but such a mechanism, it would seem, must, like repression, comprise a withdrawal of the cathexis sent out by the ego.[2]

---

[1] [This is an early hint at a problem that was to occupy Freud in his later years. It was first discussed at length in the paper on 'Fetishism' (1927e) and afterwards in two unfinished works, in 'Splitting of the Ego in the Process of Defence' (1940e [1938]) and in Chapter VIII of the *Outline* (1940a [1938]).]

[2] [This problem, too—the nature of what Freud later called '*Verleugnung*', 'disavowal'—was discussed in the later papers mentioned in the previous footnote. See an Editor's footnote to 'The Infantile Genital Organization', this volume, p. 143 above, for a fuller discussion of the question.]

THE ECONOMIC PROBLEM OF
MASOCHISM
(1924)

EDITOR'S NOTE

DAS ÖKONOMISCHE PROBLEM DES MASOCHISMUS

(a) GERMAN EDITIONS:

1924 *Int. Z. Psychoanal.*, **10** (2), 121–33.
1924 *G.S.*, **5**, 374–86.
1926 *Psychoanalyse der Neurosen*, 147–62.
1931 *Neurosenlehre und Technik*, 193–207.
1940 *G.W.*, **13**, 371–83.

(b) ENGLISH TRANSLATION:
      'The Economic Problem in Masochism'
1924 *C.P.*, **2**, 255–68. (Tr. Joan Riviere.)

The present translation, with a slightly changed title, is based on that of 1924.

This paper was finished before the end of January, 1924 (Jones, 1957, 114).

In this important work Freud gives his fullest account of the puzzling phenomenon of masochism. He had previously dealt with it, but always somewhat tentatively, in his *Three Essays on the Theory of Sexuality* (1905*d*), *Standard Ed.*, **7**, 157–60,[1] in the metapsychological paper 'Instincts and their Vicissitudes' (1915*c*), ibid., **14**, 127–30, and, at much greater length in '"A Child is Being Beaten"' (1919*e*), which he himself described in a letter to Ferenczi as 'a paper on masochism'. In all these writings masochism is derived from a previous sadism; no such thing as primary masochism is recognized. (See, for instance, *Standard Ed.*, **14**, 128 and **17**, 193–4.) In *Beyond the Pleasure Principle* (1920*g*), however, after the introduction of the 'death instinct', we find a statement that 'there *might* be such a thing as primary masochism' (ibid., **18**, 55), and in the present paper the existence of a primary masochism is taken as certain.[2]

---

[1] Much of this was in fact only added to the book in 1915; a footnote added in 1924 gives the gist of the present paper.

[2] It should perhaps be mentioned that it was only in later writings, beginning with Chapter VI of *Civilization and its Discontents* (1930*a*), that

157

The existence of this primary masochism is here accounted for chiefly on the basis of the 'fusion' and 'defusion' of the two classes of instinct—a concept which had been examined at length in *The Ego and the Id* (1923 *b*), published less than a year previously—while the apparently self-contradictory nature of an instinct which aims at unpleasure is dealt with in the interesting introductory discussion, which for the first time clearly distinguishes between the 'principle of constancy' and the 'pleasure principle'.

Freud's analysis shows that this primary or 'erotogenic' masochism leads to two derivative forms. One of these, which he terms 'feminine', is the form that Freud had already discussed in his paper on 'beating phantasies' (1919e). But the third form, 'moral masochism', gives him an opportunity of enlarging upon many points that had only been lightly touched on in *The Ego and the Id*, and of opening up fresh problems in connection with feelings of guilt and the operation of the conscience.

Freud turned his attention more particularly to the *outward* operation of the death instinct—to aggressiveness and destructiveness, though it is discussed to some extent in the later part of the present paper.

THE ECONOMIC PROBLEM OF MASOCHISM

THE existence of a masochistic trend in the instinctual life of human beings may justly be described as mysterious from the economic point of view. For if mental processes are governed by the pleasure principle in such a way that their first aim is the avoidance of unpleasure and the obtaining of pleasure, masochism is incomprehensible. If pain and unpleasure can be not simply warnings but actually aims, the pleasure principle is paralysed—it is as though the watchman over our mental life were put out of action by a drug.

Thus masochism appears to us in the light of a great danger, which is in no way true of its counterpart, sadism. We are tempted to call the pleasure principle the watchman over our life rather than merely over our mental life. But in that case we are faced with the task of investigating the relationship of the pleasure principle to the two classes of instincts which we have distinguished—the death instincts and the erotic (libidinal) life instincts; and we cannot proceed further in our consideration of the problem of masochism till we have accomplished that task.

It will be remembered that we have taken the view that the principle which governs all mental processes is a special case of Fechner's 'tendency towards stability',[1] and have accordingly attributed to the mental apparatus the purpose of reducing to nothing, or at least of keeping as low as possible, the sums of excitation which flow in upon it. Barbara Low [1920, 73] has suggested the name of 'Nirvana principle' for this supposed tendency, and we have accepted the term.[2] But we have unhesitatingly identified the pleasure-unpleasure principle with this Nirvana principle. Every unpleasure ought thus to coincide with a heightening, and every pleasure with a lowering, of mental

---

[1] *Beyond the Pleasure Principle* (1920g) [*Standard Ed.*, **18**, 9].
[2] [*Beyond the Pleasure Principle*, ibid., 56. Freud had previously given this same principle the name of 'the principle of constancy'. A full discussion of the history of Freud's use of these concepts and of their relation to the pleasure principle will be found in an Editor's footnote to 'Instincts and their Vicissitudes' (1915c), *Standard Ed.*, **14**, 121.]

tension due to stimulus; the Nirvana principle (and the pleasure principle which is supposedly identical with it) would be entirely in the service of the death instincts, whose aim is to conduct the restlessness of life into the stability of the inorganic state, and it would have the function of giving warnings against the demands of the life instincts—the libido—which try to disturb the intended course of life. But such a view cannot be correct. It seems that in the series of feelings of tension we have a direct sense of the increase and decrease of amounts of stimulus, and it cannot be doubted that there are pleasurable tensions and unpleasurable relaxations of tension. The state of sexual excitation is the most striking example of a pleasurable increase of stimulus of this sort, but it is certainly not the only one.

Pleasure and unpleasure, therefore, cannot be referred to an increase or decrease of a quantity (which we describe as 'tension due to stimulus'), although they obviously have a great deal to do with that factor. It appears that they depend, not on this quantitative factor, but on some characteristic of it which we can only describe as a qualitative one. If we were able to say what this qualitative characteristic is, we should be much further advanced in psychology. Perhaps it is the rhythm, the temporal sequence of changes, rises and falls in the quantity of stimulus.[1] We do not know.

However this may be, we must perceive that the Nirvana principle, belonging as it does to the death instinct, has undergone a modification in living organisms through which it has become the pleasure principle; and we shall henceforward avoid regarding the two principles as one. It is not difficult, if we care to follow up this line of thought, to guess what power was the source of the modification. It can only be the life instinct, the libido, which has thus, alongside of the death instinct, seized upon a share in the regulation of the processes of life. In this way we obtain a small but interesting set of connections. The *Nirvana* principle expresses the trend of the death instinct; the *pleasure* principle represents the demands of the libido; and the modification of the latter principle, the *reality* principle,[2] represents the influence of the external world.

[1] [This possibility had already been raised in *Beyond the Pleasure Principle*, Standard Ed., **18**, 8 and 63.]

[2] [Cf. 'Formulations on the Two Principles of Mental Functioning' (1911*b*), *Standard Ed.*, **12**, 219.]

None of these three principles is actually put out of action by another. As a rule they are able to tolerate one another, although conflicts are bound to arise occasionally from the fact of the differing aims that are set for each—in one case a quantitative reduction of the load of the stimulus, in another a qualitative characteristic of the stimulus, and, lastly [in the third case], a postponement of the discharge of the stimulus and a temporary acquiescence in the unpleasure due to tension.

The conclusion to be drawn from these considerations is that the description of the pleasure principle as the watchman over our life cannot be rejected.[1]

To return to masochism. Masochism comes under our observation in three forms: as a condition imposed on sexual excitation, as an expression of the feminine nature, and as a norm of behaviour.[2] We may, accordingly, distinguish an *erotogenic*, a *feminine* and a *moral* masochism. The first, the erotogenic, masochism—pleasure in pain—lies at the bottom of the other two forms as well. Its basis must be sought along biological and constitutional lines and it remains incomprehensible unless one decides to make certain assumptions about matters that are extremely obscure. The third, and in some respects the most important, form assumed by masochism has only recently been recognized by psycho-analysis as a sense of guilt which is mostly unconscious; but it can already be completely explained and fitted into the rest of our knowledge. Feminine masochism, on the other hand, is the one that is most accessible to our observation and least problematical, and it can be surveyed in all its relations. We will begin our discussion with it.

We have sufficient acquaintance with this kind of masochism in men (to whom, owing to the material at my command, I shall restrict my remarks), derived from masochistic—and therefore often impotent—subjects whose phantasies either terminate in an act of masturbation or represent a sexual satisfaction in themselves.[3] The real-life performances of masochistic perverts tally completely with these phantasies, whether

[1] [Freud took up this discussion again in Chapter VIII of his *Outline* (1940a [1938]).]   [2] [This last word is added in English in the original.]
[3] [See Section VI of ' "A Child is Being Beaten" ' (1919e), *Standard Ed.*, **17**, 196 ff.]

the performances are carried out as an end in themselves or serve to induce potency and to lead to the sexual act. In both cases—for the performances are, after all, only a carrying-out of the phantasies in play—the manifest content is of being gagged, bound, painfully beaten, whipped, in some way maltreated, forced into unconditional obedience, dirtied and debased. It is far more rare for mutilations to be included in the content, and then only subject to strict limitations. The obvious interpretation, and one easily arrived at, is that the masochist wants to be treated like a small and helpless child, but, particularly, like a naughty child. It is unnecessary to quote cases to illustrate this; for the material is very uniform and is accessible to any observer, even to non-analysts. But if one has an opportunity of studying cases in which the masochistic phantasies have been especially richly elaborated, one quickly discovers that they place the subject in a characteristically female situation; they signify, that is, being castrated, or copulated with, or giving birth to a baby. For this reason I have called this form of masochism, *a potiori* as it were [i.e. on the basis of its extreme examples], the feminine form, although so many of its features point to infantile life. This superimposed stratification of the infantile and the feminine will find a simple explanation later on. Being castrated—or being blinded, which stands for it—often leaves a negative trace of itself in phantasies, in the condition that no injury is to occur precisely to the genitals or the eyes. (Masochistic tortures, incidentally, rarely make such a serious impression as the cruelties of sadism, whether imagined or performed.) A sense of guilt, too, finds expression in the manifest content of masochistic phantasies; the subject assumes that he has committed some crime (the nature of which is left indefinite) which is to be expiated by all these painful and tormenting procedures. This looks like a superficial rationalization of the masochistic subject-matter, but behind it there lies a connection with infantile masturbation. On the other hand, this factor of guilt provides a transition to the third, moral, form of masochism.

This feminine masochism which we have been describing is entirely based on the primary, erotogenic masochism, on pleasure in pain. This cannot be explained without taking our discussion very far back.

In my *Three Essays on the Theory of Sexuality*, in the section on the sources of infantile sexuality, I put forward the proposition that 'in the case of a great number of internal processes sexual excitation arises as a concomitant effect, as soon as the intensity of those processes passes beyond certain quantitative limits'. Indeed, 'it may well be that nothing of considerable importance can occur in the organism without contributing some component to the excitation of the sexual instinct'.[1] In accordance with this, the excitation of pain and unpleasure would be bound to have the same result, too.[2] The occurrence of such a libidinal sympathetic excitation when there is tension due to pain and unpleasure would be an infantile physiological mechanism which ceases to operate later on. It would attain a varying degree of development in different sexual constitutions; but in any case it would provide the physiological foundation on which the psychical structure of erotogenic masochism would afterwards be erected.

The inadequacy of this explanation is seen, however, in the fact that it throws no light on the regular and close connections of masochism with its counterpart in instinctual life, sadism. If we go back a little further, to our hypothesis of the two classes of instincts which we regard as operative in the living organism, we arrive at another derivation of masochism, which, however, is not in contradiction with the former one. In (multicellular) organisms the libido meets the instinct of death, or destruction, which is dominant in them and which seeks to disintegrate the cellular organism and to conduct each separate unicellular organism [composing it] into a state of inorganic stability (relative though this may be). The libido has the task of making the destroying instinct innocuous, and it fulfils the task by diverting that instinct to a great extent outwards—soon with the help of a special organic system, the muscular apparatus—towards objects in the external world. The instinct is then called the destructive instinct, the instinct for mastery, or the will to power. A portion of the instinct is placed directly in the service of the sexual function, where it has an important part to play. This is sadism proper. Another portion does not share in this transposition outwards; it remains inside the organism and, with the help of the accompanying sexual excitation

[1] [*Three Essays* (1905d), *Standard Ed.*, 7, 204-5.]
[2] [Ibid., 204.]

described above, becomes libidinally bound there. It is in this portion that we have to recognize the original, erotogenic masochism.[1]

We are without any physiological understanding of the ways and means by which this taming[2] of the death-instinct by the libido may be effected. So far as the psycho-analytic field of ideas is concerned, we can only assume that a very extensive fusion and amalgamation, in varying proportions, of the two classes of instincts takes place, so that we never have to deal with pure life instincts or pure death instincts but only with mixtures of them in different amounts. Corresponding to a fusion of instincts of this kind, there may, as a result of certain influences, be a *de*fusion of them. How large the portions of the death instincts are which refuse to be tamed in this way by being bound to admixtures of libido we cannot at present guess.

If one is prepared to overlook a little inexactitude, it may be said that the death instinct which is operative in the organism —primal sadism—is identical with masochism. After the main portion of it has been transposed outwards on to objects, there remains inside, as a residuum of it, the erotogenic masochism proper, which on the one hand has become a component of the libido and, on the other, still has the self as its object. This masochism would thus be evidence of, and a remainder from, the phase of development in which the coalescence, which is so important for life, between the death instinct and Eros took place. We shall not be surprised to hear that in certain circumstances the sadism, or instinct of destruction, which has been directed outwards, projected, can be once more introjected, turned inwards, and in this way regress to its earlier situation. If this happens, a secondary masochism is produced, which is added to the original masochism.

Erotogenic masochism accompanies the libido through all its developmental phases and derives from them its changing

---

[1] [For all of this see Chapter IV of *The Ego and the Id* (p. 41 above). Cf. also another account in Chapter VI of *Beyond the Pleasure Principle*, *Standard Ed.*, 18, 50.]

[2] ['*Bändigung.*' Freud takes up the word again in the third section of his late paper on 'Analysis Terminable and Interminable' (1937c). He had much earlier applied the idea to the 'taming' of memories in Section 3 of Part III of his 'Project' of 1895 (Freud, 1950a).]

psychical coatings.[1] The fear of being eaten up by the totem animal (the father) originates from the primitive oral organization; the wish to be beaten by the father comes from the sadistic-anal phase which follows it; castration, although it is later disavowed, enters into the content of masochistic phantasies as a precipitate of the phallic stage or organization;[2] and from the final genital organization there arise, of course, the situations of being copulated with and of giving birth, which are characteristic of femaleness. The part played in masochism by the nates, too, is easily understandable,[3] apart from its obvious basis in reality. The nates are the part of the body which is given erotogenic preference in the sadistic-anal phase, like the breast in the oral phase and the penis in the genital phase. ·

The third form of masochism, moral masochism,[4] is chiefly remarkable for having loosened its connection with what we recognize as sexuality. All other masochistic sufferings carry with them the condition that they shall emanate from the loved person and shall be endured at his command. This restriction has been dropped in moral masochism. The suffering itself is what matters; whether it is decreed by someone who is loved or by someone who is indifferent is of no importance. It may even be caused by impersonal powers or by circumstances; the true masochist always turns his cheek whenever he has a chance of receiving a blow. It is very tempting, in explaining this attitude, to leave the libido out of account and to confine oneself to assuming that in this case the destructive instinct has been turned inwards again and is now raging against the self; yet there must be some meaning in the fact that linguistic usage has not given up the connection between this norm of behaviour and erotism and calls these self-injurers masochists too.

[1] ['*Psychische Umkleidungen.*' The image is an old one of Freud's. It occurs several times, for instance, in the 'Dora' case history (1905*e*), *Standard Ed.*, 7, 83, 84, and 99 *n.* 2.]

[2] See 'The Infantile Genital Organization' (1923*e*) [p. 143 above, where a footnote discussing the use of the word 'disavowal' will also be found].

[3] [Cf. a reference to this at the end of Section 4 of the second of the *Three Essays* (1905*d*), *Standard Ed.*, 7, 193.]

[4] [In a paragraph added in 1909 to *The Interpretation of Dreams* (1900*a*), Freud had proposed the term 'mental masochism' for people 'who find their pleasure, not in having *physical* pain inflicted on them, but in humiliation and mental torture'. (*Standard Ed.*, 4, 159.)]

Let us keep to a habit of our technique and consider first the extreme and unmistakably pathological form of this masochism. I have described elsewhere[1] how in analytic treatment we come across patients to whom, owing to their behaviour towards its therapeutic influence, we are obliged to ascribe an 'unconscious' sense of guilt. I pointed out the sign by which such people can be recognized (a 'negative therapeutic reaction') and I did not conceal the fact that the strength of such an impulse constitutes one of the most serious resistances and the greatest danger to the success of our medical or educative aims. The satisfaction of this unconscious sense of guilt is perhaps the most powerful bastion in the subject's (usually composite) gain from illness— in the sum of forces which struggle against his recovery and refuse to surrender his state of illness. The suffering entailed by neuroses is precisely the factor that makes them valuable to the masochistic trend. It is instructive, too, to find, contrary to all theory and expectation, that a neurosis which has defied every therapeutic effort may vanish if the subject becomes involved in the misery of an unhappy marriage, or loses all his money, or develops a dangerous organic disease. In such instances one form of suffering has been replaced by another; and we see that all that mattered was that it should be possible to maintain a certain amount of suffering.

Patients do not easily believe us when we tell them about the unconscious sense of guilt. They know only too well by what torments—the pangs of conscience—a conscious sense of guilt, a consciousness of guilt, expresses itself, and they therefore cannot admit that they could harbour exactly analogous impulses in themselves without being in the least aware of them. We may, I think, to some extent meet their objection if we give up the term 'unconscious sense of guilt', which is in any case psychologically incorrect,[2] and speak instead of a 'need for punishment', which covers the observed state of affairs just as aptly. We cannot, however, restrain ourselves from judging and localizing this unconscious sense of guilt in the same way as we do the conscious kind.

We have attributed the function of conscience to the super-ego and we have recognized the consciousness of guilt as an

---

[1] *The Ego and the Id* (1923b) [Chapter V, p. 49 f. above].
[2] [Feelings cannot properly be described as 'unconscious'. See Chapter II of *The Ego and the Id*, pp. 22-3 above.]

expression of a tension between the ego and the super-ego.[1]
The ego reacts with feelings of anxiety (conscience anxiety)[2]
to the perception that it has not come up to the demands made
by its ideal, the super-ego. What we want to know is how the
super-ego has come to play this demanding role and why the ego,
in the case of a difference with its ideal, should have to be afraid.

We have said that the function of the ego is to unite and to
reconcile the claims of the three agencies which it serves; and
we may add that in doing so it also possesses in the super-ego
a model which it can strive to follow. For this super-ego is as
much a representative of the id as of the external world.[3] It
came into being through the introjection into the ego of the
first objects of the id's libidinal impulses—namely, the two
parents. In this process the relation to those objects was desexualized; it was diverted from its direct sexual aims. Only
in this way was it possible for the Oedipus complex to be surmounted. The super-ego retained essential features of the introjected persons—their strength, their severity, their inclination
to supervise and to punish. As I have said elsewhere,[4] it is
easily conceivable that, thanks to the defusion of instinct which
occurs along with this introduction into the ego, the severity
was increased. The super-ego—the conscience at work in the
ego—may then become harsh, cruel and inexorable against the
ego which is in its charge. Kant's Categorical Imperative is thus
the direct heir of the Oedipus complex.[5]

But the same figures who continue to operate in the super-ego
as the agency we know as conscience after they have ceased to
be objects of the libidinal impulses of the id—these same figures
also belong to the real external world. It is from there that they
were drawn; their power, behind which lie hidden all the
influences of the past and of tradition, was one of the most
strongly-felt manifestations of reality. In virtue of this con-
currence, the super-ego, the substitute for the Oedipus complex,
becomes a representative of the real external world as well and
thus also becomes a model for the endeavours of the ego.

In this way the Oedipus complex proves to be—as has

---

[1] [Ibid., Chapter III, p. 37 above.]
[2] ['*Gewissensangst.*' An Editor's footnote discussing this term will be
found in Chapter VII of *Inhibitions, Symptoms and Anxiety* (1926d), *Standard
Ed.*, 20, 128.]   [3] [Cf. 'Neurosis and Psychosis' (1924b), p. 152 above.]
[4] *The Ego and the Id* [pp. 54–5 above].   [5] [Cf. ibid., pp. 35 and 48.]

already been conjectured in a historical sense[1]—the source of
our individual ethical sense, our morality. The course of childhood development leads to an ever-increasing detachment from
parents, and their personal significance for the super-ego recedes
into the background. To the imagos[2] they leave behind there
are then linked the influences of teachers and authorities, self-
chosen models and publicly recognized heroes, whose figures
need no longer be introjected by an ego which has become more
resistant. The last figure in the series that began with the parents
is the dark power of Destiny which only the fewest of us are able
to look upon as impersonal. There is little to be said against the
Dutch writer Multatuli[3] when he replaces the $Mo\tilde{\iota}\varrho a$ [Destiny]
of the Greeks by the divine pair '$\Lambda\acute{o}\gamma o\varsigma$ $\varkappa a\grave{\iota}$ '$A\nu\acute{a}\gamma\varkappa\eta$, [Reason and
Necessity]';[4] but all who transfer the guidance of the world to
Providence, to God, or to God and Nature, arouse a suspicion
that they still look upon these ultimate and remotest powers as
a parental couple, in a mythological sense, and believe themselves linked to them by libidinal ties. In The Ego and the Id
[p. 58] I made an attempt to derive mankind's realistic fear
of death, too, from the same parental view of fate. It seems
very hard to free oneself from it.

After these preliminaries we can return to our consideration
of moral masochism. We have said[5] that, by their behaviour
during treatment and in life, the individuals in question give
an impression of being morally inhibited to an excessive degree,
of being under the domination of an especially sensitive con-

---

[1] In Essay IV of Totem and Taboo (1912–13).

[2] [The term 'imago' was not often used by Freud, especially in his
later writings. Its first appearance seems to be in his technical paper on
'The Dynamics of Transference' (1912b), Standard Ed., 12, 100, where
he attributes it to Jung (1911, 164). In this latter passage Jung tells us
that he partly chose the word from the title of a novel of the same name
by the Swiss writer, Carl Spitteler; and we learn from Hanns Sachs
(1945, 63) that the psycho-analytic periodical Imago, started by him
and Rank in 1912, also owed its title to the same source.]

[3] E. D. Dekker (1820–87). ['Multatuli' had long been a favourite of
Freud's. He heads the list of 'ten good books' which he drew up in 1907,
Standard Ed., 9, 246.]

[4] ['$A\nu\acute{a}\gamma\varkappa\eta$ had been named by Freud at least as early as in the
Leonardo paper (1910c), Standard Ed., 11, 125. $\Lambda\acute{o}\gamma o\varsigma$, on the other hand,
seems to appear for the first time here. Both are discussed, and more
especially $\Lambda\acute{o}\gamma o\varsigma$, in the closing passage of The Future of an Illusion
(1927c).]   [5] [The Ego and the Id, p. 49 ff. above.]

science, although they are not conscious of any of this ultra-morality. On closer inspection, we can see the difference there is between an unconscious extension of morality of this kind and moral masochism. In the former, the accent falls on the heightened sadism of the super-ego to which the ego submits; in the latter, it falls on the ego's own masochism which seeks punishment, whether from the super-ego or from the parental powers outside. We may be forgiven for having confused the two to begin with; for in both cases it is a question of a relationship between the ego and the super-ego (or powers that are equivalent to it), and in both cases what is involved is a need which is satisfied by punishment and suffering. It can hardly be an insignificant detail, then, that the sadism of the super-ego becomes for the most part glaringly conscious, whereas the masochistic trend of the ego remains as a rule concealed from the subject and has to be inferred from his behaviour.

The fact that moral masochism is unconscious leads us to an obvious clue. We were able to translate the expression 'unconscious sense of guilt' as meaning a need for punishment at the hands of a parental power. We now know that the wish, which so frequently appears in phantasies, to be beaten by the father stands very close to the other wish, to have a passive (feminine) sexual relation to him and is only a regressive distortion of it. If we insert this explanation into the content of moral masochism, its hidden meaning becomes clear to us. Conscience and morality have arisen through the overcoming, the desexualization, of the Oedipus complex; but through moral masochism morality becomes sexualized once more, the Oedipus complex is revived and the way is opened for a regression from morality to the Oedipus complex. This is to the advantage neither of morality nor of the person concerned. An individual may, it is true, have preserved the whole or some measure of ethical sense alongside of his masochism; but, alternatively, a large part of his conscience may have vanished into his masochism. Again, masochism creates a temptation to perform 'sinful' actions, which must then be expiated by the reproaches of the sadistic conscience (as is exemplified in so many Russian character-types) or by chastisement from the great parental power of Destiny. In order to provoke punishment from this last representative of the parents, the masochist must do what is inexpedient, must act against his own interests, must ruin the prospects which open out to him in the real world and must, perhaps, destroy his own real existence.

The turning back of sadism against the self regularly occurs where a *cultural suppression of the instincts* holds back a large part of the subject's destructive instinctual components from being exercised in life. We may suppose that this portion of the destructive instinct which has retreated appears in the ego as an intensification of masochism. The phenomena of conscience, however, lead us to infer that the destructiveness which returns from the external world is also taken up by the super-ego, without any such transformation, and increases its sadism against the ego. The sadism of the super-ego and the masochism of the ego supplement each other and unite to produce the same effects. It is only in this way, I think, that we can understand how the suppression of an instinct can—frequently or quite generally—result in a sense of guilt and how a person's conscience becomes more severe and more sensitive the more he refrains from aggression against others.[1] One might expect that if a man knows that he is in the habit of avoiding the commission of acts of aggression that are undesirable from a cultural standpoint he will for that reason have a good conscience and will watch over his ego less suspiciously. The situation is usually presented as though ethical requirements were the primary thing and the renunciation of instinct followed from them. This leaves the origin of the ethical sense unexplained. Actually, it seems to be the other way about. The first instinctual renunciation is enforced by external powers, and it is only this which creates the ethical sense, which expresses itself in conscience and demands a further renunciation of instinct.[2]

Thus moral masochism becomes a classical piece of evidence for the existence of fusion of instinct. Its danger lies in the fact that it originates from the death instinct and corresponds to the part of that instinct which has escaped being turned outwards as an instinct of destruction. But since, on the other hand, it has the significance of an erotic component, even the subject's destruction of himself cannot take place without libidinal satisfaction.[3]

[1] [Cf. *The Ego and the Id*, p. 54 above.]

[2] [The subjects discussed in this paragraph were enlarged upon by Freud in Chapter VII of *Civilization and its Discontents* (1930a).]

[3] [Freud discussed masochism in relation to psycho-analytic treatment once more in Section VI of his paper on 'Analysis Terminable and Interminable' (1937c).]

THE DISSOLUTION OF THE
OEDIPUS COMPLEX
(1924)

DER UNTERGANG DES ÖDIPUSKOMPLEXES

(a) GERMAN EDITIONS:
1924   Int. Z. Psychoanal., 10 (3), 245–52.
1924   G.S., 5, 423–30.
1926   Psychoanalyse der Neurosen, 169–77.
1931   Neurosenlehre und Technik, 191–9.
1940   G.W., 13, 395–402.

(b) ENGLISH TRANSLATION:
          'The Passing of the Oedipus Complex'
1924   Int. J. Psycho-Anal., 5 (4), 419–24. (Tr. Joan Riviere.)
1924   C.P., 2, 269–76. (Reprint of above.)

The present translation, with a changed title, is based on that of 1924.

This paper, written in the early months of 1924, was in its essence an elaboration of a passage in *The Ego and the Id* (p. 31 ff. above). It further claims our special interest as laying emphasis for the first time on the different course taken by the development of sexuality in boys and in girls. This fresh line of thought was carried further some eighteen months later in Freud's paper on 'Some Psychical Consequences of the Anatomical Distinction between the Sexes' (1925*j*). The history of Freud's changing views on this subject is discussed in an Editor's Note to the latter paper (p. 243 ff. below).

THE DISSOLUTION[1] OF THE
OEDIPUS COMPLEX

To an ever-increasing extent the Oedipus complex reveals its importance as the central phenomenon of the sexual period of early childhood. After that, its dissolution takes place; it succumbs to repression, as we say, and is followed by the latency period. It has not yet become clear, however, what it is that brings about its destruction. Analyses seem to show that it is the experience of painful disappointments. The little girl likes to regard herself as what her father loves above all else; but the time comes when she has to endure a harsh punishment from him and she is cast out of her fool's paradise. The boy regards his mother as his own property; but he finds one day that she has transferred her love and solicitude to a new arrival. Reflection must deepen our sense of the importance of those influences, for it will emphasize the fact that distressing experiences of this sort, which act in opposition to the content of the complex, are inevitable. Even when no special events occur, like those we have mentioned as examples, the absence of the satisfaction hoped for, the continued denial of the desired baby, must in the end lead the small lover to turn away from his hopeless longing. In this way the Oedipus complex would go to its destruction from its lack of success, from the effects of its internal impossibility.

Another view is that the Oedipus complex must collapse because the time has come for its disintegration, just as the milk-teeth fall out when the permanent ones begin to grow.

[1] ['*Untergang.*' We learn from Ernest Jones (1957, 114) that Ferenczi, in a letter of March 24, 1924, objected to the strength of this word and suggested that it was chosen as a reaction to Rank's ideas on the importance of the 'birth trauma'. Freud, replying two days later, 'admitted that the word in the title might have been emotionally influenced by his feelings about Rank's new ideas, but said that the paper itself was quite independent of the latter' (Jones, loc. cit.). It must be pointed out, indeed, that the phrase '*Untergang des Ödipuskomplexes*' had in fact been used twice by Freud in *The Ego and the Id*, which was written before the publication of Rank's hypothesis. (See above, pp. 32 and 34.) In the same passage he had in fact also used the still stronger word '*Zertrümmerung* (demolition)'.]

Although the majority of human beings go through the Oedipus complex as an individual experience, it is nevertheless a phenomenon which is determined and laid down by heredity and which is bound to pass away according to programme when the next pre-ordained phase of development sets in. This being so, it is of no great importance what the occasions are which allow this to happen, or, indeed, whether any such occasions can be discovered at all.[1]

The justice of both these views cannot be disputed. Moreover, they are compatible. There is room for the ontogenetic view side by side with the more far-reaching phylogenetic one. It is also true that even at birth the whole individual is destined to die, and perhaps his organic disposition may already contain the indication of what he is to die from. Nevertheless, it remains of interest to follow out how this innate programme is carried out and in what way accidental noxae exploit his disposition.

We have lately[2] been made more clearly aware than before that a child's sexual development advances to a certain phase at which the genital organ has already taken over the leading role. But this genital is the male one only, or, more correctly, the penis; the female genital has remained undiscovered. This phallic phase, which is contemporaneous with the Oedipus complex, does not develop further to the definitive genital organization, but is submerged, and is succeeded by the latency period. Its termination, however, takes place in a typical manner and in conjunction with events that are of regular recurrence.

When the (male) child's interest turns to his genitals he betrays the fact by manipulating them frequently; and he then finds that the adults do not approve of this behaviour. More or less plainly, more or less brutally, a threat is pronounced that this part of him which he values so highly will be taken away from him. Usually it is from women that the threat emanates; very often they seek to strengthen their authority by a reference to the father or the doctor, who, so they say, will carry out the punishment. In a number of cases the women will themselves

---

[1] [The ideas contained in this and the preceding paragraph had been expressed by Freud in very similar terms in Section IV of ' "A Child is Being Beaten" ' (1919e), *Standard Ed.*, **17**, 188.]

[2] [See 'The Infantile Genital Organization of the Libido' (1923e), p. 141 above.]

mitigate the threat in a symbolic manner by telling the child that what is to be removed is not his genital, which actually plays a passive part, but his hand, which is the active culprit. It happens particularly often that the little boy is threatened with castration, not because he plays with his penis with his hand, but because he wets his bed every night and cannot be got to be clean. Those in charge of him behave as if this nocturnal incontinence was the result and the proof of his being unduly concerned with his penis, and they are probably right.[1] In any case, long-continued bed-wetting is to be equated with the emissions of adults. It is an expression of the same excitation of the genitals which has impelled the child to masturbate at this period.

Now it is my view that what brings about the destruction of the child's phallic genital organization is this threat of castration. Not immediately, it is true, and not without other influences being brought to bear as well. For to begin with the boy does not believe in the threat or obey it in the least. Psycho-analysis has recently attached importance to two experiences which all children go through and which, it is suggested, prepare them for the loss of highly valued parts of the body. These experiences are the withdrawal of the mother's breast—at first intermittently and later for good—and the daily demand on them to give up the contents of the bowel. But there is no evidence to show that, when the threat of castration takes place, those experiences have any effect.[2] It is not until a *fresh* experience comes his way that the child begins to reckon with the possibility of being castrated, and then only hesitatingly and unwillingly, and not without making efforts to depreciate the significance of something he has himself observed.

The observation which finally breaks down his unbelief is the sight of the female genitals. Sooner or later the child, who is so

[1] [Cf. the case history of 'Dora' (1905e), *Standard Ed.*, 7, 74 and the second of the *Three Essays* (1905d), ibid., 190.]

[2] [Cf. a footnote added, at about the time this paper was written, to the case history of 'Little Hans' (1909b), *Standard Ed.*, 10, 8, in which reference is made to papers by Andreas-Salomé (1916), A. Stärcke (1910) and Alexander (1922). A third experience of separation—that of birth —is also mentioned there, but, as in the present passage, Freud objects to the confusion with the castration complex. Cf. also a footnote to 'The Infantile Genital Organization of the Libido' (1923e), p. 144 above.]

proud of his possession of a penis, has a view of the genital region of a little girl, and cannot help being convinced of the absence of a penis in a creature who is so like himself. With this, the loss of his own penis becomes imaginable, and the threat of castration takes its deferred effect.

We should not be as short-sighted as the person in charge of the child who threatens him with castration, and we must not overlook the fact that at this time masturbation by no means represents the whole of his sexual life. As can be clearly shown, he stands in the Oedipus attitude to his parents; his masturbation is only a genital discharge of the sexual excitation belonging to the complex, and throughout his later years will owe its importance to that relationship. The Oedipus complex offered the child two possibilities of satisfaction, an active and a passive one. He could put himself in his father's place in a masculine fashion and have intercourse with his mother as his father did, in which case he would soon have felt the latter as a hindrance; or he might want to take the place of his mother and be loved by his father, in which case his mother would become superfluous. The child may have had only very vague notions as to what constitutes a satisfying erotic intercourse; but certainly the penis must play a part in it, for the sensations in his own organ were evidence of that. So far he had had no occasion to doubt that women possessed a penis. But now his acceptance of the possibility of castration, his recognition that women were castrated, made an end of both possible ways of obtaining satisfaction from the Oedipus complex. For both of them entailed the loss of his penis—the masculine one as a resulting punishment and the feminine one as a precondition. If the satisfaction of love in the field of the Oedipus complex is to cost the child his penis, a conflict is bound to arise between his narcissistic interest in that part of his body and the libidinal cathexis of his parental objects. In this conflict the first of these forces normally triumphs: the child's ego turns away from the Oedipus complex.

I have described elsewhere how this turning away takes place.[1] The object-cathexes are given up and replaced by identifications. The authority of the father or the parents is introjected into the ego, and there it forms the nucleus of the super-ego, which takes over the severity of the father and per-

[1] [In Chapter III of *The Ego and the Id*, p. 29 ff. above.]

petuates his prohibition against incest, and so secures the ego from the return of the libidinal object-cathexis. The libidinal trends belonging to the Oedipus complex are in part desexualized and sublimated (a thing which probably happens with every transformation into an identification) and in part inhibited in their aim and changed into impulses of affection. The whole process has, on the one hand, preserved the genital organ—has averted the danger of its loss—and, on the other, has paralysed it—has removed its function. This process ushers in the latency period, which now interrupts the child's sexual development.

I see no reason for denying the name of a 'repression' to the ego's turning away from the Oedipus complex, although later repressions come about for the most part with the participation of the super-ego, which in this case is only just being formed. But the process we have described is more than a repression. It is equivalent, if it is ideally carried out, to a destruction and an abolition of the complex. We may plausibly assume that we have here come upon the borderline—never a very sharply drawn one—between the normal and the pathological. If the ego has in fact not achieved much more than a *repression* of the complex, the latter persists in an unconscious state in the id and will later manifest its pathogenic effect.

Analytic observation enables us to recognize or guess these connections between the phallic organization, the Oedipus complex, the threat of castration, the formation of the super-ego and the latency period. These connections justify the statement that the destruction of the Oedipus complex is brought about by the threat of castration. But this does not dispose of the problem; there is room for a theoretical speculation which may upset the results we have come to or put them in a new light. Before we start along this new path, however, we must turn to a question which has arisen in the course of this discussion and has so far been left on one side. The process which has been described refers, as has been expressly said, to male children only. How does the corresponding development take place in little girls?

At this point our material—for some incomprehensible reason[1]—becomes far more obscure and full of gaps. The female sex, too, develops an Oedipus complex, a super-ego and a

---

[1] [Freud suggested some explanation for this in Section I of his paper on 'Female Sexuality' (1931*b*).]

latency period. May we also attribute a phallic organization
and a castration complex to it? The answer is in the affirmative;
but these things cannot be the same as they are in boys. Here
the feminist demand for equal rights for the sexes does not take
us far, for the morphological distinction is bound to find
expression in differences of psychical development.[1] 'Anatomy
is Destiny', to vary a saying of Napoleon's. The little girl's
clitoris behaves just like a penis to begin with; but, when she
makes a comparison with a playfellow of the other sex, she
perceives that she has 'come off badly'[2] and she feels this as a
wrong done to her and as a ground for inferiority. For a while
still she consoles herself with the expectation that later on, when
she grows older, she will acquire just as big an appendage as the
boy's. Here the masculinity complex of women branches off.
A female child, however, does not understand her lack of a
penis as being a sex character; she explains it by assuming that
at some earlier date she had possessed an equally large organ
and had then lost it by castration. She seems not to extend this
inference from herself to other, adult females, but, entirely on
the lines of the phallic phase, to regard them as possessing large
and complete—that is to say, male—genitals. The essential
difference thus comes about that the girl accepts castration as
an accomplished fact, whereas the boy fears the possibility of
its occurrence.

The fear of castration being thus excluded in the little girl,
a powerful motive also drops out for the setting-up of a super-
ego and for the breaking-off of the infantile genital organization. In her, far more than in the boy, these changes seem to be
the result of upbringing and of intimidation from outside which
threatens her with a loss of love. The girl's Oedipus complex
is much simpler than that of the small bearer of the penis; in my
experience, it seldom goes beyond the taking of her mother's
place and the adopting of a feminine attitude towards her
father. Renunciation of the penis is not tolerated by the girl
without some attempt at compensation. She slips—along the

---

[1] [See Freud's paper, written about eighteen months after this one,
on 'Some Psychical Consequences of the Anatomical Distinction between the Sexes' (1925*j*), p. 248 below. Much of what follows is elaborated there. The paraphrase of Napoleon's epigram had appeared
already in the second paper on the psychology of love (1912*d*), *Standard
Ed.*, 11, 189.]   [2] [Literally, 'come off too short'.]

line of a symbolic equation, one might say—from the penis to a baby. Her Oedipus complex culminates in a desire, which is long retained, to receive a baby from her father as a gift—to bear him a child.[1] One has an impression that the Oedipus complex is then gradually given up because this wish is never fulfilled. The two wishes—to possess a penis and a child—remain strongly cathected in the unconscious and help to prepare the female creature for her later sexual role. The comparatively lesser strength of the sadistic contribution to her sexual instinct, which we may no doubt connect with the stunted growth of her penis, makes it easier in her case for the direct sexual trends to be transformed into aim-inhibited trends of an affectionate kind. It must be admitted, however, that in general our insight into these developmental processes in girls is unsatisfactory, incomplete and vague.[2]

I have no doubt that the chronological and causal relations described here between the Oedipus complex, sexual intimidation (the threat of castration), the formation of the super-ego and the beginning of the latency period are of a typical kind; but I do not wish to assert that this type is the only possible one. Variations in the chronological order and in the linking-up of these events are bound to have a very important bearing on the development of the individual.

Since the publication of Otto Rank's interesting study, *The Trauma of Birth* [1924], even the conclusion arrived at by this modest investigation, to the effect that the boy's Oedipus complex is destroyed by the fear of castration, cannot be accepted without further discussion. Nevertheless, it seems to me premature to enter into such a discussion at the present time, and perhaps inadvisable to begin a criticism or an appreciation of Rank's view at this juncture.[3]

---

[1] [Cf. Freud's paper on 'Transformations of Instinct' (1917c), *Standard Ed.*, 17, 128 ff.; see also below, p. 256.]

[2] [Freud discussed this topic much more fully in his papers on the anatomical distinction between the sexes (1925j) and on female sexuality (1931b), in both of which he gave a very different account of the girl's Oedipus complex from the present one.]

[3] [The question was taken up by Freud soon afterwards in *Inhibitions, Symptoms and Anxiety* (1926d). Cf. Section (e) of the Editor's Introduction to that work, *Standard Ed.*, 20, 83 ff.]

THE LOSS OF REALITY IN NEUROSIS AND PSYCHOSIS
(1924)

DER REALITATSVERLUST BEI NEUROSE
UND PSYCHOSE

(*a*) GERMAN EDITIONS:

1924 *Int. Z. Psychoanal.*, **10** (4), 374–9.

1925 *G.S.*, **6**, 409–14.

1926 *Psychoanalyse der Neurosen*, 178–84.

1931 *Neurosenlehre und Technik*, 199–204.

1940 *G.W.*, **13**, 363–8.

(*b*) ENGLISH TRANSLATION:

'The Loss of Reality in Neurosis and Psychosis'

1924 *C.P.*, **2**, 277–82. (Tr. Joan Riviere.)

According to a statement in a footnote to the English translation (*C.P.*, **2**, 277), it was actually published before the German original. The present translation is based on that of 1924.

This paper was written by the end of May, 1924, for it was read by Abraham during that month. It continues the discussion begun in the earlier paper 'Neurosis and Psychosis' (1924*b*), p. 149 above, which it amplifies and corrects. Some doubts about the validity of the distinction drawn in these two papers were discussed by Freud later, in his paper on 'Fetishism' (1927*e*).

THE LOSS OF REALITY IN NEUROSIS
AND PSYCHOSIS

I HAVE recently[1] indicated as one of the features which differentiate a neurosis from a psychosis the fact that in a neurosis the ego, in its dependence on reality, suppresses a piece of the id (of instinctual life), whereas in a psychosis, this same ego, in the service of the id, withdraws from a piece of reality. Thus for a neurosis the decisive factor would be the predominance of the influence of reality, whereas for a psychosis it would be the predominance of the id. In a psychosis, a loss of reality would necessarily be present, whereas in a neurosis, it would seem, this loss would be avoided.

But this does not at all agree with the observation which all of us can make that every neurosis disturbs the patient's relation to reality in some way, that it serves him as a means of withdrawing from reality, and that, in its severe forms, it actually signifies a flight from real life. This contradiction seems a serious one; but it is easily resolved, and the explanation of it will in fact help us to understand neuroses.

For the contradiction exists only as long as we keep our eyes fixed on the situation at the *beginning* of the neurosis, in which the ego, in the service of reality, sets about the repression of an instinctual impulse. This, however, is not yet the neurosis itself. The neurosis consists rather in the processes which provide a compensation for the portion of the id that has been damaged —that is to say, in the reaction against the repression and in the failure of the repression. The loosening of the relation to reality is a consequence of this second step in the formation of a neurosis, and it ought not to surprise us if a detailed examination shows that the loss of reality affects precisely that piece of reality as a result of whose demands the instinctual repression ensued.

There is nothing new in our characterization of neurosis as the result of a repression that has failed. We have said this all along,[2] and it is only because of the new context in which we are viewing the subject that it has been necessary to repeat it.

[1] 'Neurosis and Psychosis' (1924*b*) [this volume, p. 149].

[2] [The notion that the 'return of the repressed' constitutes 'the illness

Incidentally, the same objection arises in a specially marked manner when we are dealing with a neurosis in which the exciting cause (the 'traumatic scene') is known, and in which one can see how the person concerned turns away from the experience and consigns it to amnesia. Let me go back by way of example to a case analysed a great many years ago,[1] in which the patient, a young woman, was in love with her brother-in-law. Standing beside her sister's death-bed, she was horrified at having the thought: 'Now he is free and can marry me.' This scene was instantly forgotten, and thus the process of regression,[2] which led to her hysterical pains, was set in motion. It is instructive precisely in this case, moreover, to learn along what path the neurosis attempted to solve the conflict. It took away from the value of the change that had occurred in reality, by repressing the instinctual demand which had emerged— that is, her love for her brother-in-law. The *psychotic* reaction would have been a disavowal[3] of the fact of her sister's death.

We might expect that when a psychosis comes into being, something analogous to the process in a neurosis occurs, though, of course, between different agencies of the mind; thus we might expect that in a psychosis, too, two steps could be discerned, of which the first would drag the ego away, this time from reality, while the second would try to make good the damage done and re-establish the subject's relations to reality at the expense of the id. And, in fact, some analogy of the sort can be observed in a psychosis. Here, too, there are two steps, the second of which has the character of a reparation. But beyond that the analogy gives way to a far more extensive similarity between the two processes. The second step of the psychosis is indeed intended to make good the loss of reality,

proper' is already stated in Draft K of the Fliess correspondence, of January 1, 1896 (Freud 1950a). A little later Freud restated this, using the actual words 'failure of defence' as equivalent to 'return of the repressed', in Section II of the second paper on 'The Neuro-Psychoses of Defence' (1896b).]

[1] In *Studies on Hysteria* (1895d). [*Standard Ed.*, **2**, 156 and 167. The words of the patient, Frau Elisabeth von R., are not here quoted verbatim.]

[2] [The German word is *'Regression'*, not *'Verdrängung'* ('repression'), in all editions.]

[3] [See Editor's footnote to 'The Infantile Genital Organization' (1923e), p. 143 above.]

not, however, at the expense of a restriction of the id—as happens in neurosis at the expense of the relation to reality—but in another, more autocratic manner, by the creation of a new reality which no longer raises the same objections as the old one that has been given up. The second step, therefore, both in neurosis and psychosis, is supported by the same trends. In both cases it serves the desire for power of the id, which will not allow itself to be dictated to by reality. Both neurosis and psychosis are thus the expression of a rebellion on the part of the id against the external world, of its unwillingness—or, if one prefers, its incapacity—to adapt itself to the exigencies of reality, to 'Aνάγκη [Necessity].[1] Neurosis and psychosis differ from each other far more in their first, introductory, reaction than in the attempt at reparation which follows it.

Accordingly, the initial difference is expressed thus in the final outcome: in neurosis a piece of reality is avoided by a sort of flight, whereas in psychosis it is remodelled. Or we might say: in psychosis, the initial flight is succeeded by an active phase of remodelling; in neurosis, the initial obedience is succeeded by a deferred attempt at flight. Or again, expressed in yet another way: neurosis does not disavow the reality, it only ignores it; psychosis disavows it and tries to replace it. We call behaviour 'normal' or 'healthy', if it combines certain features of both reactions—if it disavows the reality as little as does a neurosis, but if it then exerts itself, as does a psychosis, to effect an alteration of that reality. Of course, this expedient, normal, behaviour leads to work being carried out on the external world; it does not stop, as in psychosis, at effecting internal changes. It is no longer *autoplastic* but *alloplastic*.[2]

In a psychosis, the transforming of reality is carried out upon the psychical precipitates of former relations to it—that is, upon the memory-traces, ideas and judgements which have been previously derived from reality and by which reality was represented in the mind. But this relation was never a closed one; it was continually being enriched and altered by fresh perceptions.

[1] [See 'The Economic Problem of Masochism' (1924c), p. 168 above.]
[2] [These terms are possibly due to Ferenczi, who used them in a paper on 'The Phenomena of Hysterical Materialization' (1919a, 24; English trans., 1926, 97). But he there appears to attribute them to Freud, who, however, does not seem to have used them elsewhere than in this passage.]

Thus the psychosis is also faced with the task of procuring for itself perceptions of a kind which shall correspond to the new reality; and this is most radically effected by means of hallucination. The fact that, in so many forms and cases of psychosis, the paramnesias, the delusions and the hallucinations that occur are of a most distressing character and are bound up with a generation of anxiety—this fact is without doubt a sign that the whole process of remodelling is carried through against forces which oppose it violently. We may construct the process on the model of a neurosis, with which we are more familiar. There we see that a reaction of anxiety sets in whenever the repressed instinct makes a thrust forward, and that the outcome of the conflict is only a compromise and does not provide complete satisfaction. Probably in a psychosis the rejected piece of reality constantly forces itself upon the mind, just as the repressed instinct does in a neurosis, and that is why in both cases the consequences too are the same. The elucidation of the various mechanisms which are designed, in the psychoses, to turn the subject away from reality and to reconstruct reality —this is a task for specialized psychiatric study which has not yet been taken in hand.[1]

There is, therefore, a further analogy between a neurosis and a psychosis, in that in both of them the task which is undertaken in the second step is partly unsuccessful. For the repressed instinct is unable to procure a full substitute (in neurosis); and the representation of reality cannot be remoulded into satisfying forms (not, at least, in every species of mental illness). But the emphasis is different in the two cases. In a psychosis it falls entirely on the first step, which is pathological in itself and cannot but lead to illness. In a neurosis, on the other hand, it falls on the second step, on the failure of the repression, whereas the first step may succeed, and does succeed in innumerable instances without overstepping the bounds of health—even though it does so at a certain price and not without leaving behind traces of the psychical expenditure it has called for. These distinctions, and perhaps many others as well, are a result of the topographical difference in the initial situation of the pathogenic conflict—namely whether in it the ego

[1] [Cf., however, some beginnings made by Freud himself in the case of paranoia (*Standard Ed.*, **12**, 69–71) and of 'paraphrenia' (ibid., **14**, 86–7, 203–4 and 230).]

yielded to its allegiance to the real world or to its dependence on the id.

A neurosis usually contents itself with avoiding the piece of reality in question and protecting itself against coming into contact with it. The sharp distinction between neurosis and psychosis, however, is weakened by the circumstance that in neurosis, too, there is no lack of attempts to replace a disagreeable reality by one which is more in keeping with the subject's wishes. This is made possible by the existence of a *world of phantasy*, of a domain which became separated from the real external world at the time of the introduction of the reality principle. This domain has since been kept free from the demands of the exigencies of life, like a kind of 'reservation';[1] it is not inaccessible to the ego, but is only loosely attached to it. It is from this world of phantasy that the neurosis draws the material for its new wishful constructions, and it usually finds that material along the path of regression to a more satisfying real past.

It can hardly be doubted that the world of phantasy plays the same part in psychosis and that there, too, it is the storehouse from which the materials or the pattern for building the new reality are derived. But whereas the new, imaginary external world of a psychosis attempts to put itself in the place of external reality, that of a neurosis, on the contrary, is apt, like the play of children, to attach itself to a piece of reality— a different piece from the one against which it has to defend itself—and to lend that piece a special importance and a secret meaning which we (not always quite appropriately) call a *symbolic* one. Thus we see that both in neurosis and psychosis there comes into consideration the question not only of a *loss of reality* but also of a *substitute for reality*.

[1] [Cf. the paper on the 'Two Principles of Mental Functioning' (1911*b*), *Standard Ed.*, 12, 222 and footnote.]

A SHORT ACCOUNT OF PSYCHO-ANALYSIS
(1924 [1923])

KURZER ABRISS DER PSYCHOANALYSE

(a) GERMAN EDITIONS:
(1923   Date of Composition)
1928   *G.S.*, **11**, 183–200.
1940   *G.W.*, **13**, 403–27.

(b) ENGLISH TRANSLATION:
'Psychoanalysis: Exploring the Hidden Recesses of the Mind'
1924   In *These Eventful Years: The Twentieth Century in the Making, as Told by Many of its Makers*, Vol. II, Chap. LXXIII, 511–23, London and New York: Encyclopaedia Britannica Publishing Co. (Tr. A. A. Brill.)

The present translation, with a changed title, is a new one by James Strachey.

We learn from Ernest Jones (1957, 114) that this was written by Freud, at the request of the American publishers, in October and November, 1923. This work is to be distinguished from the article written some two years later for the *Encyclopaedia Britannica* itself (1926*f*). The original German text, with a less exciting title than the American one, was published for the first time in 1928.

A SHORT ACCOUNT OF PSYCHO-ANALYSIS

I

PSYCHO-ANALYSIS may be said to have been born with the twentieth century; for the publication in which it emerged before the world as something new—my *Interpretation of Dreams*—bears the date '1900'.[1] But, as may well be supposed, it did not drop from the skies ready-made. It had its starting-point in older ideas, which it developed further; it sprang from earlier suggestions, which it elaborated. Any history of it must therefore begin with an account of the influences which determined its origin and should not overlook the times and circumstances that preceded its creation.

Psycho-analysis grew up in a narrowly-restricted field. At the outset, it had only a single aim—that of understanding something of the nature of what were known as the 'functional' nervous diseases, with a view to overcoming the impotence which had so far characterized their medical treatment. The neurologists of that period had been brought up to have a high respect for chemico-physical and pathologico-anatomical facts; and they were latterly under the influence of the findings of Hitzig and Fritsch, of Ferrier, Goltz and others, who seemed to have established an intimate and possibly exclusive connection between certain functions and particular parts of the brain. They did not know what to make of the psychical factor and could not understand it. They left it to the philosophers, the mystics and—the quacks; and they considered it unscientific to have anything to do with it. Accordingly they could find no approach to the secrets of the neuroses, and in particular of the enigmatic 'hysteria', which was, indeed, the prototype of the whole species. As late as in 1885, when I was studying at the Salpêtrière, I found that people were content to account for hysterical paralyses by a formula which asserted that they were founded on slight functional disturbances of the same parts of the brain which, when they were severely damaged, led to the corresponding organic paralyses.

Of course this lack of understanding affected the *treatment* of

[1] [It was actually published at the beginning of November, 1899. Cf. *Standard Ed.*, 4, xii.]

these pathological conditions badly as well. In general this consisted in measures designed to 'harden' the patient—in the prescription of medicines and in attempts, mostly very ill-contrived and executed in an unfriendly manner, at bringing mental influences to bear on him by threats, jeers and warnings and by exhorting him to make up his mind to 'pull himself together'. Electrical treatment was given out as being a specific cure for nervous conditions; but anyone who has endeavoured to carry out Erb's [1882] detailed instructions must marvel at the space that phantasy can occupy even in what professes to be an exact science. The decisive turn was taken in the eighties, when the phenomena of hypnotism made one more attempt to find admission to medical science—this time with more success than so often before, thanks to the work of Liébeault, Bernheim, Heidenhain and Forel. The essential thing was that the genuineness of these phenomena was recognized. Once this had been admitted, two fundamental and unforgettable lessons could not fail to be drawn from hypnotism. First, one was given convincing proof that striking somatic changes could after all be brought about solely by mental influences, which in this case one had oneself set in motion. Secondly, one received the clearest impression—especially from the behaviour of subjects *after* hypnosis—of the existence of mental processes that one could only describe as 'unconscious'. The 'unconscious' had, it is true, long been under discussion among philosophers as a theoretical concept; but now for the first time, in the phenomena of hypnotism, it became something actual, tangible and subject to experiment. Apart from all this, hypnotic phenomena showed an unmistakable similarity to the manifestations of some neuroses.

It is not easy to over-estimate the importance of the part played by hypnotism in the history of the origin of psycho-analysis. From a theoretical as well as from a therapeutic point of view, psycho-analysis has at its command a legacy which it has inherited from hypnotism.

Hypnosis also proved a valuable aid in the study of the neuroses—once again, first and foremost, of hysteria. Charcot's experiments created a great impression. He suspected that certain paralyses which appeared after a trauma (an accident) were of a hysterical nature, and he showed that, by suggesting a trauma under hypnosis, he was able to provoke paralyses of the same sort artificially. The expectation was thus raised that traumatic influences might in all cases play a part in the production of hysterical symptoms. Charcot himself made no further efforts towards a psychological understanding of hysteria; but his pupil, Pierre Janet, took up the question and was able to show, with the help of hypnosis, that the symptoms of hysteria were firmly dependent on certain unconscious thoughts (*idées fixes*). Janet attributed to hysteria a supposed constitutional incapacity for holding mental processes together —an incapacity which led to a disintegration (dissociation) of mental life.

Psycho-analysis, however, was not in any way based on these researches of Janet's. The decisive factor in its case was the experience of a Viennese physician, Dr. Josef Breuer. In 1881, independently of any outside influence, he was able with the help of hypnosis to study and restore to health a highly-gifted girl who suffered from hysteria.[1] Breuer's findings were not given to the public until fifteen years later, after he had taken the present writer (Freud) into collaboration. This case of Breuer's retains its unique significance for our understanding of the neuroses to this day; so that we cannot avoid dwelling on it a little longer. It is essential to realize clearly in what its peculiarity consisted. The girl had fallen ill while she was nursing her father, to whom she was tenderly attached. Breuer was able to establish that all her symptoms were related to this period of nursing and could be explained by it. Thus it had for the first time become possible to obtain a complete view of a case of this puzzling neurosis, and all its symptoms had turned out to have a meaning. Further, it was a universal feature of the symptoms that they had arisen in situations involving an impulse to an action which, however, had not been carried out but had for other reasons been suppressed. The symptoms had, in fact, appeared *in place of* the actions that were not performed. Thus, to explain the aetiology of hysterical symptoms, we were led to the subject's emotional life (to affectivity) and to the interplay of mental forces (to dynamics); and since then these two lines of approach have never been dropped.

The precipitating causes of the symptoms were compared by Breuer to Charcot's traumas. Now it was a remarkable fact that all these traumatic precipitating causes, and all the mental impulses starting from them, were lost to the patient's memory,

[1] [Cf. *Standard Ed.*, **2**, 21 ff.]

as though they had never happened; while their products—the symptoms—persisted unaltered, as though, so far as they were concerned, there was no such thing as the effacing effect of time. Here, therefore, we had a fresh proof of the existence of mental processes which were unconscious but for that very reason especially powerful—processes which we had first come to know in post-hypnotic suggestion. The therapeutic procedure adopted by Breuer was to induce the patient, under hypnosis, to remember the forgotten traumas and to react to them with powerful expressions of affect. When this had been done, the symptom, which had till then taken the place of these expressions of emotion, disappeared. Thus one and the same procedure served simultaneously the purposes of investigating and of getting rid of the ailment; and this unusual conjunction was later retained in psycho-analysis.

After the present writer had, during the early nineties, confirmed Breuer's results in a considerable number of patients, the two, Breuer and Freud, together decided on a publication, *Studies on Hysteria* (1895d), which contained their findings and an attempt at a theory based on them. This asserted that hysterical symptoms arose when the affect of a mental process cathected with a strong affect was forcibly prevented from being worked over consciously in the normal way and was thus diverted into a wrong path. In cases of hysteria, according to this theory, the affect passed over into an unusual somatic innervation ('conversion'), but could be given another direction and got rid of ('abreacted'), if the experience were revived under hypnosis. The authors gave this procedure the name of 'catharsis' (purging, setting free of a strangulated affect).

The cathartic method was the immediate precursor of psycho-analysis; and, in spite of every extension of experience and of every modification of theory, is still contained within it as its nucleus. But it was no more than a new medical procedure for influencing certain nervous diseases, and nothing suggested that it might become a subject for the most general interest and for the most violent contradiction.

II

Soon after the publication of *Studies on Hysteria* the partnership between Breuer and Freud came to an end. Breuer, who was in reality a consultant in internal medicine, gave up treating nervous patients, and Freud devoted himself to the further perfection of the instrument left over to him by his elder collaborator. The technical novelties which he introduced and the discoveries which he made changed the cathartic method into psycho-analysis. The most momentous step, no doubt, was his determination to do without the assistance of hypnosis in his technical procedure. He did so for two reasons: first, because, in spite of a course of instruction with Bernheim at Nancy, he did not succeed in inducing hypnosis in a sufficient number of cases, and secondly, because he was dissatisfied with the therapeutic results of catharsis based on hypnosis. It is true that these results were striking and appeared after a treatment of short duration, but they turned out not to be permanent and to depend too much on the patient's personal relations with the physician. The abandonment of hypnosis made a breach in the course of development of the procedure up to then, and it meant a fresh start.

Hypnosis had, however, performed the service of restoring to the patient's memory what he had forgotten. It was necessary to find some other technique to replace it; and the idea occurred to Freud of substituting for it the method of 'free association'. That is to say, he pledged his patients to refrain from any conscious reflection and to abandon themselves, in a state of quiet concentration, to following the ideas which occurred to them spontaneously (involuntarily)—'to skim off the surface of their consciousness'.[1] They were to communicate these ideas to the physician even if they felt objections to doing so, if, for instance, the thoughts seemed too disagreeable, too senseless, too unimportant or irrelevant. The choice of free association as a means of investigating the forgotten unconscious material seems so strange that a word in justification of it will not be out of place. Freud was led to it by an expectation that the so-called 'free' association would prove in fact to be unfree, since, when all conscious intellectual purposes had been suppressed, the ideas that emerged would be seen to be determined by the unconscious material. This expectation was justified by experience. When the 'fundamental rule of psycho-analysis' which has

---

[1] [The reason for the inverted commas is not clear. See, however, the similar phrase in Freud's contribution on 'Psycho-Analysis' to Marcuse's encyclopaedia (1923a), *Standard Ed.*, 18, 238.]

just been stated was obeyed, the course of free association produced a plentiful store of ideas which could put one on the
track of what the patient had forgotten. To be sure, this material
did not bring up what had actually been forgotten, but it
brought up such plain and numerous hints at it that, with the
help of a certain amount of supplementing and interpreting,
the doctor was able to guess (to reconstruct) the forgotten
material from it. Thus free association together with the art of
interpretation performed the same function as had previously
been performed by hypnotism.

It looked as though our work had been made much more
difficult and complicated; but the inestimable gain was that an
insight was now obtained into an interplay of forces which had
been concealed from the observer by the hypnotic state. It
became evident that the work of uncovering what had been
pathogenically forgotten had to struggle against a constant and
very intense resistance. The critical objections which the patient
raised in order to avoid communicating the ideas which
occurred to him, and against which the fundamental rule of
psycho-analysis was directed, had themselves already been
manifestations of this resistance. A consideration of the phenomena of resistance led to one of the corner-stones of the psycho-
analytic theory of the neuroses—the theory of repression. It was
plausible to suppose that the same forces which were now
struggling against the pathogenic material being made conscious had at an earlier time made the same efforts with
success. A gap in the aetiology of neurotic symptoms was thus
filled. The impressions and mental impulses, for which the
symptoms were now serving as substitutes, had not been forgotten without reason or on account of a constitutional incapacity for synthesis (as Janet supposed); they had, through
the influence of other mental forces, met with a repression the
success and evidence of which was precisely their being debarred from consciousness and excluded from memory. It was
only in consequence of this repression that they had become
pathogenic—that, is, had succeeded in manifesting themselves
along unusual paths as symptoms.

A conflict between two groups of mental trends had to be
looked on as the ground for repression and accordingly as the
cause of every neurotic illness. And here experience taught us
a new and surprising fact about the nature of the forces that

were struggling against each other. Repression invariably proceeded from the sick person's conscious personality (his ego) and took its stand on aesthetic and ethical motives; the impulses that were subjected to repression were those of selfishness and cruelty, which can be summed up in general as evil, but above all sexual wishful impulses, often of the crudest and most forbidden kind. Thus the symptoms were a substitute for forbidden satisfactions and the illness seemed to correspond to an incomplete subjugation of the immoral side of human beings.

Advance in knowledge made ever clearer the enormous part played in mental life by sexual wishful impulses, and led to a detailed study of the nature and development of the sexual instinct.[1] But we also came upon another purely empirical finding, in the discovery that the experiences and conflicts of the first years of childhood play an unsuspectedly important part in the individual's development and leave behind them ineffaceable dispositions bearing upon the period of maturity. This led to the revelation of something that had hitherto been fundamentally overlooked by science—infantile sexuality, which, from the tenderest age onwards, is manifested both in physical reactions and in mental attitudes. In order to bring together this sexuality of children with what is described as the normal sexuality of adults and the abnormal sexual life of perverts, the concept of what was sexual had itself to be corrected and widened in a manner which could be justified by the evolution of the sexual instinct.

After hypnosis was replaced by the technique of free association, Breuer's cathartic procedure turned into psycho-analysis, which for more than a decade was developed by the author (Freud) alone. During that time psycho-analysis gradually acquired a theory which appeared to give a satisfactory account of the origin, meaning and purpose of neurotic symptoms and provided a rational basis for medical attempts at curing the complaint. I will once again enumerate the factors that go to make up this theory. They are: emphasis on instinctual life (affectivity), on mental dynamics, on the fact that even the apparently most obscure and arbitrary mental phenomena invariably have a meaning and a causation, the theory of psychical conflict and of the pathogenic nature of repression, the view that symptoms are substitutive satisfactions, the recognition of

[1] Freud, *Three Essays on the Theory of Sexuality* (1905d).

the aetiological importance of sexual life, and in particular of the beginnings of infantile sexuality. From a philosophical standpoint this theory was bound to adopt the view that the mental does not coincide with the conscious, that mental processes are in themselves unconscious and are only made conscious by the functioning of special organs (agencies or systems). By way of completing this list, I will add that among the affective attitudes of childhood the complicated emotional relation of children to their parents—what is known as the Oedipus complex—came into prominence. It became ever clearer that this was the nucleus of every case of neurosis, and in the patient's behaviour towards his analyst certain phenomena of his emotional transference emerged which came to be of great importance for theory and technique alike.

In the form which it thus assumed, the psycho-analytic theory of the neuroses already contained a number of things which ran counter to accepted opinions and inclinations and which were calculated to provoke astonishment, repugnance and scepticism in outsiders: for instance, the attitude of psycho-analysis to the problem of the unconscious, its recognition of an infantile sexuality and the stress it laid on the sexual factor in mental life generally. But more was to follow.

III

In order to reach even half way to an understanding of how, in a hysterical girl, a forbidden sexual wish can change into a painful symptom, it had been necessary to make far-reaching and complicated hypotheses about the structure and functioning of the mental apparatus. There was an evident contradiction here between expenditure of effort and result. If the conditions postulated by psycho-analysis really existed, they were of a fundamental nature and must be able to find expression in other phenomena besides hysterical ones. But if this inference were correct, psycho-analysis would have ceased to be of interest only to neurologists; it could claim the attention of everyone to whom psychological research was of any importance. Its findings would not only have to be taken into account in the field of pathological mental life but could not be overlooked either in coming to an understanding of normal functioning.

Evidence of its being of use for throwing light on other than pathological mental activity was early forthcoming in connection with two kinds of phenomena: with the very frequent parapraxes that occur in everyday life—such as forgetting things, slips of the tongue, and mislaying objects—and with the dreams dreamt by healthy and psychically normal people. Small failures of functioning, like the temporary forgetting of normally familiar proper names, slips of the tongue and of the pen, and so on, had hitherto not been considered worthy of any explanation at all or were supposed to be accounted for by conditions of fatigue, by distraction of the attention, etc. The present writer then showed from many examples, in his book *The Psychopathology of Everyday Life* (1901*b*), that events of this kind have a meaning, and arise owing to a conscious intention being interfered with by another, suppressed or actually unconscious one. As a rule, quick reflection or a short analysis is enough to reveal the interfering influence. Owing to the frequency of such parapraxes as slips of the tongue, it became easy for anyone to convince himself from his own experience of the existence of mental processes which are not conscious, but which are nevertheless operative and which at least find expression as inhibitions and modifications of other, intended acts.

The analysis of dreams led further: it was brought to public notice by the present writer as early as in 1900 in *The Interpretation of Dreams*. This showed that dreams are constructed in just the same way as neurotic symptoms. Like them, they may appear strange and senseless; but, if we examine them by a technique which differs little from the free association used in psycho-analysis, we are led from their manifest content to a secret meaning, to the latent dream-thoughts. This latent meaning is always a wishful impulse which is represented as fulfilled at the moment of the dream. But, except in young children and under the pressure of imperative physical needs, this secret wish can never be expressed recognizably. It has first to submit to a distortion, which is the work of restrictive, censoring forces in the dreamer's ego. In this way the manifest dream, as it is remembered in waking life, comes about. It is distorted, to the pitch of being unrecognizable, by concessions made to the dream-censorship; but it can be revealed once more by analysis as an expression of a situation of satisfaction or as the fulfilment of a wish. It is a compromise between two conflicting groups of mental trends, just as we have found to be the case with hysterical symptoms. The formula which, at bottom, best meets the essence of the dream is this: a dream is a (disguised) fulfilment of a (repressed) wish. The study of the process which transforms the latent dream-wish into the manifest content of the dream—a process known as the 'dream-work'—has taught us the best part of what we know of unconscious mental life.

Now a dream is not a morbid symptom but a product of the normal mind. The wishes which it represents as fulfilled are the same as those which are repressed in neuroses. Dreams owe the possibility of their genesis merely to the favourable circumstance that during the state of sleep, which paralyses man's power of movement, repression is mitigated into the dream-censorship. If, however, the process of dream-formation oversteps certain limits, the dreamer brings it to a stop and wakes up in a fright. Thus it is proved that the same forces and the same processes taking place between them operate in normal as in pathological mental life. From the date of *The Interpretation of Dreams* psycho-analysis had a twofold significance. It was not only a new method of treating the neuroses but it was also a new psychology; it claimed the attention not only of nerve-specialists but also of all those who were students of a menta lscience.

The reception given it in the scientific world was, however, no friendly one. For some ten years no one took any notice of Freud's works. About the year 1907 attention was drawn to psycho-analysis by a group of Swiss psychiatrists (Bleuler and Jung, in Zurich), and a storm of indignation, which was not precisely fastidious in its methods and arguments, thereupon broke out, particularly in Germany. In this, psycho-analysis was sharing the fate of many novelties which, after a certain lapse of time, have found general recognition. Nevertheless it lay in its nature that it should inevitably arouse particularly violent opposition. It wounded the prejudices of civilized humanity at some specially sensitive spots. It subjected every individual, as it were, to the analytic reaction, by uncovering what had by universal agreement been repressed into the unconscious; and in this way it forced its contemporaries to behave like patients who, under analytic treatment, above all else bring their resistances to the fore. It must also be admitted that it was no easy thing to become convinced of the correctness of the psycho-analytic theories, nor to obtain instruction in the practice of analysis.

The general hostility, however, did not succeed in preventing psycho-analysis from continuous expansion during the next decade in two directions: on the map, for interest in it was constantly cropping up in new countries, and in the field of the mental sciences, for it was constantly finding applications in new branches of knowledge. In 1909 President G. Stanley Hall invited Freud and Jung to give a series of lectures at Clark University in Worcester, Mass., of which he was the head and where they were given a friendly reception. Since then psycho-analysis has remained popular in America, although precisely in that country its name has been coupled with much superficiality and some abuses. As early as in 1911, Havelock Ellis was able to report that analysis was studied and practised, not only in Austria and Switzerland, but also in the United States, in England, India, Canada, and, no doubt, in Australia too.

It was in this period of struggle and of first blossoming, moreover, that the periodicals devoted exclusively to psycho-analysis were inaugurated. These were the *Jahrbuch für psychoanalytische und psychopathologische Forschungen* [*Yearbook for Psycho-Analytic and Psychopathological Researches*] (1909–1914), directed by Bleuler and Freud and edited by Jung, which ceased publication at the outbreak of the World War, the *Zentralblatt für Psychoanalyse* [*Central Journal for Psycho-Analysis*] (1911), edited by Adler and Stekel, which was soon replaced by the *Internationale Zeitschrift für Psychoanalyse* [*International Journal for Psycho-Analysis*] (1913, to-day in its tenth volume); further, since 1912, *Imago*, founded by Rank and Sachs, a periodical for the application of psycho-analysis to the mental sciences. The great interest taken in the subject by Anglo-American doctors was shown in 1913 by the founding of the still active *Psycho-Analytic Review* by White and Jelliffe. Later, in 1920, *The International Journal of Psycho-Analysis*, intended specially for readers in England, made its appearance under the editorship of Ernest Jones. The Internationaler Psychoanalytischer Verlag and the corresponding English undertaking, The International Psycho-Analytical Press, brought out a continuous series of analytic publications under the name of the Internationale Psychoanalytische Bibliothek (International Psycho-Analytical Library). The literature of psycho-analysis is, of course, not to be found only in these periodicals, which are for the most part supported by psycho-analytic societies; it appears far and wide in a great number of places, in scientific and in literary publications. Among the periodicals of the Latin world which pay special attention to psycho-analysis the *Rivista de Psiquiatria*, edited by H. Delgado in Lima (Peru), may be specially mentioned.

An essential difference between this second decade of psycho-analysis and the first lay in the fact that the present writer was no longer its sole representative. A constantly growing circle of pupils and followers had collected around him, who devoted themselves first to the diffusion of the theories of psycho-analysis and then extended them, supplemented them and carried them deeper. In the course of years, several of these supporters, as was inevitable, seceded, took their own paths, or turned themselves into an opposition which seemed to threaten the continuity of the development of psycho-analysis. Between 1911 and 1913 C. G. Jung in Zurich and Alfred Adler in Vienna produced some stir by their attempts at giving new interpretations to the facts of analysis and their efforts at a diversion from the analytic standpoint. But it soon appeared that these secessions had effected no lasting damage. What temporary success they achieved was easily accounted for by the readiness of the mass of people to have themselves set free from the pressure of the demands of psycho-analysis by whatever path might be opened to them. The great majority of co-workers remained firm and continued their work along the lines indicated to them. We shall come on their names repeatedly in the short account below of the findings of psycho-analysis in the many and various fields of its application.

IV

The noisy rejection of psycho-analysis by the medical world could not deter its supporters from developing it, to begin with, along its original lines into a specialized pathology and treatment of the neuroses—a task which has not been completely accomplished even to-day. Its undeniable therapeutic success, which far exceeded any that had previously been achieved, constantly spurred them on to fresh efforts; while the difficulties which came to light as the material was examined more deeply led to profound alterations in the technique of analysis and to important corrections in its theoretical hypotheses and postulates.

In the course of this development, the technique of psycho-analysis has become as definite and as delicate as that of any other specialized branch of medicine. A failure to understand this fact has led to many abuses (particularly in England and America) because people who have acquired only a literary knowledge of psycho-analysis from reading consider themselves capable of undertaking analytic treatments without having received any special training. The consequences of such behaviour are damaging both to the science and to the patients and have brought much discredit upon psycho-analysis. The foundation of a first psycho-analytic out-patient clinic (by Max Eitingon in Berlin in 1920) has therefore become a step of high practical importance. This institute seeks on the one hand to make analytic treatment accessible to wide circles of the population and on the other hand undertakes the education of doctors to be practical analysts by a course of training which includes as a condition that the learner shall agree to be analysed himself.

Among the hypothetical concepts which enable the doctor to deal with the analytic material, the first to be mentioned is that of 'libido'. Libido means in psycho-analysis in the first instance the force (thought of as quantitatively variable and measurable) of the sexual instincts directed towards an object—'sexual' in the extended sense required by analytic theory. Further study showed that it was necessary to set alongside this 'object-libido' a 'narcissistic' or 'ego-libido', directed to the subject's own ego; and the interaction of these two forces has enabled us to account for a great number of normal and abnormal processes in mental life. A rough distinction was soon made between what are known as the 'transference neuroses' and the narcissistic disorders. The former (hysteria and obsessional neurosis) are the objects proper of psycho-analytic treatment, while the others, the narcissistic neuroses, though they can, it is true, be examined by the help of analysis, offer fundamental difficulties to therapeutic influence. It is true that the libido theory of psycho-analysis is by no means complete and that its relation to a general theory of the instincts is not yet clear, for psycho-analysis is a young science, quite unfinished and in a stage of rapid development. Here, however, it should be emphatically pointed out how erroneous the charge of pan-sexualism is which is so often levelled at psycho-analysis. It seeks to show that psycho-analytic theory knows of no mental motive forces other than purely sexual ones and in doing so exploits popular prejudices by using the word 'sexual' not in its analytic but in its vulgar sense.

The psycho-analytic view would also have to include in narcissistic disorders all the ailments described in psychiatry as 'functional psychoses'. It could not be doubted that neuroses and psychoses are not separated by a hard and fast line, any more than health and neurosis; and it was plausible to explain the mysterious psychotic phenomena by the discoveries achieved on the neuroses, which had hitherto been equally incomprehensible. The present writer had himself, during the period of his isolation, made a case of paranoid illness partly intelligible by an analytic investigation and had pointed out in this unquestionable psychosis the same contents (complexes) and a similar interplay of forces as in the simple neuroses.[1] Bleuler [1906] followed out the indications of what he called 'Freudian mechanisms' in a whole number of psychoses, and Jung won high opinions as an analyst at a single blow when, in 1907,[2] he explained the most eccentric symptoms in the end-stages of dementia praecox from the individual life-histories of the patients. The comprehensive study of schizophrenia by Bleuler (1911) probably demonstrated once and for all the justification of a psycho-analytic angle of approach for the understanding of these psychoses.

In this way psychiatry became the first field to which psycho-analysis was applied and it has remained so ever since. The same research workers who have done most to deepen analytic knowledge of the neuroses, such as Karl Abraham in Berlin and Sándor Ferenczi in Budapest (to name only the most prominent), have also played a leading part in throwing analytic light on the psychoses. The conviction of the unity and intimate connection of all the disorders that present themselves as neurotic and psychotic phenomena is becoming more and more firmly established despite all the efforts of the psychiatrists. People are beginning to understand—best of all, perhaps, in

[1] [See Section III of Freud's second paper on the neuro-psychoses of defence (1896b).]

[2] [This is misprinted '1901' in both the German editions.]

America—that the psycho-analytic study of the neuroses is the only preparation for an understanding of the psychoses, and that psycho-analysis is destined to make possible a scientific psychiatry of the future which will not need to content itself with describing curious clinical pictures and unintelligible sequences of events and with tracing the influence of gross anatomical and toxic traumas upon a mental apparatus which is inaccessible to our knowledge.

V

But the importance of psycho-analysis for psychiatry would never have drawn the attention of the intellectual world to it or won it a place in *The History of our Times*.[1] This result was brought about by the relation of psycho-analysis to normal, not to pathological, mental life. Originally, analytic research had indeed no other aim than to establish the determinants of the onset (the genesis) of a few morbid mental states. In the course of its efforts, however, it succeeded in bringing to light facts of fundamental importance, in actually creating a new psychology, so that it became obvious that the validity of such findings could not possibly be restricted to the sphere of pathology. We have seen already when it was that the decisive proof was produced of the correctness of this conclusion. It was when dreams were successfully interpreted by analytic technique—dreams, which are a part of the mental life of normal people and which yet may in fact be regarded as pathological products that can regularly appear under healthy conditions.

If the psychological discoveries gained from the study of dreams were firmly kept in view, only one further step was needed before psycho-analysis could be proclaimed as the theory of the deeper mental processes not directly accessible to consciousness—as a 'depth-psychology'—and before it could be applied to almost all the mental sciences. This step lay in the transition from the mental activity of individual men to the psychical functions of human communities and peoples—that is, from individual to group psychology; and many surprising analogies forced this transition upon us. It had been found, for instance, that in the deep strata of unconscious mental activity contraries are not distinguished from each other but are

[1] [In English in the original—a probable allusion to the title of the publication for which this paper was written.]

expressed by the same element. But already in 1884 Karl Abel the philologist had put forward the view (in his 'Über den Gegensinn der Urworte'[1]) that the oldest languages known to us treat contraries in the same way. Thus Ancient Egyptian, for example, had in the first instance only one word for 'strong' and 'weak', and not till later were the two sides of the antithesis distinguished by slight modifications. Even in the most modern languages clear relics of such antithetical meanings are to be found. So in German '*Boden*' ['garret' or 'ground'] means the highest as well as the lowest thing in the house; similarly in Latin '*altus*' means 'high' and 'deep'. Thus the equivalence of contraries in dreams is a universal archaic trait in human thinking.

To take an instance from another field. It is impossible to escape the impression of the perfect correspondence which can be discovered between the obsessive actions of certain obsessional patients and the religious observances of believers all over the world.[2] Some cases of obsessional neurosis actually behave like a caricature of a private religion, so that it is tempting to liken the official religions to an obsessional neurosis that has been mitigated by becoming universalized. This comparison, which is no doubt highly objectionable to all believers, has nevertheless proved most fruitful psychologically. For psychoanalysis soon discovered in the case of obsessional neurosis what the forces are that struggle with one another in it till their conflicts find a remarkable expression in the ceremonial of obsessive actions. Nothing similar was suspected in the case of religious ceremonial until, by tracing back religious feeling to the relation with the father as its deepest root, it became possible to point to an analogous dynamic situation in that case too.[3] This instance, moreover, may warn the reader that even in its application to non-medical fields psycho-analysis cannot avoid wounding cherished prejudices, touching upon deeply-rooted sensibilities and thus provoking enmities which have an essentially emotional basis.

If we may assume that the most general features of unconscious mental life (conflicts between instinctual impulses, repressions and substitutive satisfactions) are present everywhere, and if there is a depth-psychology which leads to a knowledge of

---

[1] ['The Antithetical Meaning of Primal Words.' Cf. Freud, 1910*e*.]
[2] [Cf. Freud, 'Obsessive Actions and Religious Practices' (1907*b*).]
[3] [Cf. *Totem and Taboo*, 1912–13.]

those features, then we may reasonably expect that the application of psycho-analysis to the most varied spheres of human mental activity will everywhere bring to light important and hitherto unattainable results. In an exceedingly valuable study, Otto Rank and Hanns Sachs (1913) have tried to bring together what the work of psycho-analysts had been able to achieve up to that time towards fulfilling these expectations. Lack of space prevents me from attempting to complete their enumeration here. I can only select for mention the most important findings with the addition of a few details.

If we leave little-known internal urges out of account, we may say that the main motive force towards the cultural development of man has been real external exigency, which has withheld from him the easy satisfaction of his natural needs and exposed him to immense dangers. This external frustration drove him into a struggle with reality, which ended partly in adaptation to it and partly in control over it; but it also drove him into working and living in common with those of his kind, and this already involved a renunciation of a number of instinctual impulses which could not be satisfied socially. With the further advances of civilization the demands of repression also grew. Civilization is after all built entirely on renunciation of instinct, and every individual on his journey from childhood to maturity has in his own person to recapitulate this development of humanity to a state of judicious resignation. Psycho-analysis has shown that it is predominantly, though not exclusively, sexual instinctual impulses that have succumbed to this cultural suppression. One portion of them, however, exhibit the valuable characteristic of allowing themselves to be diverted from their immediate aims and of thus placing their energy at the disposal of cultural development in the form of 'sublimated' trends. But another portion persist in the unconscious as unsatisfied wishes and press for some, even if it is distorted, satisfaction.

We have seen that one part of human mental activity is directed towards obtaining control over the real external world. Psycho-analysis now tells us further that another, particularly highly-prized, part of creative mental work serves for the fulfilment of wishes—for the substitutive satisfaction of the repressed wishes which, from the days of childhood, live in the spirit of each of us, unsatisfied. Among these creations, whose connection with an incomprehensible unconscious was always suspected, are myths and works of imaginative writing and of art, and the researches of psycho-analysts have in fact thrown a flood of light on the fields of mythology, the science of literature, and the psychology of artists. It is enough to mention Otto Rank's work as an example. We have shown that myths and fairy tales can be interpreted like dreams, we have traced the convoluted paths that lead from the urge of the unconscious wish to its realization in a work of art, we have learnt to understand the emotional effect of a work of art on the observer, and in the case of the artist himself we have made clear his internal kinship with the neurotic as well as his distinction from him, and we have pointed out the connection between his innate disposition, his chance experiences and his achievements. The aesthetic appreciation of works of art and the elucidation of the artistic gift are, it is true, not among the tasks set to psycho-analysis. But it seems that psycho-analysis is in a position to speak the decisive word in all questions that touch upon the imaginative life of man.

And now, as a third point, psycho-analysis has shown us, to our growing astonishment, the enormously important part played by what is known as the 'Oedipus complex'—that is, the emotional relation of a child to its two parents—in the mental life of human beings. Our astonishment diminishes when we realize that the Oedipus complex is the psychical correlate of two fundamental biological facts: the long period of the human child's dependence, and the remarkable way in which its sexual life reaches a first climax in the third to fifth years of life, and then, after a period of inhibition, sets in again at puberty. And here, the discovery was made that a third and extremely serious part of human intellectual activity, the part which has created the great institutions of religion, law, ethics, and all forms of civic life, has as its fundamental aim the enabling of the individual to master his Oedipus complex and to divert his libido from its infantile attachments into the social ones that are ultimately desired. The applications of psycho-analysis to the science of religion and sociology (e.g. by the present writer, Theodor Reik and Oskar Pfister), which have led to these findings, are still young and insufficiently appreciated; but it cannot be doubted that further studies will only confirm the certainty of these important conclusions.

By way, as it were, of postscript, I must also mention that educationists, too, cannot avoid making use of the hints which they have received from the analytic exploration of the mental life of children; and further that voices have been raised among therapists (e.g. Groddeck and Jelliffe), maintaining that the psycho-analytic treatment of serious organic complaints shows promising results, since in many of these affections some part is played by a psychical factor on which it is possible to bring influence to bear.

Thus we may express our expectation that psycho-analysis, whose development and achievements hitherto have been briefly and inadequately related in these pages, will enter into the cultural development of the next decades as a significant ferment, and will help to deepen our understanding of the world and to fight against some things in life which are recognized as injurious. It must not be forgotten, however, that psycho-analysis alone cannot offer a complete picture of the world. If we accept the distinction which I have recently proposed of dividing the mental apparatus into an ego, turned towards the external world and equipped with consciousness, and an unconscious id, dominated by its instinctual needs, then psycho-analysis is to be described as a psychology of the id (and of its effects upon the ego). In each field of knowledge, therefore, it can make only *contributions*, which require to be completed from the psychology of the ego.[1] If these contributions often contain the essence of the facts, this only corresponds to the important part which, it may be claimed, is played in our lives by the mental unconscious that has so long remained unknown.

[1] [Freud seems, in this passage, to be imposing unusual restrictions on the scope of psycho-analysis.]

THE RESISTANCES TO
PSYCHO-ANALYSIS
(1925 [1924])

DIE WIDERSTÄNDE GEGEN DIE PSYCHOANALYSE

(*a*) GERMAN EDITIONS:

(1925   *La Revue Juive* (Geneva), March. In a French translation.)

1925   *Imago*, **11** (3), 222–33.

1925   *Almanach 1926*, 9–21.

1926   *Psychoanalyse der Neurosen*, 185–98.

1928   *G.S.*, **11**, 224–35.

1948   *G.W.*, **14**, 99–110.

(*b*) ENGLISH TRANSLATION:

      'The Resistances to Psycho-Analysis'

1950   *C.P.*, **5**, 163–74. (Tr. James Strachey.)

The present translation is a slightly corrected version of the
one published in 1950.

Freud's name was on the 'Editorial Committee' of the
periodical in which this essay first appeared in French. It was
written at the request of the actual editor, Albert Cohen,
probably in September, 1924. The German original appeared
almost simultaneously in *Imago* and in the *Almanach 1926*,
which was published in September, 1925—some six months
after the French issue.

THE RESISTANCES TO PSYCHO-ANALYSIS

A CHILD in his nurse's arms will turn away screaming at the sight of a strange face; a pious man will begin the new season with a prayer and he will also greet the first fruits of the year with a blessing; a peasant will refuse to buy a scythe unless it bears the trade-mark that was familiar to his parents. The distinction between these situations is obvious and would seem to justify one in looking for a different motive in each of them.

Nevertheless, it would be a mistake to overlook what they have in common. In each case we are dealing with unpleasure of the same kind. The child expresses it in an elementary fashion, the pious man lulls it by an artifice, while the peasant uses it as the motive for a decision. The source of this unpleasure is the demand made upon the mind by anything that is *new*, the psychical expenditure that it requires, the uncertainty, mounting up to anxious expectancy, which it brings along with it. It would be interesting to devote a whole study to mental reactions to novelty; for under certain, no longer primary, conditions we can observe behaviour of the contrary kind—a thirst for stimulation which flings itself upon anything that is new merely because it *is* new.

In scientific affairs there should be no place for recoiling from novelty. Science, in her perpetual incompleteness and insufficiency, is driven to hope for her salvation in new discoveries and new ways of regarding things. She does well, in order not to be deceived, to arm herself with scepticism and to accept nothing new unless it has withstood the strictest examination. Sometimes, however, this scepticism shows two unexpected features; it may be sharply directed against what is new while it spares what is familiar and accepted, and it may be content to reject things before it has examined them. But in behaving thus it reveals itself as a prolongation of the primitive reaction against what is new and as a cloak for the retention of that reaction. It is a matter of common knowledge how often in the history of scientific research it has happened that innovations have met with intense and stubborn resistance, while subsequent events have shown that the resistance was unjustified and that the novelty was valuable and important. What provoked the resistance was, as a rule, certain factors in the subject-matter of the novelty, while, on the other side, several factors must have combined to make the irruption of the primitive reaction possible.

A particularly bad reception was accorded to psycho-analysis, which the present writer began to develop nearly thirty years ago from the discoveries of Josef Breuer (of Vienna) on the origin of neurotic symptoms. It cannot be disputed that it possessed the quality of novelty, even though it made use of plenty of material which was well known from other sources (quite apart from Breuer's discoveries), such as the lessons from the teachings of Charcot, the great neuropathologist, and impressions derived from the sphere of hypnotic phenomena. Its original significance was purely therapeutic: it aimed at creating a new and efficient method for treating neurotic illnesses. But connections which could not be foreseen in the beginning caused psycho-analysis to reach out far beyond its original aim. It ended by claiming to have set our whole view of mental life upon a new basis and therefore to be of importance for every field of knowledge that is founded on psychology. After a decade of complete neglect it suddenly became a subject of general interest—and set loose a storm of indignant opposition.

The *forms* in which the resistance to psycho-analysis found expression need not now be considered. It is enough to say that the struggle over this innovation is by no means at an end, though it is already possible to see what direction it will take. Its opponents have not succeeded in suppressing the movement. Psycho-analysis, of which twenty years ago I was the only spokesman, has since attracted the support of numerous valuable and active workers, medical and non-medical, who make use of it as a procedure for the treatment of nervous diseases, as a method of psychological research and as an auxiliary instrument for scientific work in the most various departments of intellectual life. In the following pages our interest will be directed only to the *motives* of the resistance to psycho-analysis, with particular stress upon the composite character of that resistance and upon the differing amount of weight carried by its components.

From a clinical standpoint the neuroses must necessarily be put alongside the intoxications and such disorders as Graves' disease. These are conditions arising from an excess or a relative lack of certain highly active substances, whether produced inside the body or introduced into it from outside—in short, they are disturbances of the chemistry of the body, toxic conditions. If someone succeeded in isolating and demonstrating the hypothetical substance or substances concerned in neuroses, he would have no need to worry about opposition from the medical profession. For the present, however, no such avenue of approach to the problem is open. At the moment we can only start from the symptoms presented by a neurosis—symptoms which in the case of hysteria, for instance, consist of a combination of somatic and mental disturbances. Now Charcot's experiments as well as Breuer's clinical observations taught us that the somatic symptoms of hysteria are psychogenic too—that is, that they are precipitates of mental processes that have run their course. By putting a subject into a state of hypnosis it was possible at will to produce the somatic symptoms of hysteria artificially.

Psycho-analysis took hold of this new realization and began to consider the problem of the nature of the psychical processes which led to these unusual consequences. But the direction taken by this enquiry was not to the liking of the contemporary generation of physicians. They had been brought up to respect only anatomical, physical and chemical factors. They were not prepared for taking psychical ones into account and therefore met them with indifference or antipathy. They obviously had doubts whether psychical events allowed of any exact scientific treatment whatever. As an excessive reaction against an earlier phase during which medicine had been dominated by what was known as the 'philosophy of Nature',[1] they regarded such abstractions as those with which psychology is obliged to work as nebulous, fantastic and mystical; while they simply refused to believe in remarkable phenomena which might have been the starting-point of research. The symptoms of hysterical neuroses were looked upon as shamming and the phenomena of hypnotism as a hoax. Even the psychiatrists, upon whose attention the most unusual and astonishing mental phenomena were constantly being forced, showed no inclination to examine

[1] [A pantheistic attitude, chiefly associated with the name of Schelling, which was very prevalent in Germany during the first part of the nineteenth century.]

their details or enquire into their connections. They were content to classify the variegated array of symptoms and trace them back, so far as they could manage, to somatic, anatomical or chemical aetiological disturbances. During this materialistic or, rather, mechanistic period, medicine made tremendous advances, but it also showed a short-sighted misunderstanding of the most important and most difficult among the problems of life.

It is easy to understand why doctors, with an attitude of this kind towards the mind, should have had no liking for psycho-analysis and should have demurred to its demand for learning many things afresh and for seeing many things in a different light. But as a compensation it might be supposed that the new theory would be all the more likely to meet with applause from philosophers. For philosophers were accustomed to putting abstract concepts (or, as unkind tongues would say, hazy words) in the forefront of their explanations of the universe, and it would be impossible that they should object to the extension of the sphere of psychology for which psycho-analysis had paved the way. But here another obstacle arose. The philosophers' idea of what is mental was not that of psycho-analysis. The overwhelming majority of philosophers regard as mental only the phenomena of consciousness. For them the world of consciousness coincides with the sphere of what is mental. Everything else that may take place in the 'mind'—an entity so hard to grasp—is relegated by them to the organic determinants of mental processes or to processes parallel to mental ones. Or, more strictly speaking, the mind has no contents other than the phenomena of consciousness, and consequently psychology, the science of the mind, has no other subject-matter. And on this point the layman's view is the same.

What, then, can a philosopher say to a theory which, like psycho-analysis, asserts that on the contrary what is mental is in itself *unconscious* and that being conscious is only a *quality*, which may or may not accrue to a particular mental act and the withholding of which may perhaps alter that act in no other respect? He will naturally say that anything both unconscious and mental would be an impossibility, a *contradictio in adjecto*,[1] and he will fail to observe that in making this judgement he is merely repeating his own definition of what is mental,

[1] ['A contradiction in terms.']

a definition which may perhaps be too narrow. It is easy for philosophers to feel this certainty, since they have no acquaintance with the material whose investigation has compelled analysts to believe in unconscious mental acts. Philosophers have never taken account of hypnosis, they have not concerned themselves with the interpreting of dreams—on the contrary, like doctors, they regard dreams as the meaningless products of reduced mental activity during sleep—they are scarcely aware that there are such things as obsessions and delusions and they would find themselves in a most embarrassing situation if they were asked to explain them on the basis of their own psychological premises. Analysts, too, refuse to say what the unconscious is, but they can indicate the domain of phenomena whose observation has obliged them to assume its existence. Philosophers, who know no kind of observation other than self-observation, cannot follow them into that domain.

So it comes about that psycho-analysis derives nothing but disadvantages from its middle position between medicine and philosophy. Doctors regard it as a speculative system and refuse to believe that, like every other natural science, it is based on a patient and tireless elaboration of facts from the world of perception; philosophers, measuring it by the standard of their own artificially constructed systems, find that it starts from impossible premisses and reproach it because its most general concepts (which are only now in process of evolution) lack clarity and precision.

This state of affairs is enough to account for the reluctant and hesitant reception of analysis in scientific quarters. But it does not explain the outbursts of indignation, derision and scorn which, in disregard of every standard of logic and good taste, have characterized the controversial methods of its opponents. A reaction of such a kind suggests that resistances other than purely intellectual ones were stirred up and that powerful emotional forces were aroused. And there are indeed plenty of things to be found in the theory of psycho-analysis calculated to produce such an effect as this upon the passions of men of every kind and not of scientists alone. Above all there is the very important place in the mental life of human beings which psycho-analysis assigns to what are known as the sexual instincts. Psycho-analytic theory maintained that the symptoms of neuroses are distorted substitutive satisfactions of sexual instinctual forces, the direct satisfaction of which has been frustrated by internal resistances. Later on, when analysis had extended beyond its original field of work and began to be applied to normal mental life, it sought to show that these same sexual components, which could be diverted from their immediate aims and directed to other things, made the most important contributions to the cultural achievements of the individual and of society. These views were not entirely new. The incomparable significance of sexual life had been proclaimed by the philosopher Schopenhauer in an intensely impressive passage.[1] Moreover, what psycho-analysis called sexuality was by no means identical with the impulsion towards a union of the two sexes or towards producing a pleasurable sensation in the genitals; it had far more resemblance to the all-inclusive and all-preserving Eros of Plato's *Symposium*.

But the opponents of psycho-analysis forgot its illustrious forerunners; they fell upon it as though it had made an assault upon the dignity of the human race. They accused it of 'pansexualism', though the psycho-analytic theory of the instincts had always been strictly dualistic[2] and had at no time failed to recognize, alongside the sexual instincts, others to which it actually ascribed force enough to suppress the sexual instincts. (These mutually opposing forces were described to begin with as the sexual instincts and the ego instincts. A later theoretical development changed them into Eros and the instinct of death or destruction.) The suggestion that art, religion and social order originated in part in a contribution from the sexual instincts was represented by the opponents of analysis as a degradation of the highest cultural values. They emphatically declared that men have other interests besides this eternal one of sex, overlooking in their zeal the fact that animals too have other interests—indeed they are subject to sexuality, not permanently like men, but only in bouts occurring at specific periods—overlooking, too, the fact that the existence of these other interests in men had never been disputed and that nothing can be altered in the value of a cultural achievement by its being shown to have been derived from elementary animal instinctual sources.

[1] [See the Appendix, p. 223 below.]
[2] [Cf. an Editor's footnote near the end of Chapter IV of *The Ego and the Id* (1923b), p. 46, *n.* 2 above.]

Such a display of unfairness and lack of logic cries out for an explanation. Its origin is not hard to find. Human civilization rests upon two pillars, of which one is the control of natural forces and the other the restriction of our instincts. The ruler's throne rests upon fettered slaves. Among the instinctual components which are thus brought into service, the sexual instincts, in the narrower sense of the word, are conspicuous for their strength and savagery. Woe, if they should be set loose! The throne would be overturned and the ruler trampled under foot. Society is aware of this—and will not allow the topic to be mentioned.

But why not? What harm could the discussion do? Psycho-analysis has never said a word in favour of unfettering instincts that would injure our community; on the contrary it has issued a warning and an exhortation to us to mend our ways. But society refuses to consent to the ventilation of the question, because it has a bad conscience in more than one respect. In the first place it has set up a high ideal of morality—morality being restriction of the instincts—and insists that all its members shall fulfil that ideal without troubling itself with the possibility that obedience may bear heavily upon the individual. Nor is it sufficiently wealthy or well-organized to be able to compensate the individual for the amount of his instinctual renunciation. It is consequently left to the individual to decide how he can obtain, for the sacrifice he has made, enough compensation to enable him to preserve his mental balance. On the whole, however, he is obliged to live psychologically beyond his means, while the unsatisfied claims of his instincts make him feel the demands of civilization as a constant pressure upon him. Thus society maintains a condition of *cultural hypocrisy* which is bound to be accompanied by a sense of insecurity and a necessity for guarding what is an undeniably precarious situation by forbidding criticism and discussion. This line of thought holds good for all the instinctual impulses, including, therefore, the egoistic ones. The question whether it applies to all possible forms of civilization, and not merely to those which have evolved hitherto, cannot be discussed here. As regards the sexual instincts in the narrower sense, there is the further point that in most people they are tamed insufficiently and in a manner which is psychologically wrong and are therefore readier than the rest to break loose.

Psycho-analysis has revealed the weaknesses of this system and has recommended that it should be altered. It proposes that there should be a reduction in the strictness with which instincts are repressed and that correspondingly more play should be given to truthfulness. Certain instinctual impulses, with whose suppression society has gone too far, should be permitted a greater amount of satisfaction; in the case of certain others the inefficient method of suppressing them by means of repression should be replaced by a better and securer procedure. As a result of these criticisms psycho-analysis is regarded as 'inimical to culture' and has been put under a ban as a 'social danger'. This resistance cannot last for ever. No human institution can in the long run escape the influence of fair criticism; but men's attitude to psycho-analysis is still dominated by this fear, which gives rein to their passions and diminishes their power of logical argument.

By its theory of the instincts psycho-analysis offended the feelings of individuals in so far as they regarded themselves as members of the social community; another branch of its theory was calculated to hurt every single person at the tenderest point of his own psychical development. Psycho-analysis disposed once and for all of the fairy tale of an asexual childhood. It demonstrated the fact that sexual interests and activities occur in small children from the beginning of their lives. It showed what transformations those activities pass through, how at about the age of five they succumb to inhibition and how from puberty onwards they enter the service of the reproductive function. It recognized that early infantile sexual life reaches its peak in what is known as the Oedipus complex (an emotional attachment of the child to the parent of the opposite sex accompanied by an attitude of rivalry to the parent of the same sex) and that at that period of life this impulsion extends un-inhibited into a straightforward sexual desire. This can be con-firmed so easily that only the greatest efforts could make it possible to overlook it. Every individual has in fact gone through this phase but has afterwards energetically repressed its purport and succeeded in forgetting it. A horror of incest and an enormous sense of guilt are left over from this prehistoric epoch of the individual's existence. It may be that something quite similar occurred in the prehistoric epoch of the human species as a whole and that the beginnings of morality, religion and social order were intimately connected with the surmounting of that primaeval era. To adults their prehistory seems so inglorious that they refuse to allow themselves to be reminded of it: they were infuriated when psycho-analysis tried to lift the veil of amnesia from their years of childhood. There was only one way out: what psycho-analysis asserted must be false and what posed as a new science must be a tissue of fancies and distortions.

Thus the strongest resistances to psycho-analysis were not of an intellectual kind but arose from emotional sources. This explained their passionate character as well as their poverty in logic. The situation obeyed a simple formula: men in the mass behaved to psycho-analysis in precisely the same way as individual neurotics under treatment for their disorders. It is possible, however, by patient work to convince these latter individuals that everything happened as we maintained it did: we had not invented it ourselves but had arrived at it from a study of other neurotics covering a period of twenty or thirty years. The position was at once alarming and consoling: alarming because it was no small thing to have the whole human race as one's patient, and consoling because after all everything was taking place as the hypotheses of psycho-analysis declared that it was bound to.

If we cast our eyes once again over the various resistances to psycho-analysis that have been enumerated, it is evident that only a minority of them are of the kind which habitually arise against most scientific innovations of any considerable importance. The majority of them are due to the fact that powerful human feelings are hurt by the subject-matter of the theory. Darwin's theory of descent met with the same fate, since it tore down the barrier that had been arrogantly set up between men and beasts. I drew attention to this analogy in an earlier paper,[1] in which I showed how the psycho-analytic view of the relation of the conscious ego to an overpowering unconscious was a severe blow to human self-love. I described this as the *psychological* blow to men's narcissism, and compared it with the *biological* blow delivered by the theory of descent and the earlier *cosmological* blow aimed at it by the discovery of Copernicus.

Purely external difficulties have also contributed to strengthen the resistance to psycho-analysis. It is not easy to arrive at an

[1] 'A Difficulty in the Path of Psycho-Analysis' (1917a).

independent judgement upon matters to do with analysis without having experienced it oneself or practised it on someone else. Nor can one do the latter without having acquired a specific and decidedly delicate technique, while until recently there was no easily accessible means of learning psycho-analysis and its technique. This position has now been improved by the foundation (in 1920) of the Berlin Psycho-Analytic Clinic and Training Institute, and soon afterwards (in 1922) of an exactly similar institute in Vienna.

Finally, with all reserve, the question may be raised whether the personality of the present writer as a Jew who has never sought to disguise the fact that he is a Jew may not have had a share in provoking the antipathy of his environment to psychoanalysis. An argument of this kind is not often uttered aloud. But we have unfortunately grown so suspicious that we cannot avoid thinking that this factor may not have been quite without its effect. Nor is it perhaps entirely a matter of chance that the first advocate of psycho-analysis was a Jew. To profess belief in this new theory called for a certain degree of readiness to accept a situation of solitary opposition—a situation with which no one is more familiar than a Jew.

APPENDIX

EXTRACT FROM SCHOPENHAUER'S *THE WORLD AS WILL AND IDEA*[1]

In his later works, Freud made several references to the emphasis which Schopenhauer laid on the importance of sexuality. As well as mentioning the subject on p. 218 above, he also referred to it in the closing paragraph of 'A Difficulty in the Path of Psycho-Analysis' (1917*a*), *Standard Ed.*, **17**, 143–4, and in the Preface (written in 1920) to the fourth edition of the *Three Essays* (1905*d*), ibid., **7**, 134. It appears again in Chapter VI of *Beyond the Pleasure Principle* (1920*g*), ibid., **18**, 50—a work which Freud was revising at about the same time as he wrote the Preface just mentioned—and yet again near the end of Chapter V of the *Autobiographical Study* (1925*d*), ibid., **20**, 59.

Freud sometimes alluded specifically to 'an intensely impressive passage' or 'words of unforgettable impressiveness', though he nowhere quoted the passage or indicated its source in Schopenhauer's writings. It seems highly likely, however, that the extract printed here is from the passage Freud had in mind, and it is, therefore, perhaps of interest to reproduce it. This paragraph occurs in the Supplements to the Fourth Book of *The World as Will and Idea*, Chapter XLII, 'The Life of the Species' ['*Leben der Gattung*']. Immediately before this point, Schopenhauer has been discussing the character of sexual desire, which he declares is different from every other desire: '... it is not only the strongest but even specifically of a more powerful kind than any other.' He gives examples of the recognition accorded in antiquity to this power and continues as follows:

'To all this corresponds the important *rôle* which the relation of the sexes plays in the world of men, where it is really the invisible central point of all action and conduct, and peeps out everywhere in spite of all veils thrown over it. It is the cause of war and the end of peace, the basis of what is serious, and the aim of the jest, the inexhaustible source of wit, the key to all

[1] Translated by R. B. Haldane and J. Kemp, 1886, **3**, 313–14. The extract is printed by arrangement with Messrs. George Allen & Unwin.

allusions, and the meaning of all mysterious hints, of all un-spoken offers and all stolen glances, the daily meditation of the young, and often also of the old, the hourly thought of the un-chaste, and even against their will the constantly recurring imagination of the chaste, the ever ready material of a joke, just because the profoundest seriousness lies at its foundation. It is, however, the piquant element and the joke of life that the chief concern of all men is secretly pursued and ostensibly ignored as much as possible. But, in fact, we see it every moment seat itself, as the true hereditary lord of the world, out of the ful-ness of its own strength, upon the ancestral throne, and looking down from thence with scornful glances, laugh at the prepara-tions which have been made to bind it, imprison it, or at least to limit it and wherever it is possible to keep it concealed, or even so to master it that it shall only appear as a subordinate, secondary concern of life. But all this agrees with the fact that the sexual passion[1] is the kernel of the will to live, and conse-quently the concentration of all desire; therefore in the text I have called the genital organs the focus of the will. Indeed, one may say man is concrete sexual desire;[1] for his origin is an act of copulation and his wish of wishes is an act of copulation, and this tendency alone perpetuates and holds together his whole phenomenal existence. The will to live manifests itself indeed primarily as an effort to sustain the individual, yet this is only a step to the effort to sustain the species, and the latter endeavour must be more powerful in proportion as the life of the species surpasses that of the individual in duration, extension and value. Therefore sexual passion[1] is the most perfect manifesta-tion of the will to live, its most distinctly expressed type; and the origin of the individual in it, and its primacy over all other desires of the natural man, are both in complete agreement with this.'

[1] ['*Geschlechtstrieb*' in the original—a word which, when used by Freud, is translated 'sexual instinct' in the *Standard Edition*.]

A NOTE UPON THE 'MYSTIC WRITING-PAD'
(1925 [1924])

NOTIZ ÜBER DEN 'WUNDERBLOCK'

(a) GERMAN EDITIONS:
1925   Int. Z. Psychoanal., 11 (1), 1–5.
1925   G.S., 6, 415–20.
1931   Theoretische Schriften, 392–8.
1948   G.W., 14, 3–8.

(b) ENGLISH TRANSLATION:
        'A Note upon the "Mystic Writing-Pad" '
1940   Int. J. Psycho-Anal., 21 (4), 469–74. (Tr. James Strachey.)
1950   C.P., 5, 175–80.

The present translation is a slightly corrected reprint of the one published in 1950, with some additional notes.

This paper was probably written in the autumn of 1924, for Freud reported in a letter to Abraham that he was revising it in November of that year (Jones, 1957, 124–5). The curious little apparatus, which is the basis of this ingenious and illuminating discussion of the conscious, preconscious and perceptual-conscious systems, is still (1961) quite easily obtainable, at least in Great Britain, under the trade name of 'Printator'. The subject-matter of the paper will become much clearer if an actual specimen can be examined and dissected.

A NOTE UPON THE 'MYSTIC WRITING-PAD'

IF I distrust my memory—neurotics, as we know, do so to a remarkable extent, but normal people have every reason for doing so as well—I am able to supplement and guarantee its working by making a note in writing. In that case the surface upon which this note is preserved, the pocket-book or sheet of paper, is as it were a materialized portion of my mnemic apparatus, which I otherwise carry about with me invisible. I have only to bear in mind the place where this 'memory' has been deposited and I can then 'reproduce' it at any time I like, with the certainty that it will have remained unaltered and so have escaped the possible distortions to which it might have been subjected in my actual memory.

If I want to make full use of this technique for improving my mnemic function, I find that there are two different procedures open to me. On the one hand, I can choose a writing-surface which will preserve intact any note made upon it for an indefinite length of time—for instance, a sheet of paper which I can write upon in ink. I am then in possession of a 'permanent memory-trace'. The disadvantage of this procedure is that the receptive capacity of the writing-surface is soon exhausted. The sheet is filled with writing, there is no room on it for any more notes, and I find myself obliged to bring another sheet into use, that has not been written on. Moreover, the advantage of this procedure, the fact that it provides a 'permanent trace', may lose its value for me if after a time the note ceases to interest me and I no longer want to 'retain it in my memory'. The alternative procedure avoids both of these disadvantages. If, for instance, I write with a piece of chalk on a slate, I have a receptive surface which retains its receptive capacity for an unlimited time and the notes upon which can be destroyed as soon as they cease to interest me, without any need for throwing away the writing-surface itself. Here the disadvantage is that I cannot preserve a permanent trace. If I want to put some fresh notes on the slate, I must first wipe out the ones which cover it. Thus an unlimited receptive capacity and a retention of permanent traces seem to be mutually exclusive properties in the apparatus which we use as substitutes for our memory:

either the receptive surface must be renewed or the note must be destroyed.

All the forms of auxiliary apparatus which we have invented for the improvement or intensification of our sensory functions are built on the same model as the sense organs themselves or portions of them: for instance, spectacles, photographic cameras, ear-trumpets.[1] Measured by this standard, devices to aid our memory seem particularly imperfect, since our mental apparatus accomplishes precisely what they cannot: it has an unlimited receptive capacity for new perceptions and neverthe-less lays down permanent—even though not unalterable—memory-traces of them. As long ago as in 1900 I gave expression in *The Interpretation of Dreams*[2] to a suspicion that this unusual capacity was to be divided between two different systems (or organs of the mental apparatus). According to this view, we possess a system *Pcpt.-Cs.*, which receives perceptions but retains no permanent trace of them, so that it can react like a clean sheet to every new perception; while the permanent traces of the excitations which have been received are preserved in 'mnemic systems' lying behind the perceptual system. Later, in *Beyond the Pleasure Principle* (1920g),[3] I added a remark to the effect that the inexplicable phenomenon of consciousness arises in the perceptual system *instead of* the permanent traces.

Now some time ago there came upon the market, under the name of the 'Mystic Writing-Pad', a small contrivance that promises to perform more than the sheet of paper or the slate. It claims to be nothing more than a writing-tablet from which notes can be erased by an easy movement of the hand. But if it is examined more closely it will be found that its construction shows a remarkable agreement with my hypothetical structure of our perceptual apparatus and that it can in fact provide both an ever-ready receptive surface and permanent traces of the notes that have been made upon it.

The Mystic Pad is a slab of dark brown resin or wax with a paper edging; over the slab is laid a thin transparent sheet, the

---

[1] [This notion is expanded in Chapter III of *Civilization and its Discontents* (1930a).]

[2] [*Standard Ed.*, **5**, 540. As Freud mentions in *Beyond the Pleasure Principle* (1920g), ibid., **18**, 25, this distinction had already been drawn by Breuer in his theoretical section of *Studies on Hysteria* (1895d), ibid., **2**, 188–9 n.]   [3] [Ibid., **18**, 25.]

top end of which is firmly secured to the slab while its bottom end rests on it without being fixed to it. This transparent sheet is the more interesting part of the little device. It itself consists of two layers, which can be detached from each other except at their two ends. The upper layer is a transparent piece of celluloid; the lower layer is made of thin translucent waxed paper. When the apparatus is not in use, the lower surface of the waxed paper adheres lightly to the upper surface of the wax slab.

To make use of the Mystic Pad, one writes upon the celluloid portion of the covering-sheet which rests on the wax slab. For this purpose no pencil or chalk is necessary, since the writing does not depend on material being deposited on the receptive surface. It is a return to the ancient method of writing on tablets of clay or wax: a pointed stilus scratches the surface, the depressions upon which constitute the 'writing'. In the case of the Mystic Pad this scratching is not effected directly, but through the medium of the covering-sheet. At the points which the stilus touches, it presses the lower surface of the waxed paper on to the wax slab, and the grooves are visible as dark writing upon the otherwise smooth whitish-grey surface of the celluloid. If one wishes to destroy what has been written, all that is necessary is to raise the double covering-sheet from the wax slab by a light pull, starting from the free lower end.[1] The close contact between the waxed paper and the wax slab at the places which have been scratched (upon which the visibility of the writing depended) is thus brought to an end and it does not recur when the two surfaces come together once more. The Mystic Pad is now clear of writing and ready to receive fresh notes.

The small imperfections of the contrivance have, of course, no importance for us, since we are only concerned with its approximation to the structure of the perceptual apparatus of the mind.

If, while the Mystic Pad has writing on it, we cautiously raise the celluloid from the waxed paper, we can see the writing just as clearly on the surface of the latter, and the question may arise why there should be any necessity for the celluloid portion

[1] [The method by which the covering-sheet is detached from the wax slab is slightly different in the current form of the device; but this does not affect the principle.]

of the cover. Experiment will then show that the thin paper would be very easily crumpled or torn if one were to write directly upon it with the stilus. The layer of celluloid thus acts as a protective sheath for the waxed paper, to keep off injurious effects from without. The celluloid is a 'protective shield against stimuli'; the layer which actually receives the stimuli is the paper. I may at this point recall that in *Beyond the Pleasure Principle* [ibid., **18**, 27 ff.] I showed that the perceptual apparatus of our mind consists of two layers, of an external protective shield against stimuli whose task it is to diminish the strength of excitations coming in, and of a surface behind it which receives the stimuli, namely the system *Pcpt.-Cs*.

The analogy would not be of much value if it could not be pursued further than this. If we lift the entire covering-sheet—both the celluloid and the waxed paper—off the wax slab, the writing vanishes and, as I have already remarked, does not re-appear again. The surface of the Mystic Pad is clear of writing and once more capable of receiving impressions. But it is easy to discover that the permanent trace of what was written is retained upon the wax slab itself and is legible in suitable lights. Thus the Pad provides not only a receptive surface that can be used over and over again, like a slate, but also permanent traces of what has been written, like an ordinary paper pad: it solves the problem of combining the two functions *by dividing them between two separate but interrelated component parts or systems*. But this is precisely the way in which, according to the hypothesis which I mentioned just now, our mental apparatus performs its perceptual function. The layer which receives the stimuli—the system *Pcpt.-Cs.*—forms no permanent traces; the foundations of memory come about in other, adjoining, systems.

We need not be disturbed by the fact that in the Mystic Pad no use is made of the permanent traces of the notes that have been received; it is enough that they are present. There must come a point at which the analogy between an auxiliary apparatus of this kind and the organ which is its prototype will cease to apply. It is true, too, that once the writing has been erased, the Mystic Pad cannot 'reproduce' it from within; it would be a mystic pad indeed if, like our memory, it could accomplish that. None the less, I do not think it is too far-fetched to compare the celluloid and waxed paper cover with the system *Pcpt.-Cs.* and its protective shield, the wax slab with the unconscious behind them, and the appearance and disappearance of the writing with the flickering-up and passing-away of consciousness in the process of perception.

But I must admit that I am inclined to press the comparison still further. On the Mystic Pad the writing vanishes every time the close contact is broken between the paper which receives the stimulus and the wax slab which preserves the impression. This agrees with a notion which I have long had about the method by which the perceptual apparatus of our mind functions, but which I have hitherto kept to myself.[1] My theory was that cathectic innervations are sent out and withdrawn in rapid periodic impulses from within into the completely pervious system *Pcpt.-Cs.* So long as that system is cathected in this manner, it receives perceptions (which are accompanied by consciousness) and passes the excitation on to the unconscious mnemic systems; but as soon as the cathexis is withdrawn, consciousness is extinguished and the functioning of the system comes to a standstill.[2] It is as though the unconscious stretches out feelers, through the medium of the system *Pcpt.-Cs.*, towards the external world and hastily withdraws them as soon as they have sampled the excitations coming from it. Thus the interruptions, which in the case of the Mystic Pad have an external origin, were attributed by my hypothesis to the discontinuity in the current of innervation; and the actual breaking of contact which occurs in the Mystic Pad was replaced in my theory by the periodic non-excitability of the perceptual system. I further had a suspicion that this discontinuous method of functioning of the system *Pcpt.-Cs.* lies at the bottom of the origin of the concept of time.[3]

---

[1] [It had in fact been mentioned in *Beyond the Pleasure Principle*, ibid., 18, 28. The notion re-appears at the end of the paper on 'Negation' (1925*h*), below, p. 238. It is already present in embryo at the end of Section 19 of Part I of the 'Project' of 1895 (Freud 1950*a*).]

[2] [This is in accordance with the 'principle of the insusceptibility to excitation of uncathected systems', which is discussed in an Editor's footnote to the metapsychological paper on dreams (1917*d*), *Standard Ed.*, 14, 227.]

[3] [This also had been suggested in *Beyond the Pleasure Principle*, ibid., 28, and hinted at earlier, in 'The Unconscious' (1915*e*), ibid., 14, 187–8. It is restated in 'Negation' (1925*h*), p. 238 below, where, however, Freud attributes the sending out of feelers to the ego.]

If we imagine one hand writing upon the surface of the Mystic Writing-Pad while another periodically raises its covering-sheet from the wax slab, we shall have a concrete representation of the way in which I tried to picture the functioning of the perceptual apparatus of our mind.

NEGATION
(1925)

DIE VERNEINUNG

(*a*) GERMAN EDITIONS:
1923   *Imago*, **11** (3), 217–21.
1926   *Psychoanalyse der Neurosen*, 199–204.
1928   *G.S.*, **11**, 3–7.
1931   *Theoretische Schriften*, 399–404.
1948   *G.W.*, **14**, 11–15.

(*b*) ENGLISH TRANSLATION:
'Negation'
1925   *Int. J. Psycho-Anal.*, **6** (4), 367–71. (Tr. Joan Riviere.)
1950   *C.P.*, **5**, 181–5. (Revision of above.)

The present translation is a modified version of the one published in 1950. The translation of 1950 is reprinted in D. Rapaport, *Organization and Pathology of Thought*, New York, 1951.

We are told by Ernest Jones (1957, 125) that this was written in July, 1925. The subject had, however, evidently been in Freud's thoughts for some time, as is shown by the footnote added by him to the 'Dora' case history in 1923. (See p. 239 below.) The paper is one of his most succinct. Though primarily it deals with a special point of metapsychology, yet in its opening and closing passages it touches upon technique. It will be seen from the references in the footnotes that both of these aspects of the paper had a long previous history.

Extracts from the earlier (1925) translation of this paper were included in Rickman's *General Selection from the Works of Sigmund Freud* (1937, 63–7).

NEGATION

THE manner in which our patients bring forward their associations during the work of analysis gives us an opportunity for making some interesting observations. 'Now you'll think I mean to say something insulting, but really I've no such intention.' We realize that this is a rejection, by projection, of an idea that has just come up. Or: 'You ask who this person in the dream can be. It's *not* my mother.' We emend this to: 'So it *is* his mother.' In our interpretation, we take the liberty of disregarding the negation and of picking out the subject-matter alone of the association. It is as though the patient had said: 'It's true that my mother came into my mind as I thought of this person, but I don't feel inclined to let the association count.'[1]

There is a very convenient method by which we can sometimes obtain a piece of information we want about unconscious repressed material. 'What', we ask, 'would you consider the most unlikely imaginable thing in that situation? What do you think was furthest from your mind at that time?' If the patient falls into the trap and says what he thinks is most incredible, he almost always makes the right admission. A neat counterpart to this experiment is often met with in an obsessional neurotic who has already been initiated into the meaning of his symptoms. 'I've got a new obsessive idea,' he says, 'and it occurred to me at once that it might mean so and so. But no; that can't be true, or it couldn't have occurred to me.' What he is repudiating, on grounds picked up from his treatment, is, of course, the correct meaning of the obsessive idea.

Thus the content of a repressed image or idea can make its way into consciousness, on condition that it is *negated*.[2] Negation is a way of taking cognizance of what is repressed; indeed it is

---

[1] [Freud had drawn attention to this in (among other places) the 'Rat Man' analysis (1909*d*), *Standard Ed.*, **10**, 183 *n*.]

[2] [The German *'verneinen'* is here translated by 'to negate' instead of by the more usual 'to deny', in order to avoid confusion with the German *'verleugnen'*, which has also in the past been rendered by 'to deny'. In this edition 'to disavow' has in general been used for the latter German word. See the footnote on this point in 'The Infantile Genital Organization' (1923*e*), p. 143 above.]

already a lifting of the repression, though not, of course, an acceptance of what is repressed. We can see how in this the intellectual function is separated from the affective process. With the help of negation only one consequence of the process of repression is undone—the fact, namely, of the ideational content of what is repressed not reaching consciousness. The outcome of this is a kind of intellectual acceptance of the repressed, while at the same time what is essential to the repression persists.[1] In the course of analytic work we often produce a further, very important and somewhat strange variant of this situation. We succeed in conquering the negation as well, and in bringing about a full intellectual acceptance of the repressed; but the repressive process itself is not yet removed by this.

Since to affirm or negate the content of thoughts is the task of the function of intellectual judgement, what we have just been saying has led us to the psychological origin of that function. To negate something in a judgement is, at bottom, to say: 'This is something which I should prefer to repress.' A negative judgement is the intellectual substitute for repression;[2] its 'no' is the hall-mark of repression, a certificate of origin—like, let us say, 'Made in Germany'.[3] With the help of the symbol of negation, thinking frees itself from the restrictions of repression and enriches itself with material that is indispensable for its proper functioning.

The function of judgement is concerned in the main with two sorts of decisions. It affirms or disaffirms the possession by a thing of a particular attribute; and it asserts or disputes that a presentation has an existence in reality.[4] The attribute to be

---

[1] The same process is at the root of the familiar superstition that boasting is dangerous. 'How nice not to have had one of my headaches for so long.' But this is in fact the first announcement of an attack, of whose approach the subject is already sensible, although he is as yet unwilling to believe it. [Freud's attention had first been drawn to this explanation by one of his earliest patients, Frau Cäcilie M. Cf. the long footnote on the subject in the first of Freud's case histories in *Studies on Hysteria* (1895*d*), *Standard Ed.*, **2**, 76.]

[2] [Freud's earliest statement of this idea seems to have been in his book on jokes (1905*c*), *Standard Ed.*, **8**, 175. It re-appears in the paper on 'The Two Principles of Mental Functioning' (1911*b*), ibid., **12**, 221, and in the metapsychological paper on 'The Unconscious' (1915*e*), ibid., **14**, 186.]

[3] [In English in the original.]   [4] [This is explained below, p. 237.]

decided about may originally have been good or bad, useful or harmful. Expressed in the language of the oldest—the oral—instinctual impulses, the judgement is: 'I should like to eat this', or 'I should like to spit it out'; and, put more generally: 'I should like to take this into myself and to keep that out.' That is to say: 'It shall be inside me' or 'it shall be outside me'. As I have shown elsewhere, the original pleasure-ego wants to intrjoect into itself everything that is good and to eject from itself everything that is bad. What is bad, what is alien to the ego and what is external are, to begin with, identical.[1]

The other sort of decision made by the function of judgement —as to the real existence of something of which there is a presentation (reality-testing)—is a concern of the definitive reality-ego, which develops out of the initial pleasure-ego. It is now no longer a question of whether what has been perceived (a thing) shall be taken into the ego or not, but of whether something which is in the ego as a presentation can be rediscovered in perception (reality) as well. It is, we see, once more a question of *external* and *internal*. What is unreal, merely a presentation and subjective, is only internal; what is real is also there *outside*. In this stage of development regard for the pleasure principle has been set aside. Experience has shown the subject that it is not only important whether a thing (an object of satisfaction for him) possesses the 'good' attribute and so deserves to be taken into his ego, but also whether it is there in the external world, so that he can get hold of it whenever he needs it. In order to understand this step forward we must recollect that all presentations originate from perceptions and are repetitions of them. Thus originally the mere existence of a presentation was a guarantee of the reality of what was presented. The antithesis between subjective and objective does not exist from the first. It only comes into being from the fact that thinking possesses the capacity to bring before the mind once more something that has once been perceived, by reproducing it as a presentation without the external object having still to be there. The first and immediate aim, therefore, of reality-testing is, not to *find* an object in real perception which corresponds to the one presented, but to *refind* such an object, to

[1] See the discussion in 'Instincts and their Vicissitudes' (1915c) [*Standard Ed.*, 14, 136.—Freud took up this question again in the first chapter of *Civilization and its Discontents* (1930a).]

convince oneself that it is still there.[1] Another capacity of the power of thinking offers a further contribution to the differentiation between what is subjective and what is objective. The reproduction of a perception as a presentation is not always a faithful one; it may be modified by omissions, or changed by the merging of various elements. In that case, reality-testing has to ascertain how far such distortions go. But it is evident that a precondition for the setting up of reality-testing is that objects shall have been lost which once brought real satisfaction.

Judging is the intellectual action which decides the choice of motor action, which puts an end to the postponement due to thought and which leads over from thinking to acting. This postponement due to thought has also been discussed by me elsewhere.[2] It is to be regarded as an experimental action, a motor palpating, with small expenditure of discharge. Let us consider where the ego has used a similar kind of palpating before, at what place it learnt the technique which it now applies in its processes of thought. It happened at the sensory end of the mental apparatus, in connection with sense perceptions. For, on our hypothesis, perception is not a purely passive process. The ego periodically sends out small amounts of cathexis into the perceptual system, by means of which it samples the external stimuli, and then after every such tentative advance it draws back again.[3]

The study of judgement affords us, perhaps for the first time,

---

[1] [Much of this is foreshadowed in *The Interpretation of Dreams* (1900)*a*, *Standard Ed.*, **5**, 565–7, and, more particularly, in the 1895 'Project' (Freud, 1950*a*; Section 16 of Part I). Here the 'object' to be refound is the mother's breast. Cf., too, a sentence which occurs in a similar connection in Section 5 of the *Three Essays* (1905*d*), *Standard Ed.*, **7**, 222: 'The finding of an object is in fact a refinding of it.']

[2] [See *The Ego and the Id* (1923*b*), p. 55 above. But Freud made the point repeatedly, beginning with the 'Project' of 1895 (at the end of Section 17 of Part I). A list of references will be found in Lecture XXXII of the *New Introductory Lectures* (1933*a*). Incidentally, the whole topic of judgement is discussed at great length and on much the same lines as the present ones, in Sections 16, 17 and 18 of Part I of the 'Project'.]

[3] [See *Beyond the Pleasure Principle* (1920*g*), *Standard Ed.*, **18**, 28, and 'A Note upon the "Mystic Writing-Pad"' (1925*a*), p. 231 above. It may be remarked that in this last passage Freud suggests not that the ego but that the *unconscious* 'stretches out feelers, through the medium of the system *Pcpt.-Cs.*, towards the external world'.]

an insight into the origin of an intellectual function from the interplay of the primary instinctual impulses. Judging is a continuation, along lines of expediency, of the original process by which the ego took things into itself or expelled them from itself, according to the pleasure principle. The polarity of judgement appears to correspond to the opposition of the two groups of instincts which we have supposed to exist. Affirmation—as a substitute for uniting—belongs to Eros; negation—the successor to expulsion—belongs to the instinct of destruction. The general wish to negate, the negativism which is displayed by some psychotics, is probably to be regarded as a sign of a defusion of instincts that has taken place through a withdrawal of the libidinal components.[1] But the performance of the function of judgement is not made possible until the creation of the symbol of negation has endowed thinking with a first measure of freedom from the consequences of repression and, with it, from the compulsion of the pleasure principle.

This view of negation fits in very well with the fact that in analysis we never discover a 'no' in the unconscious and that recognition of the unconscious on the part of the ego is expressed in a negative formula. There is no stronger evidence that we have been successful in our effort to uncover the unconscious than when the patient reacts to it with the words 'I didn't think that', or 'I didn't (ever) think of that'.[2]

[1] [Cf. a remark in Chapter VI of the book on Jokes (1905c), *Standard Ed.*, 8, 175, footnote 2.]

[2] [Freud had made this point in almost the same words in a footnote added in 1923 to the 'Dora' analysis (1905e), *Standard Ed.*, 7, 57. He once more returned to it in his very late paper on 'Constructions in Analysis' (1937d).]

SOME PSYCHICAL CONSEQUENCES OF THE ANATOMICAL DISTINCTION BETWEEN THE SEXES
(1925)

EDITOR'S NOTE

EINIGE PSYCHISCHE FOLGEN DES ANATOMISCHEN GESCHLECHTSUNTERSCHIEDS

(a) GERMAN EDITIONS:

1925   Int. Z. Psychoanal., 11 (4), 401–10.
1926   Psychoanalyse der Neurosen, 205–19.
1928   G.S., 11, 8–19.
1931   Sexualtheorie und Traumlehre, 207–20.
1948   G.W., 14, 19–30.

(b) ENGLISH TRANSLATION:
   'Some Psychological Consequences of the Anatomical
              Distinction between the Sexes'
1927   Int. J. Psycho-Anal., 8 (2), 133–42. (Tr. James Strachey.)
1950   C.P., 5, 186–97. (Revised reprint of above.)

The present translation is a corrected and freshly annotated version, with a slightly modified title, of the one published in 1950.

This paper was finished by August, 1925, when Freud showed it to Ferenczi. It was read on his behalf by Anna Freud at the Homburg International Psycho-Analytical Congress on September 3, and was published in the *Zeitschrift* later in the autumn (Jones, 1957, 119).

What is in effect a first complete re-assessment of Freud's views on the psychological development of women will be found condensed in this short paper. It contains the germs of all his later work on the subject.

From early days Freud made complaints of the obscurity enveloping the sexual life of women. Thus, near the beginning of his *Three Essays on the Theory of Sexuality* (1905*d*), he wrote that the sexual life of men 'alone has become accessible to research. That of women . . . is still veiled in an impenetrable obscurity.' (*Standard Ed.*, 7, 151.) Similarly, in his discussion of the sexual theories of children (1908*c*), he wrote: 'In consequence of unfavourable circumstances, both of an external and an internal nature, the following observations apply chiefly to the sexual development of one sex only—that is, of males.' (Ibid., **9**, 211.) Again, very much later, in his pamphlet on lay analysis (1926*e*): 'We know less about the sexual life of little girls than of boys. But we need not feel ashamed of this distinction; after all, the sexual life of adult women is a "dark continent" for psychology.' (Ibid., **20**, 212.)[1]

One result of this obscurity was to lead Freud to assume very often that the psychology of women could be taken simply as analogous to that of men. There are many examples of this. In his first full account of the Oedipus situation, for instance, in *The Interpretation of Dreams* (1900*a*), he assumes that there is a complete parallel between the two sexes, that 'a girl's first affection is for her father and a boy's first childish desires are for his mother' (*Standard Ed.*, **4**, 257). Similarly, in his long description of the sexual development of children in Lecture XXI of the *Introductory Lectures* (1916–17) he writes: 'As you see, I have only described the relation of a boy to his father and mother. Things happen in just the same way with little girls, with the necessary changes: an affectionate attachment to her father, a need to get rid of her mother as superfluous . . .' Or, speaking of the early history of identification in *Group Psychology* (1921*c*): 'The same holds good, with the necessary substitutions, of the baby daughter as well' (*Standard Ed.*, **18**, 106). Even in *The Ego and the Id* (1923*b*) the complicated processes accompanying and following the dissolution of the Oedipus complex are supposed to be 'precisely analogous' in girls and boys (p. 32 above).[2] Or the account of the female Oedipus complex may

---

[1] Ernest Jones writes (1955, 468): 'There is little doubt that Freud found the psychology of women more enigmatic than that of men. He said once to Marie Bonaparte: "The great question that has never been answered and which I have not yet been able to answer, despite my thirty years of research into the feminine soul, is 'What does a woman want?'"' Unfortunately Jones gives no date for this remark. Freud himself suggests a part explanation of his difficulty in the last paragraph of Section I of his later paper on 'Female Sexuality' (1931*b*), where he attributes it to a peculiarity in his transference-relation with women.

[2] A similar position was adopted in the *Autobiographical Study* (1925*d*): 'boys concentrate their sexual wishes upon their mother and develop hostile impulses against their father as being a rival, while girls adopt an analogous attitude' (*Standard Ed.*, **20**, 36). But here Freud added a footnote in 1935 with a drastic correction of his earlier views and an explanation of how they arose: 'The information about infantile sexu-

simply be omitted, as in the article for Marcuse's encyclopaedia (1923*a*), *Standard Ed.*, **18**, 245. On the other hand, in describing the 'phallic phase' in the paper on the infantile genital organization (1923*e*) Freud writes frankly: 'Unfortunately we can describe this state of things only as it affects the male child; the corresponding processes in the little girl are not known to us' (p. 142 above).

But in fact over a long period from the time of the 'Dora' analysis in 1900, Freud's interest had not been directed to feminine psychology. It was not for fifteen years that he published any important case material dealing with a woman. Then came the case of female paranoia 'running counter to psychoanalytic theory' (1915*f*), the essence of which lay in the patient's relation to her mother. Not long after came the case of female homosexuality (1920*a*) of which the same might well be said. Between them came the study of beating phantasies (1919*e*), which was almost wholly concerned with the infantile sexual development of girls. And here already there is clear evidence of dissatisfaction with the 'precise analogy' between the two sexes: 'the expectation of there being a complete parallel was mistaken' (*Standard Ed.*, **17**, 196). Thereafter the problem of the sexual history of women was no doubt constantly in Freud's mind. And although there is little about it in *The Ego and the Id* (1923*b*), it was the theories developed there concerning the end of the Oedipus complex which, linked with fresh clinical observations, gave the key to the new thesis. Freud was already feeling his way towards it in 'The Dissolution of the Oedipus Complex' (1924*d*) but it is fully stated for the first time in the present paper. It was to be further enlarged on in the later paper on 'Female Sexuality' (1931*b*),[1] in Lecture XXXIII of the *New Introductory Lectures* (1933*a*) and finally in Chapter VII of the posthumous *Outline of Psycho-Analysis* (1940*a* [1938]).

---

ality was obtained from the study of men and the theory deduced from it was concerned with male children. It was natural enough to expect to find a complete parallel between the two sexes; but this turned out not to hold.' And he went on to give the gist of the findings first announced in the present paper.

[1] The most important addition made in this was the discovery, based on fresh case-material, of the strength and duration of the little girl's pre-Oedipus attachment to her mother.

Almost every detail is already present in a condensed form in this work. But it is remarkable that many of these details had been ready to hand long before and only required linking up. Thus certain peculiarities in the sexual development of girls had been noted and insisted upon. Already in the first edition of the *Three Essays* (1905d) Freud had maintained that in little girls the leading sexual organ was the clitoris, that, in conformity with this fact, 'the sexuality of little girls is of a wholly masculine character', and that 'a wave of repression at puberty' is required before the clitoris gives place to the vagina and masculinity to femininity (*Standard Ed.*, 7, 219–21). Most of this had, indeed, been indicated many years before in a letter to Fliess of November 14, 1897 (Freud, 1950a, Letter 75). The matter was carried further in the paper on 'The Sexual Theories of Children' (1908c), where it was brought into relation with the girl's envy for the penis and the castration complex (*Standard Ed.*, 9, 217–18).[1] The fact that the injury to her narcissism caused by this leads to resentment against her mother was pointed out in the paper on 'Some Character-Types' (1916d), ibid, 14, 315; and other grounds for this resentment had been enumerated in the paranoia case history a little earlier (1915f), ibid., 267–8.

Nor had the fundamental basis of the new thesis been unstated—though for long periods it seemed forgotten. In the *Three Essays* we find the plain statement that a child's first sexual object is the mother's breast and that this is the prototype of every later love-relation (*Standard Ed.*, 7, 222). This was clearly meant to be true of girls as well as boys, but it seems to be repeated explicitly for the first time here (p. 251).[2] The twofold change required of the little girl before she could arrive at the 'normal' Oedipus complex thus became evident: a change in her leading sexual organ and a change in her sexual object. And the path lay open for an investigation of her 'pre-Oedipus' phase, together with the differences between girls and boys implied by the hypotheses in *The Ego and the Id*—the difference

---

[1] This was further discussed in 'The Taboo of Virginity' (1918a).

[2] In the paper on narcissism (1914c), this primary fact is again stated (*Standard Ed.*, 14, 87–8), but somehow passed over; and the distinction between the early libidinal objects of boys and girls becomes concentrated on the distinction between the anaclitic and narcissistic types of object-choice.

in the relation of their castration and Oedipus complexes and the further difference in the construction of their super-egos. It is the synthesis of these various pieces of knowledge, derived from such widely separated historical strata of Freud's work, which gives its importance to the present paper.

SOME PSYCHICAL CONSEQUENCES OF THE ANATOMICAL DISTINCTION BETWEEN THE SEXES

In my own writings and in those of my followers more and more stress is laid on the necessity that the analyses of neurotics shall deal thoroughly with the remotest period of their childhood, the time of the early efflorescence of sexual life. It is only by examining the first manifestations of the patient's innate instinctual constitution and the effects of his earliest experiences that we can accurately gauge the motive forces that have led to his neurosis and can be secure against the errors into which we might be tempted by the degree to which things have become remodelled and overlaid in adult life. This requirement is not only of theoretical but also of practical importance, for it distinguishes our efforts from the work of those physicians whose interests are focused exclusively on therapeutic results and who employ analytic methods, but only up to a certain point. An analysis of early childhood such as we are considering is tedious and laborious and makes demands both upon the physician and upon the patient which cannot always be met. Moreover, it leads us into dark regions where there are as yet no signposts. Indeed, analysts may feel reassured, I think, that there is no risk of their work becoming mechanical, and so of losing its interest, during the next few decades.

In the following pages I bring forward some findings of analytic research which would be of great importance if they could be proved to apply universally. Why do I not postpone publication of them until further experience has given me the necessary proof, if such proof is obtainable? Because the conditions under which I work have undergone a change, with implications which I cannot disguise. Formerly, I was not one of those who are unable to hold back what seems to be a new discovery until it has been either confirmed or corrected. My *Interpretation of Dreams* (1900a) and my 'Fragment of an Analysis of a Case of Hysteria' (1905e) (the case of Dora) were suppressed by me—if not for the nine years enjoined by Horace—at all events for four or five years before I allowed them to be pub-

lished. But in those days I had unlimited time before me—
'oceans of time'[1] as an amiable author puts it—and material
poured in upon me in such quantities that fresh experiences
were hardly to be escaped. Moreover, I was the only worker in
a new field, so that my reticence involved no danger to myself
and no loss to others.

But now everything has changed. The time before me is
limited. The whole of it is no longer spent in working, so that
my opportunities for making fresh observations are not so
numerous. If I think I see something new, I am uncertain
whether I can wait for it to be confirmed. And further, everything that is to be seen upon the surface has already been
exhausted; what remains has to be slowly and laboriously
dragged up from the depths. Finally, I am no longer alone.
An eager crowd of fellow-workers is ready to make use of what
is unfinished or doubtful, and I can leave to them that part of
the work which I should otherwise have done myself. On this
occasion, therefore, I feel justified in publishing something
which stands in urgent need of confirmation before its value or
lack of value can be decided.

In examining the earliest mental shapes assumed by the
sexual life of children we have been in the habit of taking as
the subject of our investigations the male child, the little boy.
With little girls, so we have supposed, things must be similar,
though in some way or other they must nevertheless be different.
The point in development at which this difference lay could
not be clearly determined.

In boys the situation of the Oedipus complex is the first stage
that can be recognized with certainty. It is easy to understand,
because at that stage a child retains the same object which he
previously cathected with his libido—not as yet a genital one—
during the preceding period while he was being suckled and
nursed. The fact, too, that in this situation he regards his father
as a disturbing rival and would like to get rid of him and take
his place is a straightforward consequence of the actual state of
affairs. I have shown elsewhere[2] how the Oedipus attitude in

---

[1] [In English in the original. It is not clear what author Freud had in
mind.—The reference to Horace is to his *Ars Poetica*, 388.]

[2] 'The Dissolution of the Oedipus Complex' (1924*d*) [this volume,
p. 173. Much of what follows is an elaboration of that paper.]

little boys belongs to the phallic phase, and how its destruction is brought about by the fear of castration—that is, by narcissistic interest in their genitals. The matter is made more difficult to grasp by the complicating circumstance that even in boys the Oedipus complex has a double orientation, active and passive, in accordance with their bisexual constitution; a boy also wants to take his *mother's* place as the love-object of his *father*—a fact which we describe as the feminine attitude.[1]

As regards the prehistory of the Oedipus complex in boys we are far from complete clarity. We know that that period includes an identification of an affectionate sort with the boy's father, an identification which is still free from any sense of rivalry in regard to his mother. Another element of that stage is invariably, I believe, a masturbatory activity in connection with the genitals, the masturbation of early childhood, the more or less violent suppression of which by those in charge of the child sets the castration complex in action. It is to be assumed that this masturbation is attached to the Oedipus complex and serves as a discharge for the sexual excitation belonging to it. It is, however, uncertain whether the masturbation has this character from the first, or whether on the contrary it makes its first appearance spontaneously as an activity of a bodily organ and is only brought into relation with the Oedipus complex at some later date; this second possibility is by far the more probable. Another doubtful question is the part played by bed-wetting and by the breaking of that habit through the intervention of training measures. We are inclined to make the simple connection that continued bed-wetting is a result of masturbation and that its suppression is regarded by boys as an inhibition of their genital activity—that is, as having the meaning of a threat of castration;[2] but whether we are always right in supposing this remains to be seen. Finally, analysis shows us in a shadowy way how the fact of a child at a very early age listening to his parents copulating may set up his first sexual excitation, and how that event may, owing to its after-effects, act as a starting-point for the child's whole sexual development. Masturbation, as well as the two attitudes in the Oedipus complex, later on become attached to this early experience, the child having subsequently interpreted its meaning. It is impossible, however, to suppose that these observations

[1] [Cf. ibid., p. 176.]   [2] [Cf. ibid., p. 175.]

of coitus are of universal occurrence, so that at this point we are faced with the problem of 'primal phantasies'.[1] Thus the prehistory of the Oedipus complex, even in boys, raises all of these questions for sifting and explanation; and there is the further problem of whether we are to suppose that the process invariably follows the same course, or whether a great variety of different preliminary stages may not converge upon the same terminal situation.

In little girls the Oedipus complex raises one problem more than in boys. In both cases the mother is the original object; and there is no cause for surprise that boys retain that object in the Oedipus complex. But how does it happen that girls abandon it and instead take their father as an object? In pursuing this question I have been able to reach some conclusions which may throw light precisely on the prehistory of the Oedipus relation in girls.

Every analyst has come across certain women who cling with especial intensity and tenacity to the bond with their father and to the wish in which it culminates of having a child by him. We have good reason to suppose that the same wishful phantasy was also the motive force of their infantile masturbation, and it is easy to form an impression that at this point we have been brought up against an elementary and unanalysable fact of infantile sexual life. But a thorough analysis of these very cases brings something different to light—namely, that here the Oedipus complex has a long prehistory and is in some respects a secondary formation.

The old paediatrician Lindner [1879] once remarked that a child discovers the genital zones (the penis or the clitoris) as a source of pleasure while indulging in sensual sucking (thumb-sucking).[2] I shall leave it an open question whether it is really true that the child takes the newly found source of pleasure in exchange for the recent loss of the mother's nipple—a possibility to which later phantasies (fellatio) seem to point. Be that as it may, the genital zone is discovered at some time or

---

[1] [Cf. the discussions in the 'Wolf Man' analysis (1918*b*), *Standard Ed.*, 17, especially 48–60 and 95–7, and Lecture XXIII of the *Introductory Lectures* (1916–17).]

[2] Cf. *Three Essays on the Theory of Sexuality* (1905*d*) [*Standard Ed.*, 7, 179].

other, and there seems no justification for attributing any psychical content to the first activities in connection with it. But the first step in the phallic phase which begins in this way is not the linking-up of the masturbation with the object-cathexes of the Oedipus complex, but a momentous discovery which little girls are destined to make. They notice the penis of a brother or playmate, strikingly visible and of large proportions, at once recognize it as the superior counterpart of their own small and inconspicuous organ, and from that time forward fall a victim to envy for the penis.

There is an interesting contrast between the behaviour of the two sexes. In the analogous situation, when a little boy first catches sight of a girl's genital region, he begins by showing irresolution and lack of interest; he sees nothing or disavows[1] what he has seen, he softens it down or looks about for expedients for bringing it into line with his expectations. It is not until later, when some threat of castration has obtained a hold upon him, that the observation becomes important to him: if he then recollects or repeats it, it arouses a terrible storm of emotion in him and forces him to believe in the reality of the threat which he has hitherto laughed at. This combination of circumstances leads to two reactions, which may become fixed and will in that case, whether separately or together or in conjunction with other factors, permanently determine the boy's relations to women: horror of the mutilated creature or triumphant contempt for her. These developments, however, belong to the future, though not to a very remote one.

A little girl behaves differently. She makes her judgement and her decision in a flash. She has seen it and knows that she is without it and wants to have it.[2]

---

[1] [See Editor's footnote to 'The Infantile Genital Organization', p. 143 above.]

[2] This is an opportunity for correcting a statement which I made many years ago. I believed that the sexual interest of children, unlike that of pubescents, was aroused, not by the difference between the sexes, but by the problem of where babies come from. We now see that, at all events with girls, this is certainly not the case. With boys it may no doubt happen sometimes one way and sometimes the other; or with both sexes chance experiences may determine the event.—[The statement mentioned at the beginning of this footnote appears in more than one place: e.g. in the paper on 'The Sexual Theories of Children' 1908c), *Standard Ed.*, 9, 212, in the case history of 'Little Hans' (1909b),

Here what has been named the masculinity complex of women branches off.[1] It may put great difficulties in the way of their regular development towards femininity, if it cannot be got over soon enough. The hope of some day obtaining a penis in spite of everything and so of becoming like a man may persist to an incredibly late age and may become a motive for strange and otherwise unaccountable actions. Or again, a process may set in which I should like to call a 'disavowal',[2] a process which in the mental life of children seems neither uncommon nor very dangerous but which in an adult would mean the beginning of a psychosis. Thus a girl may refuse to accept the fact of being castrated, may harden herself in the conviction that she *does* possess a penis, and may subsequently be compelled to behave as though she were a man.

The psychical consequences of envy for the penis, in so far as it does not become absorbed in the reaction-formation of the masculinity complex, are various and far-reaching. After a woman has become aware of the wound to her narcissism, she develops, like a scar, a sense of inferiority.[3] When she has passed beyond her first attempt at explaining her lack of a penis as being a punishment personal to herself and has realized that that sexual character is a universal one, she begins to share the contempt felt by men for a sex which is the lesser in so important a respect, and, at least in holding that opinion, insists on being like a man.[4]

ibid., **10**, 133, and in a passage added in 1915 to the *Three Essays* (1905*d*), ibid., **7**, 195. In a passage earlier than any of these, however, in a paper on 'The Sexual Enlightenment of Children' (1907*c*), ibid., **9**, 135, Freud in fact takes the opposite view—the one advocated here.]

[1] [This term seems to have been introduced by Van Ophuijsen (1917). Freud adopted it in ' "A Child is Being Beaten" ' (1919*e*), *Standard Ed.*, **17**, 191. Cf. also p. 178 above.]

[2] [For the parallel process in boys, see 'The Infantile Genital Organization' (1923*e*), pp. 143–4 above.]

[3] [Cf. *Beyond the Pleasure Principle* (1920*g*), *Standard Ed.*, **18**, 20–1.]

[4] In my first critical account of the 'History of the Psycho-Analytic Movement' (1914*d*) [*Standard Ed.*, **14**, 54–5], I recognized that this fact represents the core of truth contained in Adler's theory. That theory has no hesitation in explaining the whole world by this single point ('organ-inferiority', the 'masculine protest', 'breaking away from the feminine line') and prides itself upon having in this way robbed sexuality of its importance and put the desire for power in its place! Thus the only organ which could claim to be called 'inferior' without any ambiguity

Even after penis-envy has abandoned its true object, it continues to exist: by an easy displacement it persists in the character-trait of *jealousy*. Of course, jealousy is not limited to one sex and has a wider foundation than this, but I am of opinion that it plays a far larger part in the mental life of women than of men and that that is because it is enormously reinforced from the direction of displaced penis-envy. While I was still unaware of this source of jealousy and was considering the phantasy 'a child is being beaten', which occurs so commonly in girls, I constructed a first phase for it in which its meaning was that another child, a rival of whom the subject was jealous, was to be beaten.[1] This phantasy seems to be a relic of the phallic period in girls. The peculiar rigidity which struck me so much in the monotonous formula 'a child is being beaten' can probably be interpreted in a special way. The child which is being beaten (or caressed) may ultimately be nothing more nor less than the clitoris itself, so that at its very lowest level the statement will contain a confession of masturbation, which has remained attached to the content of the formula from its beginning in the phallic phase till later life.

A third consequence of penis-envy seems to be a loosening of the girl's relation with her mother as a love-object. The situation as a whole is not very clear, but it can be seen that in the end the girl's mother, who sent her into the world so insufficiently equipped, is almost always held responsible for her lack of a penis. The way in which this comes about historically is often that soon after the girl has discovered that her genitals are unsatisfactory she begins to show jealousy of another child on the ground that her mother is fonder of it than of her, which serves as a reason for her giving up her affectionate relation to her mother. It will fit in with this if the child which has been preferred by her mother is made into the first object of the beating-phantasy which ends in masturbation.

would be the clitoris. On the other hand, one hears of analysts who boast that, though they have worked for dozens of years, they have never found a sign of the existence of a castration complex. We must bow our heads in recognition of the greatness of this achievement, even though it is only a negative one, a piece of virtuosity in the art of overlooking and mistaking. The two theories form an interesting pair of opposites: in the latter not a trace of a castration complex, in the former nothing else than its consequences.

[1] ' "A Child is Being Beaten" ' (1919*e*) [*Standard Ed.*, 17, 184–5].

There is yet another surprising effect of penis-envy, or of the discovery of the inferiority of the clitoris, which is undoubtedly the most important of all. In the past I had often formed an impression that in general women tolerate masturbation worse than men, that they more frequently fight against it and that they are unable to make use of it in circumstances in which a man would seize upon it as a way of escape without any hesitation. Experience would no doubt elicit innumerable exceptions to this statement, if we attempted to turn it into a rule. The reactions of human individuals of both sexes are of course made up of masculine and feminine traits. But it appeared to me nevertheless as though masturbation were further removed from the nature of women than of men, and the solution of the problem could be assisted by the reflection that masturbation, at all events of the clitoris, is a masculine activity and that the elimination of clitoridal sexuality is a necessary precondition for the development of femininity.[1] Analyses of the remote phallic period have now taught me that in girls, soon after the first signs of penis-envy, an intense current of feeling against masturbation makes its appearance, which cannot be attributed exclusively to the educational influence of those in charge of the child. This impulse is clearly a forerunner of the wave of repression which at puberty will do away with a large amount of the girl's masculine sexuality in order to make room for the development of her femininity. It may happen that this first opposition to auto-erotic activity fails to attain its end. And this was in fact the case in the instances which I analysed. The conflict continued, and both then and later the girl did everything she could to free herself from the compulsion to masturbate. Many of the later manifestations of sexual life in women remain unintelligible unless this powerful motive is recognized.

I cannot explain the opposition which is raised in this way by little girls to phallic masturbation except by supposing that there is some concurrent factor which turns her violently against that pleasurable activity. Such a factor lies close at hand. It

---

[1] [A reference to clitoridal masturbation in girls appeared in the first edition of the *Three Essays* (1905d), *Standard Ed.*, 7, 220. In the course of his 'Contributions to a Discussion on Masturbation' (1912 f), Freud expressed regret at the lack of knowledge about female masturbation (*Standard Ed.*, 12, 247).]

cannot be anything else than her narcissistic sense of humiliation which is bound up with penis-envy, the reminder that after all this is a point on which she cannot compete with boys and that it would therefore be best for her to give up the idea of doing so. Thus the little girl's recognition of the anatomical distinction between the sexes forces her away from masculinity and masculine masturbation on to new lines which lead to the development of femininity.

So far there has been no question of the Oedipus complex, nor has it up to this point played any part. But now the girl's libido slips into a new position along the line—there is no other way of putting it—of the equation 'penis-child'. She gives up her wish for a penis and puts in place of it a wish for a child: and *with that purpose in view* she takes her father as a love-object.[1] Her mother becomes the object of her jealousy. The girl has turned into a little woman. If I am to credit a single analytic instance, this new situation can give rise to physical sensations which would have to be regarded as a premature awakening of the female genital apparatus. When the girl's attachment to her father comes to grief later on and has to be abandoned, it may give place to an identification with him and the girl may thus return to her masculinity complex and perhaps remain fixated in it.

I have now said the essence of what I had to say: I will stop, therefore, and cast an eye over our findings. We have gained some insight into the prehistory of the Oedipus complex in girls. The corresponding period in boys is more or less unknown. In girls the Oedipus complex is a secondary formation. The operations of the castration complex precede it and prepare for it. As regards the relation between the Oedipus and castration complexes there is a fundamental contrast between the two sexes. *Whereas in boys the Oedipus complex is destroyed by the castration complex,*[2] *in girls it is made possible and led up to by the castration complex.* This contradiction is cleared up if we reflect that the castration complex always operates in the sense implied in its subject-matter: it inhibits and limits masculinity and encourages femininity. The difference between the sexual development of males and females at the stage we have been considering

---

[1] [Cf. 'The Dissolution of the Oedipus Complex', p. 179 above.]
[2] [Ibid., p. 177 above.]

is an intelligible consequence of the anatomical distinction between their genitals and of the psychical situation involved in it; it corresponds to the difference between a castration that has been carried out and one that has merely been threatened. In their essentials, therefore, our findings are self-evident and it should have been possible to foresee them.

The Oedipus complex, however, is such an important thing that the manner in which one enters and leaves it cannot be without its effects. In boys (as I have shown at length in the paper to which I have just referred [1924*d*] and to which all of my present remarks are closely related) the complex is not simply repressed, it is literally smashed to pieces by the shock of threatened castration. Its libidinal cathexes are abandoned, desexualized and in part sublimated; its objects are incorporated into the ego, where they form the nucleus of the super-ego and give that new structure its characteristic qualities. In normal, or, it is better to say, in ideal cases, the Oedipus complex exists no longer, even in the unconscious; the super-ego has become its heir. Since the penis (to follow Ferenczi [1924]) owes its extraordinarily high narcissistic cathexis to its organic significance for the propagation of the species, the catastrophe to the Oedipus complex (the abandonment of incest and the institution of conscience and morality) may be regarded as a victory of the race over the individual. This is an interesting point of view when one considers that neurosis is based upon a struggle of the ego against the demands of the sexual function. But to leave the standpoint of individual psychology is not of any immediate help in clarifying this complicated situation.

In girls the motive for the demolition of the Oedipus complex is lacking. Castration has already had its effect, which was to force the child into the situation of the Oedipus complex. Thus the Oedipus complex escapes the fate which it meets with in boys: it may be slowly abandoned or dealt with by repression, or its effects may persist far into women's normal mental life. I cannot evade the notion (though I hesitate to give it expression) that for women the level of what is ethically normal is different from what it is in men. Their super-ego is never so inexorable, so impersonal, so independent of its emotional origins as we require it to be in men. Character-traits which critics of every epoch have brought up against women—that they show less sense of justice than men, that they are less ready to submit to the great exigencies of life, that they are more often influenced in their judgements by feelings of affection or hostility—all these would be amply accounted for by the modification in the formation of their super-ego which we have inferred above. We must not allow ourselves to be deflected from such conclusions by the denials of the feminists, who are anxious to force us to regard the two sexes as completely equal in position and worth; but we shall, of course, willingly agree that the majority of men are also far behind the masculine ideal and that all human individuals, as a result of their bisexual disposition and of cross-inheritance, combine in themselves both masculine and feminine characteristics, so that pure masculinity and femininity remain theoretical constructions of uncertain content.

I am inclined to set some value on the considerations I have brought forward upon the psychical consequences of the anatomical distinction between the sexes. I am aware, however, that this opinion can only be maintained if my findings, which are based on a handful of cases, turn out to have general validity and to be typical. If not, they would remain no more than a contribution to our knowledge of the different paths along which sexual life develops.

In the valuable and comprehensive studies on the masculinity and castration complexes in women by Abraham (1921), Horney (1923) and Helene Deutsch (1925) there is much that touches closely on what I have written but nothing that coincides with it completely, so that here again I feel justified in publishing this paper.

JOSEF POPPER-LYNKEUS AND THE
THEORY OF DREAMS
(1923)

JOSEF POPPER-LYNKEUS UND DIE THEORIE DES TRAUMES

(a) GERMAN EDITIONS:
1923 *Allgemeine Nährpflicht* (Vienna), **6.**
1928 *G.S.*, **11**, 295–7.
1940 *G.W.*, **13**, 357–9.

(b) ENGLISH TRANSLATION:
'Josef Popper-Lynkeus and the Theory of Dreams'

The present translation, by James Strachey, is the first to appear in English.

Josef Popper (1838–1921) was an engineer by profession, but was well known in Austria for his writings (under the pseudonym of 'Lynkeus'), mainly on philosophical and sociological topics. An account of his schemes of social reform will be found in a book by Fritz Wittels, published in English under the title *An End to Poverty* (London, 1925). This also contains a short biography of Popper himself by the translators, Eden and Cedar Paul. The volume of short imaginative sketches, *Phantasien eines Realisten*, which is the subject of Freud's remarks, was highly popular and passed through many editions, the twenty-first having appeared in 1921. Freud's paper was no doubt written on the occasion of its author's death, for publication in a periodical which, as its title shows, called for the universal provision of subsistence and owed its inspiration to Popper. Freud wrote another and longer paper on the same subject some ten years later (1932c).

JOSEF POPPER-LYNKEUS AND THE
THEORY OF DREAMS

THERE is much of interest to be said on the subject of apparent scientific originality. When some new idea comes up in science, which is hailed at first as a discovery and is also as a rule disputed as such, objective research soon afterwards reveals that after all it was in fact no novelty. Usually the discovery has already been made repeatedly and has afterwards been forgotten, often at very long intervals of time. Or at least it has had forerunners, had been obscurely surmised or incompletely enunciated. This is too well known to call for further discussion.

But the subjective side of originality also deserves consideration. A scientific worker may sometimes ask himself what was the source of the ideas peculiar to himself which he has applied to his material. As regards some of them he will discover without much reflection the hints from which they were derived, the statements made by other people which he has picked out and modified and whose implications he has elaborated. But as regards others of his ideas he can make no such acknowledgements; he can only suppose that these thoughts and lines of approach were generated—he cannot tell how—in his own mental activity, and it is on them that he bases his claim to originality.

Careful psychological investigation, however, diminishes this claim still further. It reveals hidden and long-forgotten sources which gave the stimulus to the apparently original ideas, and it replaces the ostensible new creation by a revival of something forgotten applied to fresh material. There is nothing to regret in this; we had no right to expect that what was 'original' could be untraceable and undetermined.

In my case, too, the originality of many of the new ideas employed by me in the interpretation of dreams and in psychoanalysis has evaporated in this way. I am ignorant of the source of only one of these ideas. It was no less than the key to my view of dreams and helped me to solve their riddles, so far as it has been possible to solve them hitherto. I started out from the strange, confused and senseless character of so many dreams, and hit upon the notion that dreams were bound to become like

261

that because something was struggling for expression in them which was opposed by a resistance from other mental forces. In dreams hidden impulses were stirring which stood in contradiction to what might be called the dreamer's official ethical and aesthetic creed; the dreamer was thus ashamed of these impulses, turned away from them and refused to acknowledge them in day-time, and if during the night he could not withhold expression of some kind from them, he submitted them to a 'dream-distortion' which made the content of the dream appear confused and senseless. To the mental force in human beings which keeps watch on this internal contradiction and distorts the dream's primitive instinctual impulses in favour of conventional or of higher moral standards, I gave the name of 'dream-censorship'.

Precisely this essential part of my theory of dreams was, however, discovered by Popper-Lynkeus independently. I will ask the reader to compare the following quotation from a story called 'Träumen wie Wachen' ['Dreaming like Waking'] in his *Phantasien eines Realisten* [*Phantasies of a Realist*][1] which was certainly written in ignorance of the theory of dreams which I published in 1900, just as I myself was then in ignorance of Lynkeus's *Phantasien*:

'About a man who has the remarkable attribute of never dreaming nonsense . . . .

' "This splendid gift of yours, for dreaming as though you were waking, is a consequence of your virtues, of your kindness, your sense of justice, and your love of truth; it is the moral serenity of your nature which makes me understand all about you."

' "But when I think the matter over properly", replied the other, "I almost believe that everyone is made like me, and that no one at all ever dreams nonsense. Any dream which one can remember clearly enough to describe it afterwards—any dream, that is to say, which is not a fever-dream—must *always* make sense, and it cannot possibly be otherwise. For things that were mutually contradictory could not group themselves into a single whole. The fact that time and space are often thrown into confusion does not affect the true content of the dream, since no doubt neither of them are of significance for its real essence. We often do the same thing in waking life. Only think

[1] [First edition, Vienna, 1899.]

of fairy tales and of the many daring products of the imagination, which are full of meaning and of which only a man without intelligence could say: 'This is nonsense, for it is impossible.' "

' "If only one always knew how to interpret dreams in the right way, as you have just done with mine!" said his friend.

' "That is certainly no easy task; but with a little attention on the part of the dreamer himself it should no doubt always succeed.—You ask why it is that for the most part it does *not* succeed? In you other people there seems always to be something that lies concealed in your dreams, something unchaste in a special and higher sense, a certain secret quality in your being which it is hard to follow. And that is why your dreams so often seem to be without meaning or even to be nonsense. But in the deepest sense this is not in the least so; indeed, it cannot be so at all—for it is always the same man, whether he is awake or dreaming." '

I believe that what enabled *me* to discover the cause of dream-distortion was my moral courage. In the case of Popper it was the purity, love of truth and moral serenity of his nature.[1]

---

[1] [These were the epithets applied by Popper himself to the man in his story. Freud returned to the subject in a later paper 'My Contact with Josef Popper-Lynkeus' (1932c), where a further short quotation from the story will be found. Freud first commented on the coincidence between his views and those of Popper in his 'Postscript' added in 1909 to Chapter I of *The Interpretation of Dreams* (1900a), *Standard Ed.*, 4, 94–5, and in a footnote added in 1909 to Chapter VI (B) of the same work (ibid., 308–9), where he quoted the same passage as in the present paper.—The question of the 'originality' of his discoveries was raised by Freud in a passage also added in 1909 to Chapter II of *The Interpretation of Dreams* (1900a), ibid., 102–3, in some passages in the first section of his 'History of the Psycho-Analytic Movement' (1914d), ibid., 14, 13–20, and in 'A Note on the Prehistory of the Technique of Analysis' (1920b), ibid., 18, 263–5.]

DR. SÁNDOR FERENCZI
(ON HIS 50th BIRTHDAY)
(1923)

DR. FERENCZI SÁNDOR
(Zum 50. Geburtstag)

(a) German Editions:
1923 *Int. Z. Psychoanal.*, **9** (3), 257–9.
1928 *G.S.*, **11**, 273–5.
1940 *G.W.*, **13**, 443–5.

(b) English Translation:
'Dr. Sándor Ferenczi (on his 50th Birthday)'

The present translation by James Strachey seems to be the first into English.

This appeared first, over the signature *'Herausgeber und Redaktion* (Director and Editor)', as an introduction to a special issue of the *Zeitschrift* commemorating Ferenczi's fiftieth birthday.

DR. SÁNDOR FERENCZI

(ON HIS 50th BIRTHDAY)

Not many years after its publication (in 1900), *The Interpretation of Dreams* fell into the hands of a young Budapest physician, who, although he was a neurologist, psychiatrist and expert in forensic medicine, was eagerly in search of new scientific knowledge. He did not get far in reading the book; very soon he had thrown it aside—whether out of boredom or disgust is not known. Soon afterwards, however, the call for fresh possibilities of work and discovery took him to Zurich, and thence he was led to Vienna to meet the author of the book that he had once contemptuously cast aside. This first visit was succeeded by a long, intimate and hitherto untroubled friendship, in the course of which he too made the journey to America in 1909 to lecture at Clark University at Worcester, Mass.[1]

Such were the beginnings of Ferenczi, who has since himself become a master and teacher of psycho-analysis and who in the present year, 1923, completes alike the fiftieth anniversary of his birth and the first decade of his leadership of the Budapest Psycho-Analytical Society.

Ferenczi has repeatedly played a part, too, in the external affairs of psycho-analysis. His appearance at the Second Analytical Congress, at Nuremberg in 1910, will be remembered, where he proposed and helped to bring about the foundation of an International Psycho-Analytical Association as a means of defence against the contempt with which analysis was treated by official Medicine. At the Fifth Analytical Congress, at Budapest, in September, 1918, he was elected President of the Association. He appointed Anton von Freund as Secretary; and there is no doubt that the combined energy of the two men, together with Freund's generous schemes of endowment, would have made Budapest the analytic capital of Europe, had not political catastrophes and personal tragedy put a merciless end to these fair hopes. Freund fell ill and died in January, 1920.[2] In view of Hungary's isolation from contact with the rest of the

---

[1] [Cf. *Five Lectures on Psycho-Analysis* (Freud, 1910a).]
[2] [See Freud's obituary of him (1920c).]

world, Ferenczi had resigned his position in October, 1919, and had transferred the Presidency of the International Association to Ernest Jones in London. For the duration of the Soviet Republic in Hungary[1] Ferenczi had been allotted the functions of a University teacher, and his lectures had attracted crowded audiences. The Branch Society, which he had founded in 1913,[2] survived every storm and, under his guidance, became a centre of intense and productive work and was distinguished by an accumulation of abilities such as were exhibited in combination by no other Branch Society. Ferenczi, who, as a middle child in a large family, had to struggle with a powerful brother complex, had, under the influence of analysis, become an irreproachable elder brother, a kindly teacher and promoter of young talent.

Ferenczi's analytic writings have become universally known and appreciated. It was not until 1922 that his *Popular Lectures on Psycho-Analysis* were published by our *Verlag* [publishing house] as Volume XIII of the 'Internationale Psychoanalytische Bibliothek'. These lectures, clear and formally perfect, sometimes most fascinatingly written, offer what is in fact the best 'Introduction to Psycho-Analysis'[3] for those who are unfamiliar with it. There is still no [German] collection of his purely technical [psycho-analytic] medical writings, a number of which have been translated into English by Ernest Jones. The *Verlag* will fulfil this task as soon as more favourable times make it possible.[4] Those of his books and papers which have appeared in Hungarian have passed through many editions and have made analysis familiar to educated circles in Hungary.

Ferenczi's scientific achievement is impressive above all from its many-sidedness. Besides well-chosen case histories and acutely observed clinical communications ('A Little Chanti-

---

[1] [Under Béla Kun, March to August, 1919.]

[2] Its Inaugural General Meeting was held on May 19, 1913, with Ferenczi as President, Dr. Radó as Secretary, and Drs. Hollós, Ignotus and Lévy as members.

[3] [This is an allusion to the German title of Freud's own *Introductory Lectures*, published a few years earlier (1916–17).]

[4] [A complete German edition of Ferenczi's shorter works, *Bausteine zur Psychoanalyse*, was published in four volumes from 1927 to 1939. An equally comprehensive English edition has appeared in three volumes, of which the first, the one mentioned in the text above, was originally published in 1916.]

cleer' [1913a], 'Transitory Symptom-Constructions during the Analysis' [1912a], and shorter clinical works) we find exemplary critical writings such as those upon Jung's *Wandlungen und Symbole der Libido* [1913b], upon Régis and Hesnard's views on psycho-analysis [1915], as well as effective polemical writings such as those against Bleuler on alcohol [1911] and against Putnam on the relation between psycho-analysis and philosophy [1912b], moderate and dignified in spite of their decisiveness. But besides all these there are the papers upon which Ferenczi's fame principally rests, in which his originality, his wealth of ideas and his command over a well-directed scientific imagination find such happy expression, and with which he has enlarged important sections of psycho-analytic theory and has promoted the discovery of fundamental situations in mental life: 'Introjection and Transference', including a discussion of the theory of hypnosis [1909], 'Stages in the Development of the Sense of Reality' [1913c] and his discussion of symbolism [1912c]. Finally there are the works of these last few years—'The Psycho-Analysis of the War Neuroses' [1919b], *Hysterie und Pathoneurosen* [1919c] and, in collaboration with Hollós, *Psycho-Analysis and the Psychic Disorder of General Paresis* [1922] (in which the medical interest advances from the psychological conditions to the somatic determinants), and his approaches to an 'active' therapy.

However incomplete this enumeration may seem to be, his friends know that Ferenczi has held back even more than he has been able to make up his mind to communicate.[1] On his fiftieth birthday they are united in wishing that he may be granted strength, leisure and a frame of mind to bring his scientific plans to realization in fresh achievements.

[1] [Freud returned to this point in his obituary of Ferenczi, written just ten years later (1933c).]

PREFACE TO AICHHORN'S
WAYWARD YOUTH
(1925)

PREFACE TO AICHHORN'S *VERWAHRLOSTE JUGEND*

(*a*) GERMAN EDITIONS:
1925   In August Aichhorn, *Verwahrloste Jugend*, 5–6, Leipzig
        Vienna and Zurich: Internationaler Psychoanalyti-
        scher Verlag. (1931, 2nd ed.)
1928   *G.S.*, 11, 267–9.
1948   *G.W.*, 14, 565–7.

(*b*) ENGLISH TRANSLATIONS:
1935   In Aichhorn, *Wayward Youth*, v–vii, New York: Viking
        Press. (Reprinted 1936, London: Putnam.) (Tr.
        unspecified.)
1950   *C.P.*, 5, 98–100. (Under the title 'Psycho-Analysis and
        Delinquency'.) (Tr. James Strachey.)
1951   In Aichhorn, *Wayward Youth*, vii–ix, London: Imago
        Publishing Co. (Revised reprint of 1935 edition, but
        with Freud's Preface tr. James Strachey.)

The present translation is a very slightly corrected version
of the one first published in 1950.

A biographical study of August Aichhorn (1878–1949), by
Dr. K. R. Eissler, appears in the 1951 edition of the English
translation of *Wayward Youth*. Aichhorn's book was first
published in July, 1925. Freud made a further short reference
to it in a footnote to Chapter VII of *Civilization and its Discontents* (1930*a*).
A fuller discussion of the relations between psycho-analysis
and education was given by Freud in a long passage in the
middle of Lecture XXXIV of his *New Introductory Lectures*
(1933*a*).

PREFACE TO AICHHORN'S *WAYWARD YOUTH*

NONE of the applications of psycho-analysis has excited so much interest and aroused so many hopes, and none, consequently, has attracted so many capable workers, as its use in the theory and practice of education. It is easy to understand why; for children have become the main subject of psycho-analytic research and have thus replaced in importance the neurotics on whom its studies began. Analysis has shown how the child lives on, almost unchanged, in the sick man as well as in the dreamer and the artist; it has thrown light on the motive forces and trends which set its characteristic stamp upon the childish nature; and it has traced the stages through which a child grows to maturity. No wonder, therefore, if an expectation has arisen that psycho-analytic concern with children will benefit the work of education, whose aim it is to guide and assist children on their forward path and to shield them from going astray.

My personal share in this application of psycho-analysis has been very slight. At an early stage I had accepted the *bon mot* which lays it down that there are three impossible professions—educating, healing and governing—and I was already fully occupied with the second of them. But this does not mean that I overlook the high social value of the work done by those of my friends who are engaged in education.

The present volume by August Aichhorn is concerned with one department of the great problem—with the educational influencing of juvenile delinquents. The author had worked for many years in an official capacity as a director of municipal institutions for delinquents before he became acquainted with psycho-analysis. His attitude to his charges sprang from a warm sympathy with the fate of those unfortunates and was correctly guided by an intuitive perception of their mental needs. Psycho-analysis could teach him little that was new of a practical kind, but it brought him a clear theoretical insight into the justification of his way of acting and put him in a position to explain its basis to other people.

It must not be assumed that this gift of intuitive understanding will be found in everyone concerned with the bringing-up of children. Two lessons may be derived, it seems to me, from the experience and the success of August Aichhorn. One is that every such person should receive a psycho-analytic training, since without it children, the object of his endeavours, must remain an inaccessible problem to him. A training of this kind is best carried out if such a person himself undergoes an analysis and experiences it on himself: theoretical instruction in analysis fails to penetrate deep enough and carries no conviction.

The second lesson has a somewhat conservative ring. It is to the effect that the work of education is something *sui generis*: it is not to be confused with psycho-analytic influence and cannot be replaced by it. Psycho-analysis can be called in by education as an auxiliary means of dealing with a child; but it is not a suitable substitute for education. Not only is such a substitution impossible on practical grounds but it is also to be disrecommended for theoretical reasons. The relation between education and psycho-analytic treatment will probably before long be the subject of a detailed investigation. Here I will only give a few hints. One should not be misled by the statement— incidentally a perfectly true one—that the psycho-analysis of an adult neurotic is equivalent to an after-education.[1] A child, even a wayward and delinquent child, is still not a neurotic; and after-education is something quite different from the education of the immature. The possibility of analytic influence rests on quite definite preconditions which can be summed up under the term 'analytic situation'; it requires the development of certain psychical structures and a particular attitude to the analyst. Where these are lacking—as in the case of children, of juvenile delinquents, and, as a rule, of impulsive criminals— something other than analysis must be employed, though something which will be at one with analysis in its *purpose*. The theoretical chapters of the present volume will give the reader a preliminary grasp of the multiplicity of the decisions involved.

I will end with a further inference, and this time one which is important not for the theory of education but for the status of those who are engaged in education. If one of these has learnt

---

[1] [Freud had used this comparison as early as in his lecture 'On Psychotherapy' (1905*a* [1904]), *Standard Ed.*, 7, 267, where the word '*Nacherziehung*' is inaccurately translated 're-education' instead of 'after-education'. See also a passage towards the beginning of Lecture XXVIII of the *Introductory Lectures* (1916–17).]

analysis by experiencing it on his own person and is in a position of being able to employ it in borderline and mixed cases to assist him in his work, he should obviously be given the right to practise analysis, and narrow-minded motives should not be allowed to try to put obstacles in his way.

JOSEF BREUER
(1925)

JOSEF BREUER

(*a*) GERMAN EDITIONS:
1925 *Int. Z. Psychoanal.*, **11** (2), 255–6.
1928 *G.S.*, **11**, 281–3.
1948 *G.W.*, **14**, 562–3.

(*b*) ENGLISH TRANSLATION:
1925 *Int. J. Psycho-Anal.*, **6** (4), 459–60. (Tr. unnamed.)

The present translation is a new one by James Strachey.

The last dozen lines of this obituary were quoted at the end of the Editor's Introduction to *Studies on Hysteria* (1895*d*), *Standard Ed.*, **2**, xxviii, where a discussion will also be found of the scientific relations between the two collaborators.

JOSEF BREUER

ON June 20, 1925, there died in Vienna, in his eighty-fourth year, Josef Breuer, the creator of the cathartic method, whose name is for that reason indissolubly linked with the beginnings of psycho-analysis.

Breuer was a physician, a pupil of the clinician Oppolzer. In his youth he had worked at the physiology of respiration under Ewald Hering, and later, in the scanty hours of leisure allowed by an extensive medical practice, he occupied himself successfully with experiments on the function of the vestibular apparatus in animals. Nothing in his education could lead one to expect that he would gain the first decisive insight into the age-old riddle of the hysterical neurosis and would make a contribution of imperishable value to our knowledge of the human mind. But he was a man of rich and universal gifts, and his interests extended in many directions far beyond his professional activities.

It was in 1880[1] that chance brought into his hands an unusual patient, a girl of more than ordinary intelligence who had fallen ill of severe hysteria while she was nursing her sick father. It was only some fourteen years later, in our joint publication, *Studies on Hysteria* (1895*d*)—and even then unluckily only in a much abbreviated form, censored, too, from considerations of medical discretion—that the world learnt the nature of his treatment of this celebrated 'first case', with what immense care and patience he carried out the technique when once he had discovered it, till the patient was freed from all the incomprehensible symptoms of her illness, and what insight he obtained in the course of the work into the mental mechanisms of the neurosis.

We psycho-analysts, who have long been familiar with the idea of devoting hundreds of sessions to a single patient, can form no conception of how novel such a procedure must have seemed forty-five years ago. It must have called for a large amount of personal interest and, if the phrase can be allowed, of medical libido, but also for a considerable degree of freedom of thought and certainty of judgement. At the date of the

¹ [Breuer was born in 1842.]

publication of our *Studies* we were able to appeal to Charcot's writings and to Pierre Janet's investigations, which had by that time deprived Breuer's discoveries of some of their priority. But when Breuer was treating his first case (in 1881–2) none of this was as yet available. Janet's *Automatisme psychologique* appeared in 1889 and his second work, *L'état mental des hystériques*, not until 1892. It seems that Breuer's researches were wholly original, and were directed only by the hints offered to him by the material of his case.

I have repeatedly attempted—most recently in my *Autobiographical Study* (1925d), in Grote's series, *Die Medizin der Gegenwart* [*Contemporary Medicine*]—to define my share in the *Studies* which we published jointly. My merit lay chiefly in reviving in Breuer an interest which seemed to have become extinct, and in then urging him on to publication. A kind of reserve which was characteristic of him, an inner modesty, surprising in a man of such a brilliant personality, had led him to keep his astonishing discovery secret for so long that not all of it was any longer new. I found reason later to suppose that a purely emotional factor, too, had given him an aversion to further work on the elucidation of the neuroses. He had come up against something that is never absent—his patient's transference on to her physician, and he had not grasped the impersonal nature of the process. At the time when he submitted to my influence and was preparing the *Studies* for publication, his judgement of their significance seemed to be confirmed. 'I believe', he told me, 'that this is the most important thing we two have to give the world.'

Besides the case history of his first patient Breuer contributed a theoretical paper to the *Studies*. It is very far from being out of date; on the contrary, it conceals thoughts and suggestions which have even now not been turned to sufficient account. Anyone immersing himself in this speculative essay will form a true impression of the mental build of this man, whose scientific interests were, alas, turned in the direction of our psychopathology during only one short episode of his long life.

SHORTER WRITINGS
(1922–25)

PREFACE TO RAYMOND DE SAUSSURE'S
THE PSYCHO-ANALYTIC METHOD [1]
(1922)

IT is with great pleasure that I am able to assure the public that the present work by Dr. de Saussure is a book of value and merit. It is especially well calculated to give French readers a correct idea of what psycho-analysis is and what it contains.

Dr. de Saussure has not only conscientiously studied my writings, but in addition he has made the sacrifice of coming to me to undergo an analysis lasting several months. This has put him in a position to form his own judgement on the majority of those questions in psycho-analysis which are still undecided, and to avoid the many distortions and errors which one is accustomed to finding in French as well as in German exposi-tions of psycho-analysis. Nor has he failed to contradict certain false or negligent statements which commentators pass on from one to another: such as, for instance, that all dreams have a sexual meaning or that, according to me, the only motive force in our mental life is that of sexual libido.

Since Dr. de Saussure has said in his preface that I have corrected his work, I must add a qualification; my influence has only made itself felt in a few corrections and comments and I have in no way sought to encroach upon the author's independence. In the first, theoretical part of this work, I should have expounded a number of things differently from him: for instance, the difficult topic of the preconscious and the un-conscious. And above all, I should have treated the Oedipus complex far more exhaustively.

---

[1] [Published (in French) in R. de Saussure's *La méthode psychanalytique* Lausanne and Geneva, 1922, vii–viii. The German text has not been published and the French version seems never to have been reprinted. The work does not appear in either *G.S.* or *G.W.*; it should have been included in Volume XVIII of the *Standard Edition*, but did not come to light until that volume was in print. Through the kindness of Dr. de Saussure, we have seen the original German autograph, and it is upon this that our translation is based. Thus it differs slightly at two or three points from the French version. The present translation, the first into English, is by Angela Richards.]

The excellent dream which Dr. Odier has put at the author's disposal may give even the uninitiated an idea of the wealth of dream-associations and of the relation between the manifest dream-image and the latent thoughts concealed behind it. It demonstrates too the significance that the analysis of a dream can have in the treatment of a patient.

Finally, the remarks which the author makes in conclusion on the technique of psycho-analysis are quite excellent. They are entirely correct and, in spite of their conciseness, leave aside nothing essential. They are convincing evidence of the author's subtle understanding. The reader should not, of course, conclude that knowledge of these rules of technique alone will make him capable of undertaking an analysis.

To-day psycho-analysis is beginning to arouse in a larger measure the interest of professional men and of the lay public in France as well; it will certainly not find any fewer resistances there than it has encountered previously in other countries. Let us hope that Dr. de Saussure's book will make an important contribution to the clarification of the discussions that lie ahead.

FREUD

VIENNA, *February* 1922

PREFACE TO MAX EITINGON'S *REPORT ON THE BERLIN PSYCHO-ANALYTICAL POLICLINIC* (*MARCH 1920 to JUNE 1922*)[1]

(1923)

MY friend Max Eitingon, who created the Berlin Psycho-Analytical Policlinic and has hitherto supported it out of his own resources, has in the following pages made public his reasons for founding it and has also given an account of the Institute's organization and functions. I can only add to what he has written my wish that individuals or societies may be found elsewhere to follow Eitingon's example and bring similar institutions into existence. If psycho-analysis, alongside of its scientific significance, has a value as a therapeutic procedure, if it is capable of giving help to sufferers in their struggle to fulfil the demands of civilization, this help should be accessible as well to the great multitude who are too poor themselves to repay an analyst for his laborious work. This seems to be a social necessity particularly in our times, when the intellectual strata of the population, which are especially prone to neurosis, are sinking irresistibly into poverty.[2] Institutes such as the Berlin Policlinic are also alone in a position to overcome the difficulties which otherwise stand in the way of thorough instruction in psycho-analysis. They make possible the education of a considerable number of trained analysts, whose activity must be regarded as the sole possible protection against injury to patients by ignorant and unqualified persons, whether they are laymen or doctors.

---

[1] [First published in Max Eitingon's *Bericht über die Berliner psychoanalytische Poliklinik* (*März 1920 bis Juni 1922*), Leipzig, Vienna and Zurich, 1923, 3; reprinted *G.S.*, **11** (1928), 265 and *G.W.*, **13** (1940), 441. The present translation, the first into English, is by James Strachey. Some years later Freud wrote a preface to another pamphlet on the same subject (1930*b*).]

[2] [Freud had discussed this question at greater length in his paper at the Budapest Psycho-Analytical Congress (1919*a*), *Standard Ed.*, **17**, 166–8.]

LETTER TO FRITZ WITTELS[1]

(1924 [1923])

You have given me a Christmas present which is very largely occupied with my own personality. The failure to send a word of thanks for such a gift would be an act of rudeness only to be accounted for by very peculiar motives. Fortunately no such motives exist in this case. Your book is by no means hostile; it is not unduly indiscreet; and it manifests the serious interest in the topic which was to be anticipated in so able a writer as yourself.

I need hardly say that I neither expected nor desired the publication of such a book. It seems to me that the public has no concern with my personality, and can learn nothing from an account of it, so long as my case (for manifold reasons) cannot be expounded without any reserves whatever. But you have thought otherwise. Your own detachment from me, which you consider an advantage, entails serious drawbacks none the less. You know too little of the object of study, and you have not been able to avoid the danger of straining the facts a little in your analytic endeavours. Moreover, I am inclined to think that your adoption of Stekel's standpoint, and the fact that you

---

[1] [Fritz Wittels (1880–1950) was one of the earliest members of the Vienna Psycho-Analytical Society, but left it on some unspecified personal grounds in 1910. In 1924 he published a biography of Freud and sent him an advance copy of the work at the end of 1923. Freud acknowledged it in a letter dated December 18, 1923. Later on, in 1924, an English translation of the book, by Eden and Cedar Paul, was published: *Sigmund Freud, his Personality, his Teaching and his School* (London: Allen and Unwin; New York: Dodd, Mead). This was prefaced 'with Freud's express authorization' by a translation of extracts from his letter to Wittels. We have had access to the original German text of the letter, which never seems to have been published, and the version given here, a reprint (with two or three very small changes) of the one printed in 1924, is substantially correct. No doubt it was made by the translators of Wittels's book itself. The short omitted passage contains a further reference to Stekel and a remark about Freud's own illness. It may be added that Wittels was re-elected to the Vienna Psycho-Analytical Society in 1927. The letter appears here by arrangement with Messrs. George Allen and Unwin.]

contemplate the object of study from his outlook, cannot but have impaired the accuracy of your discernment.

In some respects, I think there are positive distortions, and I believe these to be the outcome of a preconceived notion of yours. You think that a great man must have such and such merits and defects, and must display certain extreme characteristics; and you hold that I belong to the category of great men. That is why you ascribe to me all sorts of qualities many of which are mutually conflicting. Much of general interest might be said on this matter, but unfortunately your relationship to Stekel precludes further attempts on my part to clear up the misunderstanding.

On the other hand, I am glad to acknowledge that your shrewdness has enabled you to detect some things which are well known to myself. For instance, you are right in inferring that I have often been compelled to make détours when following my own path. You are right, too, in thinking that I have no use for other people's ideas when they are presented to me at an inopportune moment. (Still, as regards the latter point, I think you might have defended me from the accusation that I am repudiating ideas when I am merely unable for the time being to pass judgement on them or to elaborate them.) But I am delighted to find that you do me full justice in the matter of my relations with Adler. . . .

I realize that you may have occasion to revise your text in view of a second edition. With an eye to this possibility, I enclose a list of suggested emendations.[1] These are based on trustworthy

[1] [A number of these are stated to have been adopted in the English translation. One such correction of Freud's is quoted in full (on pp. 251-2 of the translation). Wittels had suggested that Freud's hypothesis of the 'death instinct' in *Beyond the Pleasure Principle* (1920g) occurred to him as the result of the death of his daughter. But Freud wrote: 'That seems to me most interesting, and I regard it as a warning. Beyond question, if I had myself been analysing another person in such circumstances, I should have presumed the existence of a connection between my daughter's death and the train of thought presented in *Beyond the Pleasure Principle*. But the inference that such a sequence exists would have been false. The book was written in 1919, when my daughter was still in excellent health. She died in January, 1920. In September, 1919, I had sent the manuscript of the little book to be read by some friends in Berlin [Eitingon and Abraham]. It was finished, except for the discussion concerning the mortality or immortality of the protozoa. What seems true is not always the truth.']

data, and are quite independent of my own prepossessions. Some of them relate to matters of trifling importance, but some of them will perhaps lead you to reverse or modify certain inferences. The fact that I send you these corrections is a token that I value your work though I cannot wholly approve it.

LETTER TO SEÑOR LUIS LOPEZ-
BALLESTEROS Y DE TORRES[1]
(1923)

WHEN I was a young student, the desire to read the immortal *Don Quixote* in the original of Cervantes led me to learn, untaught, the lovely Castilian tongue. Thanks to this youthful enthusiasm, I am able to-day—at an advanced age—to test the accuracy of your Spanish version of my works, the reading of which invariably provokes in me a lively appreciation of your very correct interpretation of my thoughts and of the elegance of your style. I am above all astonished that one who, like you, is neither a doctor nor a psychiatrist by profession should have been able to obtain so absolute and precise a mastery over material which is intricate and at times obscure.

---

[1] [This letter, dated May 7, 1923, was addressed by Freud to the Spanish translator of his works. It was printed in Spanish in Volume IV of *Obras Completas del Professor S. Freud*, Madrid, 1923, 7. Reprinted *G.S.*, 11 (1928), 266 and *G.W.*, 13 (1940), 442. No German text is extant, and it is not impossible that Freud wrote it himself in Spanish, of which he had a good knowledge (cf. Jones, 1953, 180). The present translation, the first into English, is by James Strachey.]

LETTER TO *LE DISQUE VERT*[1]
(1924)

OF the many lessons lavished upon me in the past (1885–6) by the great Charcot at the Salpêtrière,[2] two left me with a deep impression: that one should never tire of considering the same phenomena again and again (or of submitting to their effects), and that one should not mind meeting with contradiction on every side provided one has worked sincerely.

FREUD

[1] In *Le Disque Vert*, 2 (3rd Series) (June), 3. This periodical, issued in Paris and Brussels by Franz Hellens (a pseudonym for Frédéric van Ermengem), published in 1924 a special number with the title 'Freud et la Psychanalyse'. It contained more than 200 pages and contributions of varying length by 36 authors. It was introduced by a short letter from Freud in French dated 'Vienna, February 26, 1924'. A detailed account of the contents of the special number will be found in *Int. Z. Psychoanal.*, **10** (1924), 206–8, where the text of Freud's letter is also printed. It was reprinted *G.S.*, **11** (1928), 266 and *G.W.*, **13** (1940), 446. No German text is extant, and the original was perhaps written in French. The present translation, the first into English, is by James Strachey.]

[2] [Cf. Freud's obituary of him (1893*f*).]

LETTER TO THE EDITOR OF THE
JEWISH PRESS CENTRE IN ZURICH[1]
(1925)

... I CAN say that I stand as far apart from the Jewish religion as from all other religions: that is to say, they are of great significance to me as a subject of scientific interest, but I have no part in them emotionally. On the other hand I have always had a strong feeling of solidarity with my fellow-people, and have always encouraged it in my children as well. We have all remained in the Jewish denomination.

In the time of my youth our free-thinking religious instructors set no store by their pupils' acquiring a knowledge of the Hebrew language and literature. My education in this field was therefore extremely behindhand, as I have since often regretted.

[1] [This was first published in the *Jüdische Presszentrale Zürich* on February 26, 1925. Reprinted *G.S.*, 11 (1928), 298 and *G.W.*, 14 (1948), 556. There is no explanation of the apparent omission at the beginning. The present translation, the first into English, is by James Strachey.]

ON THE OCCASION OF THE OPENING
OF THE HEBREW UNIVERSITY[1]
(1925)

HISTORIANS have told us that our small nation withstood the destruction of its independence as a State only because it began to transfer in its estimation of values the highest rank to its spiritual possessions, to its religion and its literature.

We are now living in a time when this people has a prospect of again winning the land of its fathers with the help of a Power that dominates the world, and it celebrates the occasion by the foundation of a University in its ancient capital city.

A University is a place in which knowledge is taught above all differences of religions and of nations, where investigation is carried on, which is to show mankind how far they understand the world around them and how far they can control it.

Such an undertaking is a noble witness to the development to which our people has forced its way in two thousand years of unhappy fortune.

I find it painful that my ill-health prevents me from being present at the opening festivities of the Jewish University in Jerusalem.

[1] [This was originally published, along with similar messages from other well-known people, in the fortnightly periodical *The New Judaea*, 1 (14), 227, on March 27, 1925. Reprinted *G.S.*, 11 (1928), 298–9, and *G.W.*, 14 (1948), 556–7. No German text is extant, and the original English is therefore reprinted here without alteration, except for a change in the title, which in the earlier versions read 'To the Opening of the Hebrew University'.—The University was inaugurated by Lord Balfour in April, 1925.]

EDITORIAL CHANGES IN THE
ZEITSCHRIFT [1]
(1924)

DR. OTTO RANK has acted as editor of this journal ever since its foundation in 1913, even though it is only since 1920 that he has been named on its title-page as sole editor. During his period of military service in the War, his place was taken by Dr. Hanns Sachs, who was at that time in Vienna. Since the beginning of the current volume Dr. S. Ferenczi has also had a share in the editing.

At Easter, 1924, Dr. Rank accepted an invitation which took him to New York. On his return home he announced that he had decided to transfer his activity as a teaching and practising analyst to America—at least for a part of the year. Thus it became necessary to place the editorship of the *Zeitschrift* in other hands. It is not within the rights of the Director to give public expression to his opinion of the level and achievements of this journal. No one who is inclined to appreciate them should overlook or forget how much of its success is due to the tireless devotion and exemplary work of the retiring editor.

Dr. Rank's place will now be taken by Dr. S. Radó of Berlin. He will be supported as advisers and collaborators by Dr. M. Eitingon (Berlin) and Dr. S. Ferenczi (Budapest). All communications and contributions for the editor should be addressed to Dr. Sándor Radó, Berlin-Schöneberg, Am Park, 20. The business side of the *Zeitschrift* will be conducted as before at the offices of the Internationaler Psychoanalytischer Verlag in Vienna (Manager: A. J. Storfer).

---

[1] ['Mitteilung des Herausgebers' ('Announcement by the Director'), *Int. Z. Psychoanal.*, **10** (1924), 373. This has never been reprinted. The present translation, the first into English, is by James Strachey.]

BIBLIOGRAPHY
AND AUTHOR INDEX

[Titles of books and periodicals are in italics; titles of papers are in inverted commas. Abbreviations are in accordance with the *World List of Scientific Periodicals* (London, 1952). Further abbreviations used in this volume will be found in the List at the end of this bibliography. Numerals in thick type refer to volumes; ordinary numerals refer to pages. The figures in round brackets at the end of each entry indicate the page or pages of this volume on which the work in question is mentioned. In the case of the Freud entries, the letters attached to the dates of publication are in accordance with the corresponding entries in the complete bibliography of Freud's writings to be included in the last volume of the *Standard Edition*.

For non-technical authors, and for technical authors where no specific work is mentioned, see the General Index.]

ABEL, K. (1884) *Über den Gegensinn der Urworte*, Leipzig. (206)

ABRAHAM, K. (1921) 'Aüsserungsformen des weiblichen Kastrationskomplezes', *Int. Z. Psychoan.*, 7, 422. (258)
  [*Trans.:* 'Manifestations of the Female Castration Complex', *Selected Papers on Psycho-Analysis*, London, 1927, Chap. XXII.]

AICHHORN, A. (1925) *Verwahrloste Jugend*, Vienna. (272-5)
  [*Trans.: Wayward Youth*, New York, 1935; London, 1936; revised reprint, London, 1951.]

ALEXANDER, F. (1922) 'Kastrationskomplex und Charakter', *Int. Z. Psychoan.*, 8, 121. (175)
  [*Trans.:* 'The Castration Complex in the Formation of Character', *Int. J. Psycho-Anal.*, 4 (1923), 11.]

ANDREAS-SALOMÉ, L. (1916) ' "Anal" und "Sexual" ', *Imago*, 4, 249. (175)

BLEULER, E. (1906) 'Freudsche Mechanismen in der Symptomatologie von Psychosen', *Psychiat.-neurol. Wschr.*, 8, 323, 338. (204)
  (1911) *Dementia Praecox, oder Gruppe der Schizophrenien*, Leipzig and Vienna. (204)
  [*Trans.: Dementia Praecox, or the Group of Schizophrenias*, New York, 1950.]

DEUTSCH, H. (1925) *Psychoanalyse der weiblichen Sexualfunktionen*, Vienna. (258)

EITINGON, M. (1923) *Bericht über die Berliner psychoanalytische Poliklinik (März 1920 bis Juni 1922)*, Leipzig, Vienna, Zurich. (285)

ELLIS, HAVELOCK (1911) 'Die Lehren der Freud-Schule', *Zbl. Psychoan.*, 2, 61. (201)

ERB, W. (1882) *Handbuch der Elektrotherapie*, Leipzig. (192)
  [*Trans.: Handbook of Electro-Therapeutics*, London, 1883.]

295

FERENCZI, S. (1909) 'Introjektion und Übertragung', *Jb. psychoan. psychopath. Forsch.*, 1, 422. (269)
[*Trans.:* 'Introjection and Transference', *First Contributions to Psycho-Analysis*, London, 1952, Chap. II.]
(1911) 'Alkohol und Neurosen. Antwort auf die Kritik von Prof. Eugen Bleuler', *Jb. psychoan. psychopath. Forsch.*, 3, 853. (269)
(1912a) 'Über passagère Symptombildung während der Analyse', *Zbl. Psychoan.*, 2, 588. (269)
[*Trans.:* 'Transitory Symptom-Constructions during the Analysis', *First Contributions to Psycho-Analysis*, London, 1952, Chap. VII.]
(1912b) 'Philosophie und Psychoanalyse. Bemerkungen zu einem Aufsatz des Herrn Prof. James J. Putnam', *Imago*, 1, 519. (269)
[*Trans.:* 'Philosophy and Psycho-Analysis (Comments on a paper by Professor J. J. Putnam of Harvard University)', *Final Contributions to the Problems and Methods of Psycho-Analysis*, London and New York, 1955, Chap. XXXV.]
(1912c) 'Symbolische Darstellung des Lust- und Realitätsprinzips im Ödipus-Mythos', *Imago*, 1, 276. (269)
[*Trans.:* 'The Symbolic Representation of the Pleasure and Reality Principles in the Oedipus Myth', *First Contributions to Psycho-Analysis*, London, 1952, Chap. X.]
(1913a) 'Ein kleiner Hahnemann', *Int. Z. (ärztl.) Psychoanal.*, 1, 240. (268-9)
[*Trans.:* 'A Little Chanticleer', *First Contributions to Psycho-Analysis*, London, 1952, Chap. IX.]
(1913b) Review of C. G. Jung's *Wandlungen und Symbole der Libido* (Leipzig and Vienna, 1912), *Int. Z. (ärztl.) Psychoanal.*, 1, 391. (269)
(1913c) 'Entwicklungsstufen des Wirklichkeitssinnes', *Int. Z. (ärztl.) Psychoanal.*, 1, 124. (35, 269)
[*Trans.:* 'Stages in the Development of the Sense of Reality', *First Contributions to Psycho-Analysis*, London, 1952, Chap. VIII.]
(1915) 'Die psychiatrische Schule von Bordeaux über die Psychoanalyse', *Int. Z. (ärztl.) Psychoanal.*, 3, 352. (269)
(1919a) Contribution to a Symposium published as *Zur Psychoanalyse der Kriegsneurosen*, Leipzig and Vienna. (269)
[*Trans.:* In *Psycho-Analysis and the War Neuroses*, London, Vienna and New York, 1921.]
(1919b) *Hysterie und Pathoneurosen*, Leipzig and Vienna. (Includes 'Hysterische Materializationsphänomene'.) (185, 269)
[*Trans.:* In *Further Contributions to the Theory and Technique of Psycho-Analysis*, London, 1926, Chaps. V, VI, IX, X, XI, XV.]
(1922) *Populäre Vorträge über Psychoanalyse*, Vienna. (268)
(1923) 'Zur Symbolik des Medusenhauptes', *Int. Z. Psychoan.*, 9, 69. (144)
[*Trans.:* 'On the Symbolism of the Head of Medusa', *Further Contributions to the Theory and Technique of Psycho-Analysis*, London, 1926, Chap. LXVI.]

(1924) *Versuch einer Genitaltheorie*, Vienna. (257)
[*Trans.: Thalassa, a Theory of Genitality*, New York, 1938.]
(1927–39) *Bausteine zur Psychoanalyse* (4 vols.), Vienna. (268)
FERENCZI, S., and HOLLÓS, S. (1922) *Zur Psychoanalyse der paralytischen Geistesstörung*, Vienna. (148, 269)
[*Trans.: Psycho-Analysis and the Psychic Disorder of General Paresis*, New York and Washington, 1925.]
FREUD, S. (1886f) Translation with Preface and Footnotes of J.-M. Charcot's *Leçons sur les maladies du systéme nerveux*, 3, Paris, 1887, under the title *Neue Vorlesungen über die Krankheiten des Nervensystems insbesondere über Hysterie*, Vienna. (69)
[*Trans.:* Preface and Footnotes to Charcot's *Neue Vorlesungen über die Krankheiten des Nervensystems insbesondere über Hysterie*, *Standard Ed.*, 1.]
(1891b) *Zur Auffassung der Aphasien*, Vienna. (20–1)
[*Trans.: On Aphasia*, London and New York, 1953.]
(1892–93a) Translation with Preface and Footnotes of J.-M. Charcot's *Leçons du mardi (1887–8)*, Paris, 1888, under the title *Poliklinische Vorträge*, 1, Vienna. (70)
[*Trans.:* Preface and Footnotes to Charcot's *Poliklinische Vorträge*, 1, *Standard Ed.*, 1.]
(1893f) 'Charcot', *G.S.*, 1, 243; *G.W.*, 1, 21. (70, 290)
[*Trans.:* 'Charcot', *C.P.*, 1, 9; *Standard Ed.*, 3.]
(1894a) 'Die Abwehr-Neuropsychosen', *G.S.*, 1, 290; *G.W.*, 1, 59. (27, 57, 148)
[*Trans.:* 'The Neuro-Psychoses of Defence', *C.P.*, 1, 59; *Standard Ed.*, 3.]
(1895d) With BREUER, J., *Studien über Hysterie*, Vienna. *G.S.*, 1, 3; *G.W.*, 1, 77 (omitting Breuer's contributions). (5, 20, 184, 193–4, 228, 236, 278, 279–80)
[*Trans.: Studies on Hysteria, Standard Ed.*, 2. Including Breuer's contributions.]
(1896b) 'Weitere Bemerkungen über die Abwehr-Neuropsychosen', *G.S.*, 1, 363; *G.W.*, 1, 379. (6, 18, 184, 204)
[*Trans.:* 'Further Remarks on, the Neuro-Psychoses of Defence', *C.P.*, 1, 155; *Standard Ed.*, 3.]
(1900a) *Die Traumdeutung*, Vienna. *G.S.*, 2–3; *G.W.*, 2–3. (4–5, 24, 25, 26, 89, 109, 111, 112, 114, 118–19, 120, 125–6, 127, 129, 130, 131–2, 135, 136, 165, 191, 199–200, 228, 238, 244, 248–9, 262–3, 267)
[*Trans.: The Interpretation of Dreams*, London and New York, 1955; *Standard Ed.*, 4–5.]
(1901b) *Zur Psychopathologie des Alltagslebens*, Berlin, 1904. *G.S.*, 4, 3; *G.W.*, 4. (98, 127, 136, 199)
[*Trans.: The Psychopathology of Everyday Life, Standard Ed.*, 6.]
(1905a) 'Über Psychotherapie', *G.S.*, 6, 11; *G.W.*, 5, 13. (274)
[*Trans.:* 'On Psychotherapy', *C.P.*, 1, 249; *Standard Ed.*, 7, 257.]
(1905c) *Der Witz und seine Beziehung zum Unbewussten*, Vienna. *G.S.*, 9, 5; *G.W.*, 6. (45, 236, 239)

[*Trans.*: *Jokes and their Relation to the Unconscious*, Standard Ed., **8.**]

(1905*d*) *Drei Abhandlungen zur Sexualtheorie*, Vienna. *G.S.*, **5**, 3; *G.W.*, **5**, 29. (33, 47, 63, 140, 141–2, 145, 157, 163, 165, 175, 197, 223, 238, 243, 246, 251, 253, 255)
[*Trans.*: *Three Essays on the Theory of Sexuality*, London, 1949; Standard Ed., **7**, 125.]

(1905*e* [1901]) 'Bruchstück einer Hysterie-Analyse', *G.S.*, **8**, 3; *G.W.*, **5**, 163. (165, 175, 234, 239, 248–9)
[*Trans.*: 'Fragment of an Analysis of a Case of Hysteria', *C.P.*, **3**, 13; Standard Ed., **7**, 3.]

(1907*b*) 'Zwangshandlungen und Religionsübung', *G.S.*, **10**, 210; *G.W.*, **7**, 129. (9, 27, 206)
[*Trans.*: 'Obsessive Actions and Religious Practices', *C.P.*, **2**, 25; Standard Ed., **9**, 116.]

(1907*c*) 'Zur sexuellen Aufklärung der Kinder', *G.S.*, **5**, 134; *G.W.*, **7**, 19. (253)
[*Trans.*: 'The Sexual Enlightenment of Children', *C.P.*, **2**, 36; Standard Ed., **9**, 131.]

(1907*d*) Antwort auf eine Rundfrage *Vom Lesen und von guten Büchern*, Vienna. (168)
[*Trans.*: Contribution to a Questionnaire on Reading, *Int. J. Psycho-Anal.*, **32**, 319; Standard Ed., **9**, 245.]

(1908*b*) 'Charakter und Analerotik', *G.S.*, **5**, 261; *G.W.*, **7**, 203. 29, 70, 119)
[*Trans.*: 'Character and Anal Erotism', *C.P.*, **2**, 45; Standard Ed., **9**, 169.]

(1908*c*) 'Über infantile Sexualtheorien', *G.S.*, **5**, 168; *G.W.*, **7**, 171. (140, 243–4, 246, 252)
[*Trans.*: 'On the Sexual Theories of Children', *C.P.*, **2**, 59; Standard Ed., **9**, 207.]

(1909*b*) 'Analyse der Phobie eines fünfjährigen Knaben', *G.S.*, **8**, 129; *G.W.*, **7**, 243. (88, 142, 144, 175, 252–3)
[*Trans.*: 'Analysis of a Phobia in a Five-Year-Old Boy', *C.P.*, **3**, 149; Standard Ed., **10**, 3.]

(1909*d*) 'Bemerkungen über einen Fall von Zwangsneurose', *G.S.*, **8**, 269; *G.W.*, **7**, 381. (235)
[*Trans.*: 'Notes upon a Case of Obsessional Neurosis', *C.P.*, **3**, 293; Standard Ed., **10**, 155.]

(1910*a* [1909]) *Über Psychoanalyse*, Vienna. *G.S.*, **4**, 349; *G.W.*, **8**, 3. (267)
[*Trans.*: 'Five Lectures on Psycho-Analysis', *Amer. J. Psychol.*, **21** (1910), 181; Standard Ed., **11**, 3.]

(1910*c*) *Eine Kindheitserinnerung des Leonardo da Vinci*, Vienna. *G.S.*, **9**, 371; *G.W.*, **8**, 128. (8, 10, 91, 168)
[*Trans.*: *Leonardo da Vinci and a Memory of His Childhood*, Standard Ed., **11**, 59.]

(1910*e*) ' "Über den Gegensinn der Urworte" ', *G.S.*, **10**, 221; *G.W.*, **8**, 214. (206)

[*Trans.:* ' "The Antithetical Meaning of Primal Words" ', *C.P.*, **4**, 184; *Standard Ed.*, **11**, 155.]

(1910*i*) 'Die psychogene Sehstörung in psychoanalytischer Auffassung', *G.S.*, **5**, 310; *G.W.*, **8**, 94. (8)
[*Trans.:* 'The Psycho-Analytic View of Psychogenic Disturbance of Vision', *C.P.*, **2**, 105; *Standard Ed.*, **11**, 211.]

(1911*b*) 'Formulierungen über die zwei Prinzipien des psychischen Geschehens', *G.S.*, **5**, 409; *G.W.*, **8**, 230. (8, 55, 143, 160, 187, 236)
[*Trans.:* 'Formulations on the Two Principles of Mental Functioning', *C.P.*, **4**, 13; *Standard Ed.*, **12**.]

(1911*c*) 'Psychoanalytische Bemerkungen über einen autobiographisch beschrieben Fall von Paranoia (Dementia Paranoides)', *G.S.*, **8**, 355; *G.W.*, **8**, 240. (8, 70, 91, 135, 151, 186)
[*Trans.:* 'Psycho-Analytic Notes on an Autobiographical Account of a Case of Paranoia (Dementia Paranoides)', *C.P.*, **3**, 387; *Standard Ed.*, **12**, 3.]

(1911*e*) 'Die Handhabung der Traumdeutung in der Psychoanalyse', *G.S.*, **6**, 45; *G.W.*, **8**, 350. (115, 127)
[*Trans.:* 'The Handling of Dream-Interpretation in Psycho-Analysis', *C.P.*, **2**, 305; *Standard Ed.*, **12**, 91.]

(1912*b*) 'Zur Dynamik der Übertragung', *G.S.*, **6**, 53; *G.W.*, **8**, 364. (168)
[*Trans.:* 'The Dynamics of Transference', *C.P.*, **2**, 312; *Standard Ed.*, **12**, 99.]

(1912*c*) 'Über neurotische Erkrankungstypen', *G.S.*, **5**, 400; *G.W.*, **8**, 322. (151)
[*Trans.:* 'Types of Onset of Neurosis', *C.P.*, **2**, 113; *Standard Ed.*, **12**, 229.]

(1912*d*) 'Über die allgemeinste Erniedrigung des Liebeslebens', *G.S.*, **5**, 198; *G.W.*, **8**, 78. (178)
[*Trans.:* 'On the Universal Tendency to Debasement in the Sphere of Love', *C.P.*, **4**, 203; *Standard Ed.*, **11**, 179.]

(1912*f*) 'Zur Onanie-Diskussion', *G.S.*, **3**, 324; *G.W.*, **8**, 332. (255)
[*Trans.:* 'Contributions to a Discussion on Masturbation', *Standard Ed.*, **12**, 241.]

(1912*g*) 'A Note on the Unconscious in Psycho-Analysis' [in English], *C.P.*, **4**, 22; *Standard Ed.*, **12**, 257. (5, 6, 14, 16)
[*German Trans.* (by Hanns Sachs): 'Einige Bemerkungen über den Begriff des Unbewussten in der Psychoanalyse', *G.S.*, **5**, 433; *G.W.*, **8**, 430.]

(1912–13) *Totem und Tabu*, Vienna, 1913. *G.S.*, **10**, 3; *G.W.*, **9**. (29, 37, 63, 85, 168, 206)
[*Trans.: Totem and Taboo*, London, 1950; New York, 1952; *Standard Ed.*, **13**, 1.]

(1913*i*) 'Die Disposition zue Zwangsneurose', *G.S.*, **5**, 277; *G.W.*, **8**, 442. (140)
[*Trans.:* 'The Disposition to Obsessional Neurosis', *C.P.*, **2**, 122; *Standard Ed.*, **12**, 313.]

(1914c) 'Zur Einführung des Narzissmus', *G.S.*, **6**, 155; *G.W.*, **10**, 138. (8, 9, 28, 30, 31, 63, 186, 246)
[*Trans.*: 'On Narcissism: an Introduction', *C.P.*, **4**, 30; *Standard Ed.*, **14**, 69.]

(1914d) 'Zur Geschichte der psychoanalytischen Bewegung', *G.S.*, **4**, 411; *G.W.*, **10**, 44. (112, 253, 263)
[*Trans.*: 'On the History of the Psycho-Analytic Movement', *C.P.*, **1**, 287; *Standard Ed.*, **14**, 3.]

(1915c) 'Triebe und Triebschicksale', *G.S.*, **5**, 443; *G.W.*, **10**, 210. (42, 46, 157, 159, 237)
[*Trans.*: 'Instincts and their Vicissitudes', *C.P.*, **4**, 60; *Standard Ed.*, **14**, 111.]

(1915e) 'Das Unbewusste', *G.S.*, **5**, 480; *G.W.*, **10**, 264. (6, 8–9, 13, 16, 18–20, 21, 23, 55, 186, 231, 236)
[*Trans.*: 'The Unconscious', *C.P.*, **4**, 98; *Standard Ed.*, **14**, 161.]

(1915f) 'Mitteilung eines der psychoanalytischen Theorie widersprechenden Falles von Paranoia', *G.S.*, **5**, 288; *G.W.*, **10**, 234. (245, 246)
[*Trans.*: 'A Case of Paranoia Running Counter to the Psycho-Analytic Theory of the Disease', *C.P.*, **2**, 150; *Standard Ed.*, **14**, 263.]

(1916d) 'Einige Charaktertypen aus der psychoanalytischen Arbeit', *G.S.*, **10**, 287; *G.W.*, **10**, 364. (52, 246)
[*Trans.*: 'Some Character-Types Met with in Psycho-Analytic Work', *C.P.*, **4**, 318; *Standard Ed.*, **14**, 311.]

(1916–17) *Vorlesungen zur Einführung in die Psychoanalyse*, Vienna. *G.S.*, **7**; *G.W.*, **11**. (63–4, 114, 117, 244, 251, 268, 274)
[*Trans.*: *Introductory Lectures on Psycho-Analysis*, revised ed., London, 1929 (*A General Introduction to Psychoanalysis*, New York, 1935); *Standard Ed.*, **15–16**.]

(1917a) 'Eine Schwierigkeit der Psychoanalyse', *G.S.*, **10**, 347; *G.W.*, **12**, 3. (63, 221, 223)
[*Trans.*: 'A Difficulty in the Path of Psycho-Analysis', *C.P.*, **4**, 347; *Standard Ed.*, **17**, 137.]

(1917c) 'Über Triebumsetzungen insbesondere der Analerotik', *G.S.*, **5**, 268; *G.W.*, **10**, 402. (179)
[*Trans.*: 'On Transformations of Instinct as Exemplified in Anal Erotism', *C.P.*, **2**, 164; *Standard Ed.*, **17**, 127.]

(1917d) 'Metapsychologische Ergänzung zur Traumlehre', *G.S.*, **5**, 520; *G.W.*, **10**, 412. (28, 130, 151, 186, 231)
[*Trans.*: 'A Metapsychological Supplement to the Theory of Dreams', *C.P.*, **4**, 137; *Standard Ed.*, **14**, 219.]

(1917e [1915]) 'Trauer und Melancholie', *G.S.*, **5**, 535; *G.W.*, **10**, 428. (9, 10, 28, 87)
[*Trans.*: 'Mourning and Melancholia', *C.P.*, **4**, 152; *Standard Ed.*, **14**, 239.]

(1918a) 'Das Tabu der Virginität', *G.S.*, **5**, 212; *G.W.*, **12**, 161. (246)
[*Trans.*: 'The Taboo of Virginity', *C.P.*, **4**, 217; *Standard Ed.*, **11**, 193.]

(1918*b* [1914]) 'Aus der Geschichte einer infantilen Neurose', *G.S.*, 8, 439; *G.W.*, 12, 29. (86, 119–20, 129, 251)
[*Trans.:* 'From the History of an Infantile Neurosis', *C.P.*, 3, 473; *Standard Ed.*, 17, 3.]

(1919*a* [1918]) 'Wege der psychoanalytischen Therapie', *G.S.*, 6, 136; *G.W.*, 12, 183. (285)
[*Trans.:* 'Lines of Advance in Psycho-Analytic Therapy', *C.P.*, 2, 392; *Standard Ed.*, 17, 159.]

(1919*e*) ' "Ein Kind wird geschlagen" ', *G.S.*, 5, 344; *G.W.*, 12, 197. (92, 157–8, 161, 174, 245, 253, 254)
[*Trans.:* ' "A Child is Being Beaten" ', *C.P.*, 2, 172; *Standard Ed.*, 17, 177.]

(1920*a*) 'Über die Psychogenese eines Falles von weiblicher Homosexualität', *G.S.*, 5, 312; *G.W.*, 12, 271. (112, 245)
[*Trans.:* 'The Psychogenesis of a Case of Female Homosexuality', *C.P.*, 2, 202; *Standard Ed.*, 18, 147.]

(1920*b*) 'Zur Vorgeschichte der analytischen Technik', *G.S.*, 6, 148; *G.W.*, 12, 309. (263)
[*Trans.:* 'A Note on the Prehistory of the Technique of Analysis', *C.P.*, 5, 101; *Standard Ed.*, 18, 263.]

(1920*c*) 'Dr. Anton von Freund', *G.S.*, 11, 280; *G.W.*, 13, 435. (267)
[*Trans.:* 'Dr. Anton von Freund', *Standard Ed.*, 18, 267.]

(1920*g*) *Jenseits des Lustprinzips*, Vienna. *G.S.*, 6, 191; *G.W.*, 13, 3. (6, 12, 17–18, 19, 22, 28, 40, 41, 46, 47, 57, 64, 108, 117–18, 157, 159, 160, 164, 223, 228, 230, 231, 238, 253, 287)
[*Trans: Beyond the Pleasure Principle*, Lond on, 1950; *Standard Ed.* 18, 3.]

(1921*b*) Introduction [in English] to J. Varendonck's *The Psychology of Day-Dreams*, London; *Standard Ed.*, 18, 271. (21)
[*German Text* (part only): *G.S.*, 11, 264; *G.W.*, 13, 439.]

(1921*c*) *Massenpsychologie und Ich-Analyse*, Vienna. *G.S.*, 6, 261; *G.W.*, 13, 73. (9–10, 28, 29, 31, 32, 37, 108, 244)
[*Trans.: Group Psychology and the Analysis of the Ego*, London, 1959; *Standard Ed.*, 18, 67.]

(1922*a*) 'Traum und Telepathie', *G.S.*, 3, 278; *G.W.*, 13, 165. (135, 138)
[*Trans.:* 'Dreams and Telepathy', *C.P.*, 4, 408; *Standard Ed.*, 18, 197.]

(1922*b*) 'Über einige neurotische Mechanismen bei Eifersucht, Paranoia und Homosexualität', *G.S.*, 5, 387; *G.W.*, 13, 195. (37, 108, 112)
[*Trans.:* 'Some Neurotic Mechanisms in Jealousy, Paranoia and Homosexuality', *C.P.*, 2, 232; *Standard Ed.*, 18, 223.]

(1922*e*) Preface [in French] to Raymond de Saussure's *La méthode psychanalytique*, Geneva.
[*Trans.: Standard Ed.*, 19, 283.]

(1922*f*) 'Etwas vom Unbewussten' (Author's Abstract of Congress Address), *Int. Z. Psychoan.*, 8, 486.
[*Trans.:* Included in 1923*b*, *Standard Ed.*, 19, 3.]

(1923*a*) ' "Psychoanalyse" und "Libido Theorie" ', *G.S.*, **11**, 201;
G.W., **13**, 211. (30, 64, 195, 244–5)
   [*Trans.*: 'Two Encyclopaedia Articles', *C.P.*, **5**, 107; *Standard Ed.*,
   18, 235.]
(1923*b*) *Das Ich und das Es*, Vienna. *G.S.*, **6**, 353; *G.W.*, **13**, 237,
   (133, 134, 145, 148, 149, 158, 164, 166–9, 170, 172, 173, 176, 218,
   238, 244, 245, 246–7)
   [*Trans.*: *The Ego and the Id*, London, 1927; *Standard Ed.*, **19**, 3.]
(1923*c* [1922]) 'Bemerkungen zur Theorie und Praxis der Traumdeutung', *G.S.*, **3**, 305; *G.W.*, **13**, 301.
   [*Trans.*: 'Remarks on the Theory and Practice of Dream-
   Interpretation' *C.P.*, **5**, 136 *Standard Ed.*, **19**, 109.]
(1923*d* [1922]) 'Eine Teufelsneurose im siebzehnten Jahrhundert',
   G.S., **10**, 409; *G.W.*, **13**, 317. (174)
   [*Trans.*: 'A Seventeenth Century Demonological Neurosis',
   C.P., **4**, 436; *Standard Ed.*, **19**, 69.]
(1923*e*) 'Die infantile Genitalorganisation', *G.S.*, **5**, 232; *G.W.*, **13**,
   293. (31, 153, 165, 174, 175, 184, 235, 245, 252, 253)
   [*Trans.*: 'The Infantile Genital Organization,' *C.P.*, **2**, 244;
   Standard Ed., **19**, 141.]
(1923*f*) 'Josef Popper-Lynkeus und die Theorie des Traumes',
   G.S., **11**, 295; *G.W.*, **13**, 357.
   [*Trans.*: 'Joseph Popper-Lynkeus and the Theory of Dreams',
   Standard Ed., **19**, 261.]
(1923*g*) Preface to Max Eitingon's *Bericht über die Berliner psycho-
   analytisch Poliklinik*, Vienna. *G.S.*, **11**, 265; *G.W.*, **13**, 441.
   [*Trans.*: Preface to Max Eitingon's *Report on the Berlin Psycho-
   Analytical Policlinic, Standard Ed.*, **19**, 285.]
(1923*h*) Letter [in Spanish] to Señor Luis Lopez-Ballesteros y de
   Torres, *G.S.*, **11**, 266; *G.W.*, **13**, 442.
   [*Trans.*: *Standard Ed.*, **19**, 289.]
(1923*i*) 'Dr. Ferenczi Sándor', *G.S.*, **11**, 273; *G.W.*, **13**, 443.
   [*Trans.*: 'Dr. Sándor Ferenczi (on his 50th Birthday)', *Standard
   Ed.* **19**, 267.]
(1924*a*) Letter [in French] to *Le Disque Vert*, *G.S.*, **11**, 266; *G.W.*,
   13, 446.
   [*Trans.*: *Standard Ed.*, **19**, 290.]
(1924*b* [1923]) 'Neurose und Psychose', *G.S.*, **5**, 418; *G.W.*, **13**, 387.
   (11, 167, 182, 183)
   [*Trans.*: 'Neurosis and Psychosis', *C.P.*, **2**, 250; *Standard Ed.*, **19**,
   149.]
(1924*c*) 'Das ökonomische Problem des Masochismus', *G.S.*, **5**, 374;
   G.W., **13**, 371. (11, 41, 50, 54, 134, 143, 152, 185)
   [*Trans.*: 'The Economic Problem of Masochism', *C.P.*, **2**, 255;
   Standard Ed., **19**, 157.]
(1924*d*) 'Der Untergang des Ödipuskomplexes', *G.S.*, **5**, 423; *G.W.*,
   13, 395. (11, 32, 144, 245, 249–50, 256–7)
   [*Trans.*: 'The Dissolution of the Oedipus Complex', *C.P.*, **2**, 269;
   Standard Ed., **19**, 173.]

(1924*e*) 'Die Realitätsverlust bei Neurose und Psychose', *G.S.*, 6, 409; *G.W.*, 13, 363. (11, 143, 148)
[*Trans.*: 'The Loss of Reality in Neurosis and Psychosis', *C.P.*, 2, 277; *Standard Ed.*, 19, 183.]

(1924*f* [1923]) 'A Short Account of Psycho-Analysis' [published as 'Psychoanalysis: Exploring the Hidden Recesses of the Mind'], Chap. 73, Vol. 2 of *These Eventful Years*, London and New York; *Standard Ed.*, 19, 191.
[*German Text*: 'Kurzer Abriss der Psychoanalyse', *G.S.*, 11, 183; *G.W.*, 13, 405. German original first appeared in 1928.]

(1924*g* [1923]) Extracts from a Letter to Wittels, in Wittels's *Sigmund Freud*, London. *Standard Ed.*, 19, 286. German original unpublished.

(1924*h*) 'Mitteilung des Herausgebers', *Int. Z. Psychoan.*, 10, 373.
[*Trans.*: 'Editorial Changes in the *Zeitschrift*', *Standard Ed.*, 19, 293.]

(1925*a* [1924]) 'Notiz über den "Wunderblock" ', *G.S.*, 6, 415; *G.W.*, 14, 3. (238)
[*Trans.*: 'A Note upon the "Mystic Writing-Pad" ', *C.P.*, 5, 175; *Standard Ed.*, 19, 227.]

(1925*b*) Letter to the Editor of the *Jüdische Presszentrale, Zürich, G.S.*, 11, 298; *G.W.*, 14, 556.
[*Trans.*: *Standard Ed.*, 19, 291.]

(1925*c*) Message on the Opening of the Hebrew University [in English], *G.S.*, 11, 298; *G.W.*, 14, 556; *Standard Ed.*, 19, 292.

(1925*d* [1924]) *Selbstdarstellung*, Vienna, 1934. *G.S.*, 11, 119; *G.W.*, 14, 33. (64, 223, 244–5, 280)
[*Trans.*: *An Autobiographical Study*, London, 1935 (*Autobiography*, New York, 1935); *Standard Ed.*, 20, 3.]

(1925*e* [1924]) 'Die Widerstände gegen die Psychoanalyse', *G.S.*, 11, 224; *G.W.*, 14, 99.
[*Trans.*: 'The Resistances to Psycho-Analysis', *C.P.*, 5, 163; *Standard Ed.*, 19, 213.]

(1925*f*) Preface to August Aichhorn's *Verwahrloste Jugend*, Vienna. *G.S.*, 11, 267; *G.W.*, 14, 565.
[*Trans.*: Preface to Aichhorn's *Wayward Youth*, *C.P.*, 5, 98; *Standard Ed.*, 19, 273.]

(1925*g*) 'Josef Breuer', *G.S.*, 11, 281; *G.W.*, 14, 562.
[*Trans.*: 'Josef Breuer', *Int. J. Psycho-Anal.*, 6, 459; *Standard Ed.*, 19, 279.]

(1925*h*) 'Die Verneinung', *G.S.*, 11, 3; *G.W.*, 14, 11. (143, 231)
[*Trans.*: 'Negation', *C.P.*, 5, 181; *Standard Ed.*, 19, 235.]

(1925*i*) 'Einige Nachträge zum Ganzen der Traumdeutung', *G.S.*, 3, 172; *G.W.*, 1, 561. (8, 54)
[*Trans.*: 'Some Additional Notes upon Dream-Interpretation as a Whole', *C.P.*, 5, 150; *Standard Ed.*, 19, 125.]

(1925*j*) 'Einige psychische Folgen des anatomischen Geschlechtsunterschieds', *G.S.*, 11, 8; *G.W.*, 14, 19. (11, 32, 143, 172, 178, 179)

[*Trans.:* 'Some Psychical Consequences of the Anatomical Distinction between the Sexes', *C.P.*, **5**, 186; *Standard Ed.*, **19**, 243.]

(1926*d*) *Hemmung, Symptom und Angst*, Vienna. *G.S.*, **11**, 23; *G.W.*, **14**, 113. (11, 35, 42, 57, 58, 167, 179)
[*Trans.: Inhibitions, Symptoms and Anxiety*, London, 1960; *Standard Ed.*, **20**, 77.]

(1926*e*) *Die Frage der Laienanalyse*, Vienna. *G.S.*, **11**, 307; *G.W.*, **14**, 209. (13, 244)
[*Trans.: The Question of Lay Analysis*, London, 1947; *Standard Ed.*, **20**, 179.]

(1926*f*) An Article in the *Encyclopaedia Britannica* [published as 'Psycho-Analysis: Freudian School'], *Encyclopaedia Britannica*, 13th ed., New Vol. 3, 253; *Standard Ed.*, **20**, 261. (190)
[*German Text:* 'Psycho-Analysis', *G.S.*, **12**, 372; *G.W.*, **14**, 299. German original first appeared in 1934.]

(1927*c*) *Die Zukunft einer Illusion*, Vienna. *G.S.*, **11**, 411; *G.W.*, **14**, 325. (168)
[*Trans.: The Future of an Illusion*, London and New York, 1928; *Standard Ed.*, **21**, 3.]

(1927*d*) 'Der Humor', *G.S.*, **11**, 402; *G.W.*, **14**, 383. (28)
[*Trans.:* 'Humour', *C.P.*, **5**, 215; *Standard Ed.*, **21**, 161.]

(1927*e*) 'Fetischismus', *G.S.*, **11**, 395; *G.W.*, **14**, 311. (143, 153, 182)
[*Trans.:* 'Fetishism', *C.P.*, **5**, 198; *Standard Ed.*, **21**, 149.]

(1928*b*) 'Dostojewski und die Vatertötung', *G.S.*, **12**, 7; *G.W.*, **14**, 399. (41)
[*Trans.:* Dostoevsky and Parricide', *C.P.*, **5**, 222; *Standard Ed.*, **21**, 175.]

(1929*b*) Letter [in French] to Maxime Leroy on Some Dreams of Descartes', *G.S.*, **12**, 403; *G.W.*, **14**, 558. (111)
[*Trans.: Standard Ed.*, **21**, 199.]

(1930*a*) *Das Unbehagen in der Kultur*, Vienna. *G.S.*, **12**, 29; *G.W.*, **14**, 421. (8, 11, 42, 50, 54, 134, 157–8, 170, 228, 237, 272)
[*Trans.: Civilization and its Discontents*, London and New York, 1930; *Standard Ed.*, **21**, 59.]

(1930*b*) Preface to *Zehn Jahre Berliner Psychoanalytisches Institut*, Vienna. *G.S.*, **12**, 388; *G.W.*, **14**, 572. (285)
[*Trans.:* In 'Personal Memories', in *Max Eitingon In Memoriam*, Jerusalem, 1951; *Standard Ed.*, **21**, 257.]

(1931*b*) 'Über die weibliche Sexualität', *G.S.*, **12**, 120; *G.W.*, **14**, 517. (177, 179, 244, 245)
[*Trans.:* 'Female Sexuality', *C.P.*, **5**, 252; *Standard Ed.*, **21**, 223.]

(1932*c*) 'Meine Berührung mit Josef Popper-Lynkeus', *G.S.*, **12**, 415; *G.W.*, **16**, 261. (260, 263)
[*Trans.:* 'My Contact with Josef Popper-Lynkeus', *C.P.*, **5**, 295; *Standard Ed.*, **22**.]

(1933*a*) *Neue Folge der Vorlesungen zur Einführung in die Psychoanalyse*, Vienna. *G.S.*, **12**, 151; *G.W.*, **15**, 207. (6, 10, 24, 36, 62, 64, 65, 109, 135, 137, 238, 245, 272)

[*Trans.: New Introductory Lectures on Psycho-Analysis*, London and New York, 1933; *Standard Ed.*, **22**.]

(1933*c*) 'Sándor Ferenczi', *G.S.*, **12**, 397; *G.W.*, **16**, 267. (269)
[*Trans.*: 'Sándor Ferenczi', *Int. J. Psycho-Anal.*, **14**, 297; *Standard Ed.*, **22**.]

(1937*c*) 'Die endliche und die unendliche Analyse', *G.W.*, **16**, 59. (164, 170)
[*Trans.*: 'Analysis Terminable and Interminable', *C.P.*, **5**, 316; *Standard Ed.*, **23**.]

(1937*d*) 'Konstruktionen in der Analyse', *G.W.*, **16**, 43. (115, 239)
[*Trans.*: 'Constructions in Analysis', *C.P.*, **5**, 358; *Standard Ed.*, **23**.]

(1939*a* [1937–39]) *Der Mann Moses und die monotheistische Religion*, *G.W.*, **16**, 103. (7)
[*Trans.*: *Moses and Monotheism*, London and New York, 1939; *Standard Ed.*, **23**.]

(1940*a* [1938]) *Abriss der Psychoanalyse*, *G.W.*, **17**, 67. (64, 143, 150, 153, 161, 245)
[*Trans.*: *An Outline of Psycho-Analysis*, London and New York, 1949; *Standard Ed.*, **23**.]

(1940*c* [1922]) 'Das Medusenhaupt', *G.W.*, **17**, 47. (144)
[*Trans.*: 'Medusa's Head', *C.P.*, **5**, 105; *Standard Ed.*, **18**, 273.]

(1940*e* [1938]) 'Die Ichspaltung im Abwehrvorgang', *G.W.*, **17**, 59. (143, 153)
[*Trans.*: 'Splitting of the Ego in the Process of Defence', *C.P.*, **5**, 372; *Standard Ed.*, **23**.]

(1941*c* [1899]) 'Eine erfüllte Traumahnung', *G.W.*, **17**, 21. (136)
[*Trans.*: 'A Premonitory Dream Fulfilled', *C.P.*, **5**, 70; *Standard Ed.*, **5**, 623.]

(1941*d* [1921]) 'Psychoanalyse und Telepathie', *G.W.*, **17**, 21. (108, 135, 137–8)
[*Trans.*: 'Psycho-Analysis and Telepathy', *Standard Ed.*, **18**, 177.]

(1950*a* [1887–1902]) *Aus den Anfängen der Psychoanalyse*, London. Includes 'Entwurf einer Psychologie' (1895). (4–5, 8, 24, 33, 57, 70, 164, 184, 231, 238, 246)
[*Trans.*: *The Origins of Psycho-Analysis*, London and New York, 1954. (Partly, including 'A Project for a Scientific Psychology', in *Standard Ed.*, **1**.)]

(1955*c* [1920]) 'Memorandum on the Electrical Treatment of War Neuroses', *Standard Ed.*, **17**, 211. (113)
[*German Text* (unpublished): 'Gutachten über die elektrische Behandlung der Kriegsneurotiker.']

(1956*a* [1886]) 'Report on my Studies in Paris and Berlin, on a Travelling Bursary Granted from the University Jubilee Fund, 1885–6', *Int. J. Psycho-Anal.*, **37**, 2; *Standard Ed.*, **1**. (69)
[*German Text* (unpublished): 'Bericht über meine mit Universitäts-Jubiläums Reisestipendium unternommene Studienreise nach Paris und Berlin.']

(1957a [1911]) With OPPENHEIM, D. E., 'Träume im Folklore', *Dreams in Folklore*, New York, 1958, Part II. (89)
[*Trans.: Dreams in Folklore*, New York, 1958, Part I; *Standard Ed.*, 12, 177.]

GRODDECK, G. (1923) *Das Buch vom Es*, Vienna. (23)

HOLLÓS, S., and FERENCZI, S. *See* FERENCZI, S., and HOLLÓS, S.

HORNEY, K. (1923) 'Zur Genese des weiblichen Kastrationskomplexes', *Int. Z. Psychoan.*, 9, 12. (258)
[*Trans.*: 'On the Genesis of the Castration Complex in Women', *Int. J. Psycho-Anal.*, 5 (1924), 50.]

HUNTER, R. A., and MACALPINE, I. *See* MACALPINE, I., and HUNTER, R. A.

JANET, PIERRE (1889) *L'automatisme psychologique*, Paris. (280)
(1892) *État mental des hystériques*, Paris. (280)

JONES, E. (1912) *Der Alptraum in seiner Beziehung zu gewissen Formen des mittelalterlichen Aberglaubens*, Leipsig and Vienna. (86, 87)
[*English Text*: In *On the Nightmare*, London, 1931.]
(1953) *Sigmund Freud: Life and Work*, Vol. 1, London and New York. (Page reference is to the English edition.) (289)
(1955) *Sigmund Freud: Life and Work*, Vol. 2, London and New York. (Page references are to the English edition.) (108, 244)
(1957) *Sigmund Freud: Life and Work*, Vol. 3, London and New York. (Page references are to the English edition.) (3, 10, 69, 70, 108, 126, 140, 157, 173, 190, 226, 234, 243)

JUNG, C. G. (1907) *Über die Psychologie der Dementia praecox*, Halle. (204)
[*Trans.: The Psychology of Dementia Praecox*, New York, 1909.]
(1911) 'Wandlungen und Symbole der Libido', Part I, *Jb. psychoan. psychopath. Forsch.*, 3, 120. (168)
[*Trans.: Psychology of the Unconscious*, New York, 1916; London, 1919.]

LINDNER, S. (1879) 'Das Saugen an den Fingern, Lippen, etc. bei den Kindern (Ludeln)', *Jb. Kinderheilk.*, N. F., 14, 68. (251)

LOW, B. (1920) *Psycho-Analysis*, London. (159)

MACALPINE, I., and HUNTER, R. A. (1954) 'Observations on the Psychoanalytic Theory of Psychosis', *Brit. J. Med. Psychol.*, 27, 175. (70)
(1956) *Schizophrenia 1677*, London. (70–1, 75)

MÜNSTERBERG, H. (1908) *Philosophie der Werte; Grundzüge einer Weltanschauung*, Leipzig. (10)

OPHUIJSEN, J. H. W. VAN (1917) 'Beiträge zum Männlichkeitskomplex der Frau', *Int. Z. Psychoan.*, 4, 241. (253)
[*Trans.*: 'Contributions to the Masculinity Complex in Women', *Int. J. Psycho-Anal.*, 5 (1924), 39.]

OPPENHEIM, D. E., and FREUD, S. *See* FREUD, S. (1957a)

PAYER-THURN, R. (1924) 'Faust in Mariazell', *Chronik des Wiener Goethe-Vereins*, 34, 1. (70, 73)

POPPER, J. ('LYNKEUS') (1899) *Phantasien eines Realisten*, Vienna. (260, 262–3)

RANK, O. (1913) 'Der "Familienroman" in der Psychologie des Attentäters', *Int. Z. (ärztl.) Psychoanal.*, 1, 565. (45)

(1924) *Das Trauma der Geburt*, Vienna. (173, 179)
[*Trans.: The Trauma of Birth*, London, 1929.]

RANK, O., and SACHS, H. (1913) *Die Bedeutung der Psychoanalyse für die Geisteswissenschaften*, Wiesbaden. (207)
[*Trans.: The Significance of Psychoanalysis for the Mental Sciences*, New York, 1916.]

RAPAPORT, D. (1951) *Organization and Pathology of Thinking*, New York. (234)

REIK, T. (1919) *Probleme der Religionspsychologie*, Vienna. (85)
(1923) *Der eigene und der fremde Gott*, Vienna. (86)

RICKMAN, J. (ed.) (1937) *General Selection from the Works of Sigmund Freud*, London. (234)

SACHS, H., and RANK, O. *See* RANK, O., and SACHS, H.

SAUSSURE, R. DE (1922) *La méthode psychanalytique*, Lausanne and Geneva. (283–4)

SCHOPENHAUER, A. (1949) *Die Welt als Wille und Vorstellung, Sämtliche Werke* (ed. Hübscher) (2nd ed.), **3**, Wiesbaden. (218, 223–4)
[*Trans.: The World as Will and Idea*, London, 1886.]

SCHREBER, D. P. (1903) *Denkwürdigkeiten eines Nervenkranken*, Leipzig. (91)

STÄRCKE, A. (1910) 'Der Kastrationskomplex', *Int. Z. (ärztl.) Psychoanal.*, 1, 9. (175)

STEKEL, W. (1908) *Nervöse Angstzustände und ihre Behandlung*, Vienna. (57)

VARENDONCK, J. (1921) *The Psychology of Day-Dreams*, London. (21)

WITTELS, F. (1924) *Sigmund Freud, his Personality, his Teaching and his School*, London and New York. (286–8)
(1925) *An End to Poverty*, London. (260)

LIST OF ABBREVIATIONS

G.S. = Freud, *Gesammelte Schriften* (12 vols.), Vienna, 1924–34
G.W. = Freud, *Gesammelte Werke* (18 vols.), London, from 1940
C.P. = Freud, Collected Papers (5 vols.), London, 1924–50
Standard Ed. = Freud, *Standard Edition* (24 vols.), London, from 1953
Neurosenlehre und Technik = Freud, *Schriften zur Neurosenlehre und zur
   psychoanalytischen Technik (1913–1926)*, Vienna, 1931
Psychoanalyse der Neurosen = Freud, *Studien zur Psychoanalyse der Neurosen
   aus den Jahren 1913–1925*, Vienna, 1926
Sexualtheorie und Traumlehre = Freud, *Kleine Schriften zur Sexualtheorie und
   zur Traumlehre*, Vienna, 1931
Theoretische Schriften = Freud, *Theoretische Schriften (1911–1925)*, Vienna,
   1931
Traumlehre = Freud, *Kleine Beiträge zur Traumlehre*, Vienna, 1925

GENERAL INDEX

This index includes the names of non-technical authors. It also includes the names of technical authors where no reference is made in the text to specific works. For references to specific technical works, the Bibliography should be consulted.—The compilation of the index was undertaken by Mrs. R. S. Partridge.

309

www.vintage-books.co.uk